TO HOLKHAM
FAKENHAM
RAYNHAM HALL FARM
GREAT RYBURGH
ST. ANDREWS
TESTERTON HALL
STABLE YARD
HIGH STREET
BUTCHER
THE MALTINGS
B1145
TO GRESSENHALL
MILEHAM
Here's where it happened!
B1146
Breach
TO DEREHAM

FULL CIRCLE

My mother, Rose May Joice née Bailey.

FULL CIRCLE

Dick Joice

THE BOYDELL PRESS

First published 1991 by The Boydell Press, Woodbridge

The Boydell Press is an imprint of
Boydell & Brewer Ltd
PO Box 9, Woodbridge, Suffolk IP12 3DF

ISBN 0 85115 288 0

British Library Cataloguing-in-Publication Data
Joice, Dick
Full circle.
I. Title
920
ISBN 0–85115–288–0

This publication is printed on acid-free paper

Printed in Great Britain by
St Edmundsbury Press Ltd, Bury St Edmunds, Suffolk

Contents

Acknowledgements

After hearing me speak at a Farmers' meeting many years ago, my father remarked, 'Never start a speech with an apology.' The late Richard Dimbleby gave me the same advice after seeing one of my early television programmes. If after reading *Full Circle* you should notice any inaccuracies, please put it down to tricks of memory and the ravages of time on the brain cells! Writing the book has given me great pleasure; you might say it has caused me to live my life again. My thanks to everyone who helped; I wish I could mention them all.

My thanks to my mother and father for their advice and encouragement (it was very difficult to disagree with them).

My thanks to my contemporaries in Ryburgh and Raynham who jogged my memory of various events, to Lord Townshend who shoved me in front of the cameras, to all the T.V. experts and technicians who kept me there for close on thirty years and thanks to the viewers who seemed to like most of it and kept the ratings up.

Margaret and our three children and other members of the family who kept all our family photos and press cuttings and gave me something to write about. Jean who gave me great encouragement to keep writing despite the dyslexia!

Dick Burgis who has always been there when I got into a tight spot and who is a 'born' grower of good crops, and Harry Reed who understands the breeding of the right sort of hens.

Lord Coke who allowed us to put the Bygones collection on show in the magnificent coach houses and stables adjoining Holkham Hall. Sally who made sense of and edited my scribblings. Pam who typed from my dictation, tapes and notes on scribbled pieces of paper.

My thanks also to Peter Wright who loves this little farm and who has helped me to find time for writing by doing much of the heavy work.

Chapter One

Early Childhood

'Always have a good reason for doing anything', my father used to say. My mother always insisted that *I* was the good reason he found for buying his first motor car.

I was born at Bridge Farm, Great Ryburgh, on 30th January 1921, the second child in what was to become a family of three. My brother, Jack, was seven years older than me and my sister, Betty, was born eight years later. The village of Great Ryburgh lies a little to the north-west in the county of Norfolk, and I understand from reports that the county was in the grip of a very cold spell in January that year. Indeed it was snowing steadily when, at about 1.00 a.m. in the morning, my mother announced that something had to be done about me. So, Father got out his bicycle and pedalled smartly up to the village to fetch the midwife.

Although called *Great* Ryburgh, the village was actually quite small and didn't merit the permanent presence of a doctor. However, I believe Dr Palin from Fakenham paid regular visits on Tuesday afternoons, using a spare front room in someone's house as a rudimentary surgery. As the night drew on and I hadn't actually appeared, my father, in consultation with the midwife, decided that Dr Palin should be called. Out came the bicycle again and off he sped – this time to Fakenham, some four-and-a-half miles away. This epic journey – recounted many times during the next fifty years until he died – became part of family folklore, as Father not only had to cycle to Fakenham to call out a none-too-pleased doctor, but he had to cycle back again behind the doctor's one-man gig drawn by his high-stepping pony. Father always said that he would never have got back if it hadn't been for the fact that unbeknown to Dr Palin he occasionally attached himself by one hand to the tail-board of the gig. It must have been a very frustrating journey as the doctor, who was fond of his pony, insisted on stopping frequently to give it a rest. The doctor was also very fond of a tipple, and the refreshment that he had had earlier on in the evening didn't help matters: he tended to take the wrong route whenever the road forked! Father then had to shout above the wind, whilst pedalling furiously to get ahead of him, to put him back on the right road. Most of the main roads were tarred and gritted, but what are now graded 'C' roads were unmettled and very rough. The road from Fakenham back to Great Ryburgh, via Little Ryburgh, was particularly bad and made worse by the inclement weather and the pony frequently stumbled. Each time this happened Dr Palin would call a halt and descend from the vehicle, having unwrapped himself from several rugs and waterproof covers, to see if there was any damage to the hooves. The only light available was from the candle-lamps on the gig and Father's bicycle gas-lamp.

The story got better as I grew older for later versions recount that soon after Father left I put in an appearance, which made a mockery of the whole journey. Salt was also rubbed in by the midwife who was quoted by my mother as saying: 'I managed perfectly well on my own, and I do like to have the fathers out of the way.' Meanwhile the doctor apparently ate a hearty breakfast washed down with stout to fortify him for the journey back, and Father had to go most of the way with him to dig him out wherever the snow had blown into drifts. Little wonder, therefore, that he felt that this experience was the best possible justification for buying his first motor car! As far as I'm concerned I believe the reason why I like getting up early, and prefer winter-time to summer, is because my first encounter with the world was in the early hours of the morning, during a snowstorm in January, 1921.

I can't truthfully say that I remember very much, if anything, of the next four years. Of course, one has heard the tales of one's early days so often that imagination sometimes tricks you into thinking you actually remember. My memories of Bridge Farm therefore are not crystal clear but it was here that my father started to farm in 1912, before his marriage. The farm, with its 400 acres, was part of the Sennowe Estate which belonged to Thomas Cook, son of the Thomas Cook of travel agent fame. Thomas Cook, senior, had come to settle down at Sennowe Park in Norfolk following the great success of his famous travel firm, which he started by running two horse-drawn coaches daily between Norfolk and London. As the coaches started near the coast, one going to the capital via Norwich and the other via Yarmouth and Ipswich, they were called the *Crab Pot* and the *Lobster Pot*. The coaches are still at Sennowe Park, and are carefully maintained by the present Tom Cook.

My father was born in 1888 and began farmwork as soon as he left school. In 1907, when he was nineteen years old, he decided to take up an offer made to lads of that age by the Canadian government to emigrate to Canada with a subsidised sea passage to farm a quarter of a 'square' mile (160 acres) of land. I only wish I had the diary he kept, which told of the traumatic conditions and what proved to be insurmountable problems he found when he arrived on site near Winnipeg. The acreage being offered by the Canadian government was uncleared, recently-felled forest with thousands of tree stumps, all very large, from felled trees upwards of one hundred years old. Father had no equipment, not even a pick or shovel, nowhere to live, no

My Grandfather James Joice; well known cob breaker.

My Father, Charles Thomas Joice at Stibbard.

help and very little money, even if there had been labour available to pay. The task was tremendous and he soon realised that to get the land into a workable, arable, state would take much too long and run him too far into debt. So, although he had set off with tremendous enthusiasm, he decided to put the venture down to experience, swallowed his pride and loss of grant (which was never paid) and took the next boat home on a working passage back to Liverpool. There he bought himself a bicycle and cycled back to Great Ryburgh. In later years he often told me that he had worked his passage home looking after the cows. I thought this meant that there had been cows on board to provide milk for the passengers. This may have been the case, but I have since discovered that in fact the cows on the boat were of the Canadian Holstein breed, whose forebears had been taken to Canada by the early Dutch settlers. They had improved the breed so much that they were better than the ones from Friesland and were being exported back to England. These must have been some of the ones that my father looked after, for they were sold on the docks at Liverpool straight off the boat. It is interesting, too, that some were actually bought by the Alston family who brought them back to Norfolk. Apart from missing the detail of the journey and the description of his great disappointment, the other reason why I am so sorry that his diary is lost is that it contained a most marvellous description of a shipboard romance that he had on the passage out with a fellow lady immigrant. I sometimes felt that had there not been so many tree stumps to dig out in Winnipeg I might have been born Canadian. As to the fate of the diary, it is significant that it disappeared from a drawer in her bedroom the day after my mother found me reading it. Perhaps she didn't feel that the details of Father's romantic journey were suitable reading for his young son.

By the time Father arrived home, his father – my grandfather – had moved to Blue Tile Farm, Stibbard, in the next village to Ryburgh. My grandparents had previously lived in a very small house at the Heath Farm, Fakenham, where my grandfather had been employed as bailiff after starting as a farmworker and rising through the ranks. My grandparents brought up a family of nine (Father came roughly in the middle) in a four-roomed cottage, with no piped water (just a well outside), no electricity or gas and the usual 'office' – a two-seater up the garden! Blue Tile Farm, Stibbard, though, was quite a large farmhouse with 300 acres. For the next three years Father worked with his father at Blue Tile Farm. During this time he also started his very first business venture, hiring and working a smallholding of a few acres at Little Ryburgh and a small set of premises from the Sennowe Estate to keep pigs. In 1912 my grandfather and father persuaded Thomas Cook to let my father have Bridge Farm. He moved in immediately, catering for himself as he hadn't yet met my mother. They were obviously all very short of capital, but by a system of cross-guaranteed overdrafts, shared implements, comparatively cheap labour, physical effort and enthusiasm, together with credit from the merchants on feedstuffs set against future harvests, and obliging vets (who usually only sent their bills out once a year knowing that it was a waste of time to submit them more often) they all did quite well.

Father soon grew tired of his diet of boiled eggs and not much else, and was fortunate enough to meet my mother, Rose Bailey, who was a shop assistant at Roy's Stores in the village of Helhoughton, about eight miles from Great Ryburgh. In those days young lady shop assistants 'lived in', so the courting was done by bicycle (no doubt the one bought in Liverpool) on a bi-weekly basis; and always under the eagle eye of Mrs Roy, the postmistress, who never once, or so she thought, let my mother or any of her protégées out of her sight in daylight, or when my father was around. She had apparently given all the mothers of her girls a pledge that she would see to it that no boys ever spoke to any of her girls. As far as she was able, Mrs Roy kept her side of the bargain. But on one notable occasion my mother's father caught her very late one night, on the outskirts of the village, being pushed through the ford of the River Wensum on the cross-bar of Father's bicycle. History never related how Mother broke the curfew, but there is still a lean-to roof below the window of the room where Mrs Roy's girls slept. This occasion was my father's first, inauspicious, meeting with James Bailey, my mother's father, and head gamekeeper on another estate.

My two grandfathers, James Joice and James Bailey, were both great fellows, but very different from each other, particularly in stature. Grandfather Joice only stood 5ft 4in in his socks, but Grandfather Bailey was a very big man. They both came from working stock locally, the Joices on farms and the Baileys in blacksmithing and general farm work, with a bit of dealing thrown in. Grandfather Bailey also did some estate game-keepering. He was obviously a good keeper for at the turn of the century he became head keeper on the estate of Colonel Scott-Chad at Pynkney. As with Grandfather Joice on the Sennowe Estate, his landlord gave him a start in farming by letting him have the tenancy of a small farm.

In spite of his very small stature Grandfather Joice was renowned throughout the area for his prowess in breaking-in awkward horses. It's sometimes said that these old-timers were unkind because they used strange-shaped bits, often known as cruel bits, in the bridles of difficult horses. The reverse was the case, for they had to show the horse who was master and in so doing saved the lives of a great many animals. If you couldn't make a horse manageable then usually there was no other use for it, and many met a sorry end at the knacker's yard. One might perhaps think that even awkward mares could have been used for breeding. Some were, of course, but it was usually the policy only to breed from good-tempered mares in case the bad temper was transmitted to future generations.

I have very clear memories of seeing Grandad Joice breaking-in young horses weighing up to half-a-ton by first of all trotting them round on a long rein, then doing the same thing with a sack of straw on their backs. A piece of equipment called a 'dumb jockey' was used for the next stage. This was a saddle with a short vertical arm sticking up from the centre which carried weights varying in size. First of all he would try the horse with a weight of, say, 2 or 3lb, increasing it gradually to weights of a stone or two. The exercise was then repeated with an agile lad aboard. When they were quiet enough to put full harness on they were walked round and round a field pulling a heavy log. Finally, Grandfather would tie the horse to a tree on a halter, stand back a few yards, then sprint towards the horse, grab the collar and hurl himself into the saddle. On some occasions we were treated to the sight of Grandfather misjudging his leap, vaulting clear over the top and landing in a heap on the other side!

Many stories about 'horse magic' have been written, and perhaps there is a good scientific explanation for some of them. They are usually connected with the horse's sense of taste or smell, for some people just don't smell right to horses. There is a tale that I well remember an old horseman telling me about 'horse magic' that I think sums it all up. This old chap, Lankester by name, lived in Suffolk and was said to understand 'horse magic'. The story goes that he once moved into a new house next to a fellow he heartily disliked, and who wasn't too fond of him either. They quarrelled about everything and constantly threw their garden refuse over the fence into each other's plots. Lankester told me that an old horseman he knew said it would be quite easy to put a stop to all the arguments between them if he took half-a-pint of mare's urine, mixed with some other chemicals (I know not what), and painted the mix on the door jambs of his neighbour's house during the night of the full moon. After a pause I said to him, 'Well, did it work?' He said, 'Yes – he were dead in a week!'

Grandfather Bailey, too, was a great storyteller and his tales often had a twist to them which kept a young audience guessing. One that had me worried was about the River Wensum. I must have been about six years old, and occasionally I spent the night with my grandparents. One day, out with my grandfather in his pony and trap dealing (after he got a start farming he used to buy animals, mostly pigs, from local farmers and either take them to market or sell them to people with larger herds), we stopped at Tatterset to give the horse a drink in the pit beside the road. Most roadside ponds were dug out for this purpose. It was evening and as we sat there in the trap he suddenly said, 'This pond is the start of the River Wensum, and the finish is at Yarmouth where it helps to fill the North Sea'. I am supposed to have asked the question, 'What would happen if the pond went dry?' And he said, 'Well, there would no water going through all the places on the way to Yarmouth; all the watermills would stop working and the North Sea would dry up, so if you wanted to you could drive straight across to Holland.' He

Grandpa and Grandma Joice, father, and two of his sisters, Hettie and Dolly.

had me worried for years – even my father couldn't convince me that I was having my leg pulled.

My grandmothers were on about the same scale as their husbands. Grandma Joice was apparently tiny as a girl and in early adult life, but by the time I first remember her, although her height hadn't increased, she had become very rotund. Grandma Bailey on the other hand was tall and slim until the last few years of her life. By modern standards they both had very little education, leaving village schools at twelve years old or soon after, but they were both very intelligent, wrote with very clear hands and were extremely good with figures. In those days education really was a case of learning to read, write and add. They both had large families. There were eleven Baileys, six boys and five girls; and nine Joices, six boys and three girls. Two children in the Bailey family died soon after birth – I think from measles. In the Joice family one twin, brother to my Uncle George, also died at birth. Both ladies, as far as I remember, were always clad completely in black to the ankles: mostly dresses but occasionally a white blouse with a black skirt. They nearly always wore aprons which changed according to the job. Plain white cotton with a bib for the dairy and butter-making, baize for cleaning special items (not that they had many) like brass and silver, a sacking apron with holdall bib for the garden, and appliqué-patterned white fine linen for afternoons. There is no record that they had white weddings, for photography was still rare in the nineteenth century.

They did have their photographs taken, but as studio portraits, and these are all a bit faded now, I'm afraid. I never saw them in anything but full-length dresses and remember how shocked they were when my parents took them to the beach in the early thirties and they saw my mother in a bathing costume. It was at Cromer and Father had hired one of those four-wheeled bathing huts for my mother to change in. These huts were pulled up and down the beach as the tide went in or out, but were always left at the point where ladies could emerge and step down a little ladder straight into the water. My grandparents sat in deckchairs some distance away from the hut and according to my mother's version were very boot-faced about the whole thing, particularly when Father emerged from under several large towels with a cotton bathing costume that had little short trousers, like the boy scouts wore. I don't think either of my parents immersed themselves entirely in the sea, but I do remember them splashing about and obviously enjoying it. I can't think why it was but we children were not allowed to bathe with them and were not allowed to go very far 'out'. My father, having changed back into his grey flannels, white open-necked shirt and trilby, would stand in the sea as far as we were allowed to go, which was knee-deep for him. Consequently I didn't learn to swim until I went away to school years later. Whether it was the influence of my grandparents' black looks or whether he really believed it I don't know, but Father always said that the sea was unhealthy because fish died in it, so we didn't go very often. But every year there was a special outing to Yarmouth where we didn't swim but paddled, and were treated to a visit to the Fair or the Hippodrome.

My mother was one of the tidiest people I have ever known. It was a good job she was because my father was exactly the opposite – except in his dress. He was one of the few people I have ever known who could muck out a stable or cowhouse, or set a sheep fold, and still look as though he was dressed up to go to the annual flower show. Strange that, for he wasn't tidy around the farmyard and in the premises – although he always knew where everything was. But Mother was meticulously tidy. She not only insisted on having everything in exactly the place that she had selected for it, but even the planning of the family 'menus' was very precise. This didn't mean that because there was an exact pattern to what we ate on any one day it was monotonous and boring. Far from it, for she was a wonderful cook and although it was always roast beef, potatoes, Yorkshire pudding and two veg. on Sundays, the sweet course would vary. Because Monday was wash-day, and busy, we always had cold roast beef and pickles. The pickles were made by her as the seasons came round, and would vary from walnuts and onions, to red cabbage and chutneys, all delicious! We always had Aberdeen sausage (known as faggots in some areas) on Tuesday. On Wednesday it was hash or shepherd's pie, or the rest of the cold beef with gravy and 'swimmers' (suet dumplings which started off the size of golf balls but after being cooked in the gravy ended up the size of ducks' eggs). There was boiled ham or salt beef on Thursday, fish on Friday and beef pattie on Saturday. There was one variant on Sundays: if the joint was small or a whole lot of cousins came to lunch we would always be given the other variety of dumplings made with just flour and water and steamed; they rose like bread. These were given to us by the slice with gravy before the meat and veg. They were delicious and it never occurred to us at the time that it was a cunning way of filling us up before the meat course – and much more economical. Breakfast was always porridge first, to fill us up, then eggs of some sort (fried, poached, boiled, scrambled or coddled), except on Sundays when it was toast and honey or home-made marmalade. A great deal of my mother's time went into the preparation of food – not only daily, but often seasonally months ahead.

The bi-annual killing of a pig was traditionally treated as a great event. It usually took place in March and October and involved a great deal of preparation from the initial choosing of a pig from the sties where they were fattened, through to the rendering down of the fat days later. The butcher who came to actually perform the slaughter and cutting up was usually my Uncle George, who had a butcher's business at Melton Constable some twenty miles away. He always stayed the previous night, as the pig was dealt with after the day's work on the farm and when milking had finished. This went on for many years through my teens and eventually when my uncle had aged, my brother and I helped Father and Mother for we had learned the art from watching. The old saying that you can use all of the pig with the exception of its squeal is very true. The whole thing was quite a performance. After the pig was slaughtered, bled and eviscerated in the dairy, it was scalded by pouring boiling water from the copper on to the outside of the carcass. You couldn't see across the room for steam! Afterwards it was scraped and scrubbed until all the bristles were off. Father always said that the bristles were used by builders to mix into the plaster to strengthen ceilings and whether or not this was true I can't say, for I never saw it put into practice. However, together with horsehair, it was apparently used to bind the fine mortar (sand and chalk) which, when pressed up between the laths nailed to the joists for the purpose, would make a very strong ceiling. In fact, it sounds similar to wattle and daub. I suppose the bristles from abattoirs were also used in the manufacture of brushes. The meat, of course, was for our consumption . . . at least most of it. The trotters made the jelly for the pork cheese (brawn); the intestines would end up as sausages; the bladder filled with run-down fat for future use as lard. A comparatively small amount of meat would be consumed fresh, but the majority was cured and smoked for ham and bacon. The curing took place at home and the process involved putting the legs of the pig and the bellies into wooden butts, which were barrels sawn in half. The butts contained a mixture of brown sugar, stout, salt and molasses. The joints were left there to soak through and every now and again were pricked with a two-tined sharp carving fork. After several weeks the pieces of meat were carefully packed in wooden crates and despatched to Yarmouth to be smoked in one of the many smoke-houses where herrings were turned into kippers. They came back a few weeks later. It was the most delicious ham and bacon imaginable! The dogs had the lights or lungs, boiled into a pudding so that it would last for some time; strips of the thicker skin and odd bits like the ears would be hung up for the small birds or fed to the ferrets. Nothing was wasted. All the skills that went into the operation were handed down from generation to generation. One of the problems was that various so-called friends would always arrive, quite by chance, on pig day. Perhaps this is why it mostly took place at night, although the squealing was always a good indication of what was going on.

In Mother's regular timetable Monday was, of course, wash-day. This meant breakfast was at 5.30 a.m. instead of 6.30 a.m. and everybody who wasn't involved kept out of the way. My father's duty was to fill the copper from the well with twenty pails of water and light the fire at 5.00 a.m. He was then excused from anything else to do with the operation. When the water was boiling, soap and soda were added and then the clothes were put in and 'dollied'. They did this by using a washing 'posher' or 'dolly', a wooden contraption about 30in long with a 6in wooden circular base which had five wooden prongs on it. On the top of the shaft was a 'T' handle. The blunt prongs were pushed into the copper and worked about so that all the clothes were subjected to the boiling liquid. When Mother pronounced them clean they were taken out with a copper stick (a round piece of wood about 2ft long), held up for a few minutes to let some of the water drain out and then plunged into a large galvanised iron bath for rinsing, with a little 'blue' to bring out the whiteness and/or starch for certain items like tablecloths and napkins and Father's collars, or anything else that needed stiffening up. The rinsing over, the larger items like sheets, pillowcases and occasionally blankets were twisted to squeeze out the water and put through the large wooden-rollered wringer. After that they were 'pulled', which meant that they were folded in four lengthways and, with one person at each end, pulled to get them straight. They were then hung on the line in the garden to dry. Tuesday was the folding-day when everything was brought indoors and hung over lines in the kitchen to air. When exactly the right amount of moisture had evaporated they were ironed, usually on Wednesday, unless Monday and Tuesday had been very wet days, in which case a certain gloom descended on the house. It seemed permanently damp because the linen was hanging in the kitchen in front of an open fire.

It wasn't until Thursday or Friday that the 'linen' side was back to normal – which didn't give much time before we all shed our weekly washing clothes on Sunday, ready for Monday's wash-day. After the wash each week beds had to be remade with clean sheets, which again was quite an operation as the feather beds had to be turned and pummelled. This gave me terrible sneezing fits and, as allergies hadn't yet become fashionable, no one realised that the feathers were making me sneeze. I didn't really enjoy the laundering side of family hygiene, except for the mechanics of the wooden-rollered mangle. The counter-rotating rollers driven by a system of cog wheels always intrigued me and probably helped to influence my interest in all types of mechanics at a very young age. There was a hitch when I fed one of my cousin's hands through the roller – which was, to say the least, painful for her! Having wound the hand in, neither of us was tall enough to unscrew the tensioning spring on the top of the roller, so we had to wind it out again. On reflection I don't ever remember her coming to stay with us again. Perhaps her parents thought the risk too great, although after all I was only turning the handle and if she had been paying attention and hadn't hung on to the sheet that she was feeding in between the rollers she would have been quite safe. After a few weeks, and a certain amount of discomfort, her nails returned to their normal pink hue.

With luck, and it usually seemed to happen, Friday was given over to cooking. I liked this very much, not only because there was always the odd basin to clean out and titbit to be had, but also because Mother taught us to cook, influenced, I expect, by the fact that before their marriage when he lived alone she knew my father lived on boiled eggs. I liked the special events and celebrations that went with cooking, the best of which for me was jam and marmalade time. Jamming in September meant that the blackberries had to be gathered and although this could be an uncomfortable job battling with nettles and brambles, it also meant that we all went out picking, wearing wellies to save our legs from prickles and stings, and taking walking sticks to pull the brambles down to get the fruit, the biggest of which were always at the top. Although the jamming and bottling saga was a very necessary element in my mother's year, and I enjoyed the picking and gathering, I didn't find the actual process very interesting as the whole place smelled of boiling fruits, and sealing the jars was always such a business. I reckon the failure rate was about twenty-five to thirty per cent, but it was always interesting to see how many had to be done again. It was the same with jam. If it didn't set, meaning that it wouldn't run off a cold saucer, it was necessary to boil the whole lot again. I was never quite sure why my father disapproved of factory jam, and if he really *could* taste the difference. The marmalade operation always started with a message from the local grocer to say that Sevilles were in and should he send a crate of them. On the appointed day they would arrive together with the 'slicer'. This was free on loan, conditional on buying the oranges from the grocer. It saved a great deal of time and was actually a machine which at first glance looked like a mincer. It sliced the oranges as they were pushed down the funnel at the top, whilst a handle which was attached to a very sharp blade was worked vigorously backwards and forwards. Again it was the mechanical device that intrigued me, and I don't ever remember either cutting anybody else's fingers off or damaging my own.

Christmas pudding day was quite an event. The box of raisins arrived in season, and Mother always bought unstoned as she said that the stoned ones were far too expensive and the de-pipping had been done by the Arabs! Consequently she sat for hours patiently cutting every one and taking out the stones. Then the suet had to be prepared. I liked pushing suet through the mincer because it was wound through with an auger, which forced the suet through a fine grid so that it came out like a mass of white worms. We still use the same machine today for making sausages. Mother made the puddings in an evening some weeks before Christmas. I helped by turning the mincer, sorting out the suet, and stoning some of the sticky raisins. My part in the actual mixing was less strenuous. I knelt on a chair, elbows on the table, and watched Mama's wooden spoon go round and round, seeing the eggs, nuts, dried mixed fruit, raisins, milk and sugar disappear as if by magic. When Mother's back was turned I remember always having a crafty fingerful off the side of the basin. The mix was left to prove in the larder overnight, and everyone around was invited to stir in the brandy the following day and make a wish before the puddings were clothed-up in basins and set to boil, it seemed for hours. When they had cooled they were hung up on hooks from the beams in the larder together with the hams and bacon. If I was absolutely honest I would admit that I preferred the uncooked pudding mix to that we actually ate on Christmas Day. By then it had turned almost black and I always thought it bitter, although this was probably the brandy. But there was an incentive to eat a lot of the pudding, of course, and this was to find the threepenny pieces. These were real threepenny pieces. I don't remember the actual date but they were certainly Victorian and silver. Although we won them by finding them, we weren't allowed to keep them. They were bought back from us by Mother for sixpence and then put in a very small suede bag and kept for the following year. I didn't discover the reason for this until I had grown up, but apparently the bag of threepenny pieces came from Grandma Joice who always said that it wasn't safe to use new, cheap, threepenny pieces that she thought weren't made of genuine silver, so every year the same threepenny pieces were kept, re-sterilised and used again. On reflection two things were strange, one that only we children ever found the coins, and the other that my father always managed to trump everyone's ace by finding a five-shilling piece in his – although how it got in there we never knew.

My father was a very jolly man and, like most Joices, his face would screw up when he was amused. This was perhaps an endearing feature in males, but the same expression used by my aunts always showed exactly where you stood. None of the men were tall but the ladies in the family were all short, plump, and walked with small steps. They always seemed to be in a hurry! They, too, were very jolly and seemed to move around in a bunch like starlings. Someone once said of them that they were very like those sets of Russian wooden dolls. Although my father had what appeared to be a placid nature, he also had a sharp temper which would flare up and die down almost as quickly. This happened when I was with him one day in Norwich cattle market. He bumped into the representative of an engineering firm who, for some reason, hadn't pleased him – probably spare parts he had ordered hadn't arrived on time. During the course of their conversation Father lost his temper and ticked the man off, and I shall never forget the phrase he used at the end of his 'raspberry'. Looking straight at the man he said, 'What is your position in your firm?' The man said he was the manager. My father pulled himself up to his full height of 5ft 6in, looked him in the eye, or very nearly because the man was taller than Father, pointed to the cockle stall nearby and said, 'You call yourself a manager of an engineering firm – you couldn't manage a cockle stall.' He then turned, grabbed my hand and walked briskly away, but stopped almost immediately and went back to the chap, prodded him in the chest and said, 'I'm sorry, I've done you an injustice, for that's just about what you could do, manage a cockle stall.' The incident stuck, and for years after that anyone in the family speaking about Father getting upset would say he gave him a 'cockle stall'!

Father was also a great one for finding ways of doing things that would save money and time for him, although often other people involved would be called to pay a price. A traveller used to come from Norwich by train in those days, bringing his bicycle in the guard's van complete with samples on the rear carrier. This splendid chap would pedal round all the farms near Great Ryburgh touting for business, which was selling bar metal to make horseshoes, and ready-made horseshoes which came more expensive, nails to hold them on, hoof-paring knives with bone handles, claw hammers, frost studs that screwed in the horseshoe itself to stop horses slipping in bad weather, and many other requisites for general farm maintenance like staples, bolts, washers, nuts, door fasteners, hinges et al. This type of thing had to be new, of course, second-hand simply wouldn't do, but a great deal of wood that Father used *was* second-hand and a lot of it came from the grocers, strange though it may seem. Wooden crates for oranges were exactly the right dimensions for nesting boxes in chicken houses, and packing cases that were made to contain motor cars and tractors imported from America were also very handy. In fact, I remember all Father's chicken houses had Chrysler, Buick or Dodge in large letters on the side. Although these cases which contained cars to save damage on the boats made very good chicken houses, sometimes they weren't exactly the right shape – in which case Father would take them to pieces and was then faced with the problem of lots of very good serviceable timber that was full of used nails. I remember a day when the traveller came from Norwich with his samples and Father was busy in the barn turning packing cases into poultry houses. He asked if we needed anything and Father said he would have to think about it, but whilst he was waiting would the chap mind de-nailing some of the boards. Father then disappeared and didn't return for an hour, by which time the poor fellow had a whole lot of clean boards and a pail full of nails. At this point Father asked him if he would like to stay for lunch, which would be in about half-an-hour, and whilst he waited perhaps he would like to straighten the nails out on the anvil. The point of the story, of course, is that the traveller got his order for bar metals, etc., for the blacksmith to use, but Father got the tedious job of de-nailing the wood done free. It was the sort of trick you could only pull once and I can't remember whether it happened again with other travellers, but I wouldn't mind betting that it did.

I was reminded of this story about the traveller later on, when I heard my Father, aged over eighty, talking to a friend of his, George Cushing, about the incident. George said, 'You're right. All my life I've been used to picking up bent nails and straightening them. Nowadays they chuck away the new straight ones.' George Cushing repeats that remark in his book, *Steam at Thursford* (David & Charles, 1982). He is a man who has had a great influence on me, which started before I can actually remember, in about 1922. George Cushing in those days worked for the council, repairing roads with the steamroller. The parish council was responsible for the minor roads, but very shortly after that date the roads became the responsibility of the county council. At the change-over George bought the steamroller he had used for years driving for the council and started work on his own. However, at about mid-morning on a particular day, my mother had put me in the pram in the garden in front of the house next to the road, where apparently I sat quite happily watching George going up and down rolling in the stones. Shortly afterwards, Father arrived home in his new car and said that he was going to Fakenham and asked if she would like to accompany him. They hit on the idea of asking friend George to keep an eye not only on me, but on a hawk which Father had seen hovering over some newly-hatched chickens he had in the pasture next to the garden and the road and he left his gun with George. When they got back from their very short shopping excursion George had seen the hawk and shot it. However, the sound of the gun had disturbed *me* so he had taken me out of the pram and put me in the coal tender of the steamroller! I was perfectly happy, but needless to say had changed colour and my white woollen combinations were covered in oil, coal dust and 'blacks' from George's hands and his beautiful roller. Perhaps this is the reason why I have always been devoted to both the Cushings and steam engines. I am not sure whether I approve of shooting hawks now, but in those days life was much harder and I suppose it was justified.

CHAPTER TWO

Childhood Memories: Great Ryburgh

Great Ryburgh in the twenties was much as it is today – a long straggling village narrowly peopled on either side of its then unclassified street. Bridge Farm, where I was born, was at the very eastern end. Going west from that point you came first of all to the neat little bridge over the River Wensum and then the church, the Boar public house, the school, and the foundry. Crossing the railway to the maltings you found the Methodist Chapel, the Crown public house, a series of smallholdings, the village hall and playing field, and all the other cottages and houses which since the 1920s have either been renovated or have suffered the fate of many dwellings in this type of Norfolk village and been replaced by modern houses and bungalows. There are actually many more new houses now as a result of infilling and council housing estates, but surprisingly this has brought the population down from 540 in 1920 to 514 today. Modern living standards now dictate that there are fewer people per bed! I always used to think that Great Ryburgh had all the ingredients necessary for a growing town. It had the maltings, which were once reputed to be the largest in Europe, the foundry, and the Great Eastern railway, Dereham to Wells. The LNER, Kings Lynn to Great Yarmouth, crossed at Fakenham four miles away and, I suppose, put paid to that as the two railways (with stations) actually crossed *in* the town.

Bridge Farm, Great Ryburgh, was where Father really started farming in 1912. It was about 400 acres, not much of it good land in the arable sense. It was hilly and there were lots of patches of sand and gravel, some of it even gaulty, and almost one-third water meadows. According to my father it had not been farmed very well and was not in good heart, but he had been brought up on the traditional four-course system of rotational cropping and soon improved the fertility. He was young and enthusiastic and keen to get on, having had his baptism of fire on the trip to Canada; and on 1st October 1913 he married my mother.

Until Michaelmas 1912 the Bridge Farm farmhouse had served its purpose as two attached cottages. They were small and conventional, two rooms and a larder downstairs, two bedrooms upstairs. But when my parents married, the Sennowe Estate put a bay window in one end and shuffled the walls around inside to make it a house of three good-sized bedrooms upstairs. Downstairs a central passage ran straight through which acted as a hall with a staircase and gave access to a sitting room, dining room, kitchen and large larder/ pantry. The house stood on the north side of the entrance to the farm from the road, and on the other side of the yard were the farm premises. These consisted of all the buildings necessary for a farm run on the Norfolk four-course system: an open yard for the cattle, standings for milking fifty cows, loose boxes for a dozen or so bullocks, calf pens, and a turnip house next to a mixing house, where some of the grain grown on the farm was milled and mixed with turnips and chaff for the cattle. Immediately adjoining this was the stable with standings for one team of eight horses, a chaff house and tack (harness) room, and a couple of loose boxes which doubled up for calving or foaling. Backing on to this was an open shed and yard for pigs. Across one end of the yard was a large Norfolk barn with double doors opening either side which, before Father's time, was used for hand threshing the corn. This was done on days when there was a good breeze, so that by opening the doors the wind automatically winnowed the corn after it had been threshed from the ears by hand flails. The only threshing by flail that I remember was for small quantities of specially grown crops like turnip and kale seed. The main threshing was all done by a travelling thresher with traction engines. It wasn't until much later, when my father was farming a larger acreage, that to have a steam engine set of his own was justified.

The enterprises running simultaneously on the farm to make up the rotation to build fertility were wheat, barley, hay and roots or vegetables. Some of the barley was sold to a firm in the village, F. & G. Smith, for making into malt, and the lower quality kept and ground for feeding to the pigs, cattle and poultry. The latter was my mother's enterprise. The straw was used for bedding, and the husks of the oats, called cholder, and from the wheat and barley were mixed with chopped turnip for the cattle. The diet for the horses was hay, made and grown for the purpose on the farm the reason being that the clover in the hay mixture fixed nitrogen in the soil and helped increase the yield of the crops that followed. Every bit of muck was kept each year. It was carted out on to a heap and turned and eventually spread by hand prior to ploughing in, usually for subsequent wheat crops. The roots, in the form of mangolds, swedes and turnips, were also used for animal feed, the mangolds being harvested and haled or clamped and kept for the winter. The swedes and turnips were folded off by the sheep. The sheep, of course, helped to fertilise the land by dropping the muck where it was required after 'conversion'.

The labour requirement by today's standards was very high and I think my father's initial labour force was big. There were always three people more or less permanently involved with the cows. As well as being pulled out of all those udders the milk had to be carried by pails from the cowhouse across to the dairy, which was on the other side of the yard, adjacent to the back door of the house some 150 yards away. Here it was cooled by running it over a Lister milk cooler, which consisted of a corrugated water jacket with fresh water running through it. The water was first pumped by hand into a holding tank from the well near the back door. The milk was then run through a cotton strainer, which caught the odd pieces of straw and dust, before being stood in churns until it was taken by milk float, drawn by a pony, to the railway station. It was subsequently delivered the next morning to the creamery at North Elmham some ten miles away.

The milk churns were conical in shape, double the top circumference at the bottom, standing about 4ft high and holding 17 gallons. I could never really understand why they held an odd amount, but I can see that the reason why they were a larger diameter at the bottom than the top was so that they didn't fall over when the train shunted or pulled up with a jolt. The weight of the churn with milk was over 300lb and although there were convenient handles on either side of the churn they were still man-killers. It took two people to get them onto the churn platform in the yard, but the lad who took them to the station had to struggle alone to get them off the churn platform on to the milk float and from the float onto the railway platform.

Father's first account book begins when, with the help of the bank and with his father as guarantor (although the latter had very few assets to cover the guarantee), he officially took over the Ryburgh farm at Michaelmas 1912. The very first item details the wages paid in the first week. They were:

To:	William Nobes	10s 0d
	Robert Fenn	10s 0d
	William Crab	3s 6d
	Walter Fenn	3s 4d
	James Fenn	4s 0d
	Total	£1 10s 10d

The equivalent today is £1.50. The second week was the same plus 2s 11d for insurance stamps to cover the five people. As far as I can gather Robert Fenn was team-man, William Nobes was stockman, and there were three boys. The labour force didn't change until the spring-time when it increased by another man, a boy, and Mrs Fenn. This brought the working wage bill to £5 17s 11d. It stayed at this figure except at harvest-time, when each man got £1 extra for four weeks from the last week in August until the last week in September. The boys got an increase amounting to slightly less than the men. In fact, the extra pay for harvest above the total weekly wage covering the month was £7 17s 0d.

Father was managing to pay his way and no doubt the war coming along in 1914 didn't hinder his financial position, although towards the end of the war many of his best horses and some of the fodder were requisitioned for army use. There was a bonus to the cash flow, too, when a unit of the Royal Bucks Hussars was stationed under compulsory order at Bridge Farm and part of the farm premises taken over for horses and men. Two officers were billeted in the house; NCOs and men ate and slept with the horses. Father was paid 7s 0d a week for the use of the barn and granary and had to provide about a ton of straw a day, so there must have been several horses involved. In fact, the army's presence brought in quite a lot of money – £427 17s 10d in the year – which included the blacksmith's account of £46, damage to hurdles and crops of £4, and damage to mangers £2 15s 0d. It looks as if the horses broke down a gate and trampled through the crops. My mother often talked about having the army billeted. There is no account of her being paid for this, although presumably she was and no doubt the rations provided for the men also helped. She also told us about the time when my father received his call-up papers and was sent to Norwich for a medical. Apparently he was down-graded because of a heart complaint, attributed to having pleurisy as a child which left him with a weak chest. It is strange to think that history was to be repeated in my own case twenty-four years later. They had decided that if Father passed the army medical Mother would go on with the farm and my father's younger brother would help her. As it turned out the age of conscription was lowered and it was the same brother, my uncle Arthur, who actually went into the Royal Flying Corps – but stayed on the ground and looked after the engines of the flying machines. So all in all the family were extremely lucky.

The cropping records on the farm for the first year are a bit vague, but it would seem that on the 270 acres or arable land he grew approximately 140 acres of wheat and barley, which were sold for cash, and 70 acres of oats and roots which were consumed on the farm. The rest was down to leys for hay and a certain amount of vegetables for sale locally. A note in the back of his book gives an account of what he paid to the outgoing tenant for covenant, horses, cattle and implements that he took over.

9 horses	£360
9 colts	£400
1 hackney (carriage horse)	£35
8 cows	£200
14 head of stock – big	£280
10 head of stock – small	£100
55 ewes	£220
Pigs	£590
Implements	£330
Total	£2,035

This seems to be the capital he required to get a start, plus an unspecified amount for seeds and smaller items.

For their own personal daily requirements and for food there was a small income from eggs from my mother's poultry, and each Thursday Father took vegetables, eggs and dressed chickens to Fakenham market to supply some of the stalls. Seasonal poultry were also supplied in the shape of geese at Michaelmas and turkeys at Christmas. Father was a very fast plucker and Mother dressed poultry beautifully. In those days, although birds were eviscerated, the feet and heads were left on, no doubt to increase weight. The gizzard, heart and liver were laced into the wing membranes, which all added to the weight and was also decorative. The 'Parson's nose' was wrapped in the fat from inside the bird.

My very first recollection of the village of Great Ryburgh was really nothing at all to do with Ryburgh itself, but concerned the effluent drain that took the goo and liquids from the cowhouse to the river. The drain was really little more than a shallow ditch where the combined efforts of the cows during the night before was pushed with slurry pushers from the concrete standings that they slept on, through a hole in the wall and into this shallow drain. There the liquids made their way down the centre and the solids built up round the edges until such time as they had to be 'hoed' to the banks. It was not a pretty sight or smell but rats seemed to like it and so did our terrier, Tip, whom my father had spent a great deal of time training to outwit the rodent residents. Most farms in those days had dogs of various types for different purposes: dogs for coursing (which probably covered poaching as well), working sheep-dogs, and the sporting dogs and terriers (often mongrels) for ratting. Strychnine could be bought at the chemist but many farmers, my father amongst them, wouldn't use it to kill rats for fear of poisoning other farm animals and so a dog for this purpose was essential. I am certain that there were many more rats then as grain was stored either in stacks or, after threshing, in sacks. The floors were not nearly as good as they are today, as concrete was expensive, and rammed chalk for floors could easily become riddled with rats.

The reason why I remember the cow drain so distinctly was because I had been got ready by my mother for the Sunday visit of one of my more formidable – or so she appeared to me – aunts. Although these visits seldom took place as she had to come by pony and trap, they were always treated as an event. Quite a lot of extra cooking was done on the Friday, and it was all put away out of everybody's reach until Sunday afternoon. The early high tea consisted of ham, salad and pickles and, as a special treat, tinned pineapple with cream. Lunch, which was served as soon as my aunt arrived, was not a particularly 'weighty' affair as nobody was ever quite certain what time she was coming, so high tea, prior to her going was, I suppose, meant to cover both lunch and supper! On this particular day I had been well prepared and told to stay clean, but I had decided to take Tip for a walk. Who led whom I am not quite certain but we arrived at the point where the slurry emerged from the cowhouse and was the playground for rats. It seems that, meaning to be helpful and with the aid of a broom handle, I tried to disturb a rat in order that Tip could get at it. The inevitable happened. Luckily I had been missed, but I still have a vision of my mother screaming to my father to come and help. Apparently I was not very concerned and, holding my broom handle which was keeping me from complete submersion, was pointing at a hole and saying, 'Tip, Tip, wat, wat'. At some cost to their own 'Sunday-best' clothes my father and mother hauled me out and the three of us emerged; and, as if exactly on cue, so did my formidable aunt and her jovial husband, who from that day on brought the subject up whenever he saw me, including the last time we met just before he died. I can't remember whether or not I suffered any actual punishment, but I certainly wasn't allowed to forget it and have often wondered how the public health authorities today would view the cowhouse sanitation of the 1920s.

Great Ryburgh was a marvellous village to be brought up in; at least I thought so. It had so many potential sources of interest and wonder for a child, and I am certain it had a great influence on me. The foundry, the railway station and the maltings were all in close proximity to each other. As well as farming, I have always been interested in the railway and it ran right through the centre of the parish. The line not only served a large catchment area of farms and carried the crops produced, but also, as there were no bulk deliveries in those days, brought a great deal of barley in sacks to the Ryburgh maltings, at one time reported to be the largest single block of maltings in the country. The railway also brought coal, pig iron and scrap to the adjacent Farmers' Foundry, serving the foundry with a siding to the east. Directly opposite, on the west side, a siding served the maltings. Except at the stations, the railway from Wells to Dereham was single track so that engines would bring in a train of trucks which were then pulled into a siding so that a train coming the other way could pass. The station had a complement of up to three horses, which had their own stables and pasture at the back of the station buildings and were used for shunting. A lot of the grain for the maltings came by rail, not in bulk, but always in 2-coomb sacks weighing 2cwt. Something that confused me for years was that they were always calculated and counted in quarters which were two sacks, 4cwt but 20 coombs to the ton.

Railway rolling stock was always built to a high standard, of very heavy wood and iron. The heavy sliding doors ran very easily and could be helpfully managed by us lads – not so the coombs of barley that all had to be man-handled. It is always salutary to look back on the amount of physical work needed to achieve anything in those days. What a knack the men had and how fast they could run with the sacks full of barley across their shoul-

Left to right. Me, Mack, Tip and brother Jack 1922.

ders. They took great pride in their prowess at the job – sometimes taking it to extreme lengths. One very well-proportioned chap called Fon Waller, who worked at the maltings, accepted a bet that he could jog a mile from the Boar public house to the Stibbard crossroads with a sack of barley (2cwt 16 stone) on his back during his lunch-time, all for a gallon of ale. History doesn't relate how the sack of barley got back, but he did it. However, years later he took on a similar wager, this time carrying a sack of peas which weighed 2½cwt, 20 stone. He did it this time too, but he never worked again as he suffered an enormous rupture.

Not all the grain came to the maltings by rail. Some, like my father's, came from local farms by horse-and-cart and some from other merchants' granaries or, from the few farmers who had one, by petrol lorry. Bridge Farm was only a mile from the maltings so all ours came by horse-and-wagon; two horses in shafts and one or two trace horses at the front. What marvellous fun it was to rattle along on the top of twenty to thirty coombs of barley from home up to the maltings and wait in the queue to unload. Working at the maltings, however, was an arduous job. The days were long and a minimum of six days a week was worked, all for 45s 0d. Indirectly there was quite a source of income for the older boys at the village school who at lunchtime would go and hold the heads of the horses bringing the wagons loaded with barley, while the waggoners nipped into the Crown or one of the other three pubs in Ryburgh. It was always worth a penny.

The grain that arrived in the railway trucks was unloaded, truck by truck, straight into the maltings' steeping tanks. These were large brick tanks lined with glazed tiles and watertight. Here it stayed for a period of about sixty to seventy hours, and during that time the water was drained off twice. Any chaff, dross or trash that came to the top as 'swimmings' was cleared off with a large hoe called a dowshie. When the grain had taken in enough water to make it grow it was transferred on to the floors above by pulley and skip, or by hand in a square box or hod carried by two men. For the next seven or eight days it had to be levelled and moved every few hours so that the shoots would continue to grow and convert the starches in the grain to sugars. The men worked in gangs of six or twelve in the vast low-ceilinged malt-houses, constantly turning and raking and hoeing the grain to keep it on the move and level. The buildings at Ryburgh were five stories high and the grain gradually worked its way along each floor, changing in appearance as it went from a rich golden colour at the outset to a pale yellow as the germination and drying out process took place. At this point, when the shoot was as long as the kernel itself, it was reckoned to be ready for the kilns. The heat on the floors was uniform and steadily increased from 60 degrees at the beginning, to 200 degrees four to five days later. During this time the men, working mostly in only trousers and boots, had to put up with terrible conditions. If the process became too dry, the grain had to be hand-watered from cans.

The next stage in the process was the loading of the kilns. The dried grain, called green malt by then, was shovelled into large skips which were hauled by hand and hoisted up into the kilns. Four companies of men worked at this in gangs of twelve and it was always a race between them, usually with pints for the winners! In the kilns the barley had to be turned frequently, the same as it had been on the growing floors in its 'green' stage, and wooden shovels were used for this purpose. The heat from the furnaces below through the slatted or perforated floors was almost beyond endurance and could only be tolerated for short periods at a time. These conditions also applied to the stokers who constantly shovelled a mixture of coal and coke on to the fires to keep up the steady temperature, increasing it as the malt-master, who kept his eye on the whole process, directed. The end result of all this truly 'sweated' labour was that the dry, and by now very dark brown, shoots were bagged up and sold back to farmers as malt culms for use in cattle feed. The malt itself was sent off to the maltings by rail, most of it to be made into beer or, if the quality was high enough, whisky and several other products.

It always seemed strange to me, and an odd bit of planning, that although the railway siding ran quite close to the maltings and the barley could be off-loaded and loaded semi-mechanically with the chain hoists direct from railway trucks, the Farmers' Foundry was built about 100yd back on the other side of the track. This meant the coal for smelting pig iron and scrap had to be hand-loaded from railway trucks on to carts just to be taken this very short distance to the Foundry. It was not the only time it was moved either, as furnaces in the smelting process had to be very carefully hand-filled. It was a great delight for us children to watch the white-hot liquid metal running down the little channels into the moulds, and twenty-four hours later, after cooling, see the moulds split. Out of the sand would appear large items like plough wheels, roll rings and pig troughs and very small pieces like plough points and the hundreds of gadgets and parts required in the building of machinery, mostly for farms. They also made doors for bread ovens, complete cast-iron cooking stoves, decorative fireplaces and flat irons, and door-knobs and knockers.

The Farmers' Foundry was a very far-sighted venture, started in 1890 by a few progressive farmers. I have since learned that the Universal 10 nhp engine was made by Edward Everett, Adams & Co. at Ryburgh. The works then were known as St Andrew's Works, after the church, and the founder and patentee, Mr Everett, also patented station slot machines, weighing machines and ice skates. He later emigrated to America taking his patents with him but died there penniless. It was at that time, in 1890, that it was taken over and its name changed to the Farmers' Foundry. By 1925 it was a limited company and the directors were all either engineers or farmers. Frank Perowne, a leading local farmer and great friend of my father's, was Chairman and one of the directors was Thomas Cooper of the famous Kings Lynn roller-bearing firm. Hector Middleton, whom I have known all my life, left school in 1925 and went there to work as an apprentice moulder. He has recently added to my already very vivid memories of the FFC. The men working there during Hector's time were twelve in the foundry, four in the machine shop, three employed on lathe work, four blacksmiths, three boiler-smiths, four painters and sundry others. Mr Harry Ely was the manager.

The machine shop at the works entrance was an absolute dream to any mechanically-minded lad and I shall never forget the sight, smell and sound of it. A steam engine drove the long overhead shaftings and the whole place was festooned with slapping, whirling belts, each one terminating at whatever machine it drove, be it drilling machine, mill, lathe, guillotine, blower or grinding wheel. All this, together with the faint puff, hiss and chug of the engine, produced a most marvellous cacophony of sound: and then there was that unforgettable smell of hot oil, steam and carborundum dust. A modern factory inspector's nightmare perhaps – but heaven to me! Next to the machine shop was the large shed where most of the implements made there were assembled. Some of the cultivating machinery I found boring – the horse-drawn rib and/or flat rolls for crushing the clods on the fields held no excitement as they were always the same. So were the ploughs, cultivators, water carts or four-wheeled iron hurdles for penning up sheep. However, some of the other machinery made there, like the steam engines, was very exciting.

Annexed to the assembly shop was the foundry itself. My mental picture is of a large low building that always seemed to be ankle deep in heaps of sand of various colours, from light fawn to jet black when it had been used in the moulds. Squatting over core boxes were the figures of the moulders, very carefully putting the patterns into the sand to make the necessary indents to receive the molten metal. They all used their own sets of tools which looked rather like a slightly larger than normal collection of dentist's tools, with a few culinary items thrown in. Most of the tools were hand-made by the owners and each had his own idea of what was a satisfactory tool for the job. The giant crucible where the ingredients were brought to a molten state had to be loaded. This was done laboriously by hand, from the top, as the crucible itself stood just outside the building and was about 10ft high; 6ft up was a platform on to which was thrown scrap, pig iron, coke and chalk in alternate layers according to what quality or type of metal was to be the end product. When the fire had been lit and blown with a mechanical fan running from the main machine shop shafting, the whole thing gradually got hotter and hotter until it became molten and ready for pouring. At the crucial moment the foundry master would pick out the clay plug at the bottom of the crucible and a small stream of molten metal would gurgle out. Two men would be ready with a receptacle to catch it, with others waiting their turn in line. When the cup was full they would walk as quickly as possible to the mould, pour the molten metal in through the blow-hole, get back into line and wait their turn for the next cup. This went on until the casting was finished or the crucible empty.

The other impressive part of the foundry was the elevator and paint shop. Here they made from timber and castings the vast elevators which were used on farms for taking the sheaves of corn from the ground up on to the stack. They were driven by gearing from a 'horse-works' and one of the jobs that boys like me got at harvest-time was to see that the horse kept going round and round underneath the elevator until it got too tired, or needed to stop for natural relief. The paint shop was also the social area of the foundry where the men had their lunches. It had a tortoise stove with a large pail on the top full of hot water which the men used to heat their bottles of cold tea.

Between the end of the nineteenth century and 1929 the Farmers' Foundry also produced twenty-nine portable engines in twice as many years. It took about two years to complete an engine from boiler plate to finished product, and what a magnificent sight they were in green and black livery, lined out in gold leaf. For the technically minded they were 7 nhp and as far as is known they were all sold locally; of the two remaining the last one, No. 29 made in 1929, is in the Bygones Museum at Holkham Hall and still works as smoothly as ever. The other is also still in this country somewhere. Although the majority of the work was done at Ryburgh some of the parts, like the drop-forged crankshafts, came from Dodman's or Savage's of Kings Lynn. The engines were used by those farmers who had sufficient acreage to justify keeping a set of threshing tackle on their farms, and who owned the necessary threshing machine to go with the engine. The description 'portable' was really a misnomer. Portable they certainly were in so far as they were on four wheels and could be moved from site to site or stack to stack, but they needed four horses to pull them about as they had no traction mechanism between the power unit on the engine and its wheels. They were much simpler to build and cheaper than a traction engine, but not really satisfactory for contract work when it was necessary to travel from farm to farm. Short distances within the limits of a farm could be coped with.

I was banned from the foundry at least once by my mother when I came back with my clothes as dirty and as black as the founders', with two of my fingers bent by passing them through a machine. One of them still is. But it was a magical place for a boy with my inclinations, and I couldn't be kept away. It was an experience which was to influence and nurture my interest in engineering, steam, and 'things mechanical' for the rest of my life.

CHAPTER THREE

Schooldays

My parents never explained to me why they decided to send me to school at the tender age of four, but I imagine that they were probably tired of looking for me in cow drains, or finding me perched precariously on the top of haystacks telling the world that I was thatching. I think my mother took far greater risks retrieving me from these alarming situations than I perhaps deserved. Leaving me to come in and eat when I was hungry might have been a wiser course. Their decision may also have been hastened by the fact that the school at Great Ryburgh was less than half-a-mile away from the farm, and the milk float passed it every morning as the school bell went. Whatever the reasons behind it I was duly enrolled at the Great Ryburgh Village School and started in the September before my fifth birthday. For the next twelve years I thought that schools were a great nuisance and from the beginning resented the interruption to my daily ritual of poking about the farm and being alternately Robin Hood or Rob Roy as the mood took me.

I am afraid that most of my school days were spent looking out of the window, but not at Great Ryburgh where the windows were sensibly put too high for gazing out of when the Victorians put up the building. The desks, which I am sure were made for three but sat six, were uncomfortable and the seats very hard. From the word 'go' I think more than anything I resented the lack of privacy. We didn't have desks with lids, but each had a small shelf underneath. This was quite satisfactory for slate and chalk and the odd book, but stopping bullseyes and apples from rolling out did present problems. Indeed, one of my first memories was seeing my bag of bullseyes disappearing into the coke-fired Tortoise stove which stood in the middle of the infants' classroom after being discovered by the Mistress. The cold classroom was another thing that I disliked intensely. Although the stove was capable of becoming red hot, the thrifty (not to say penny-pinching) outlook of Mr Skipper, the headmaster, ensured that it was usually only just warm. He seldom visited the infants, but when he did he invariably said, 'It is much too hot in here', and opened the windows and closed the flap controlling the draught which deadened down the fire. On wet days the guard surrounding the fire was festooned with the wet coats of those children who had them:

those who were unfortunate enough to come from families who couldn't afford a top coat sat in their wet woollen guernseys and the whole place steamed like a 'Turkish' bath. I only had one term at Ryburgh school whilst we lived in the village, but it was followed by two more when we moved to Testerton some two miles away. The ubiquitous milk float still went to Ryburgh Station most days, but when it didn't those of us from Testerton trotted to school in a little 'gaggle' on foot. There was one family of two girls and a boy who lived in a cottage in the Testerton farmyard who, on dry days, would sling their shoes round their necks and canter down the grass verge of the road barefoot to the outskirts of the village to save shoe leather!

Eventually my parents decided that I wasn't learning anything that would be of subsequent benefit to me at Ryburgh; although I was successfully acquiring a lot of bad language and unsavoury habits, not to mention doses of impetigo and head lice. Father didn't seem to mind about the complaints or the treatment, which was horrid, but he took great exception to a letter from the District Nurse with instructions on how to clean me up with Lysol disinfectant and sulphur paste. So they taught me to ride a bicycle and bought a second-hand one, which I rode to 'Miss' Applegate's private school in Fakenham. The bicycle was much too big and heavy for me and had to have 4 inch blocks screwed to the pedals so that I could reach them until I grew to fit it. The bicycle was a Wensum, made by the Hercules company, and it transported me every weekday morning to Fakenham as far as the gas-works on the outskirts of the town, some four-and-a-half miles. The manager of the gas-works was a bowls-playing friend of my father's and, as my parents thought that riding into the town was dangerous, I had to park my bicycle there. I liked this because on coking days when the burning coal was pushed out of the vats and sprayed with water it gave a magnificent show of sparks, like a tremendous firework display. How the men worked in the sulphur-laden air I shall never know, but I loved the smell of the coal tar, carcinogens and all! The thought, more than sixty years later, of a five-year-old cycling four-and-a-half miles morning and evening on a cycle that was much too large is horrifying, but the volume of traffic on the roads then was very small. If I did encounter anything it would be a very noisy lorry, a horse-and-cart or another bicycle, and only occasionally a car. Sometimes I was lucky enough to meet Ernie Betts, the postman, who was a very kind and gentle man. Although this was company for me he had to do a round trip from Fakenham to Stibbard, via Little and Great Ryburgh and Testerton – about twelve miles – so he needed to go at about twice my top speed. I can't think how my fat little legs stood it. However, I was able to catch him up when he stopped to deliver letters and, in fact, I used to deliver to some houses for him. My mother always said it helped me to learn to read.

'Miss' Applegate's – my new private school – had five other pupils of virtually the same age. John and Barbara Chapman, the butcher's children,

Kenneth Sinclair, the son of the headmaster of the local secondary school, Robert and Barbara Simpson, and me. 'Miss' Applegate lived in a bungalow in Radcliffe Road and used her living room as a school-room during term-time. She really was the kindest person imaginable, and although we always referred to her as 'Miss' Applegate, she was in fact married. Her husband Appy (Happy) Applegate was one of the funniest men I remember. He worked for the local Ford agent and 'did turns' at village concerts for charity. He was usually on our side and it's just as well he was for I think if his wife had known of half the pranks we got up to she would have closed the school. But he never 'split' on our gang. 'Miss' Applegate taught us reading, writing, arithmetic, and not much else, but playtime, after lunch at midday when we were let out, was a most memorable time. John and Barbara Chapman, children of the town's largest butcher, usually led the way to their father's slaughterhouse or we went to where Kenneth Sinclair lived and were allowed free range of the secondary school gymnasium if it wasn't being used. The other delight was to find 'Mr Appy' and mess around at Southgates where he worked. Southgates were coach builders as well as engineers and we were able to watch the cars and lorries being repaired and occasionally a body being built to special order. This idyllic existence for me, except when the wind was in the wrong direction for cycling, came to an end after just four months when 'Miss' Applegate's school closed, and I was transferred to Miss Dewing's at the 'Park Lane' end of Fakenham. Academically I didn't seem to do any better there and when Father had a good harvest in 1929 it was decided, on the advice of another bowls friend, to send me to the East Anglian School for Boys at Bury St Edmunds. The fact that I hadn't learned much by my seventh birthday didn't stand me in very good stead when my parents took me to see the headmaster of the East Anglian School for Boys, Dr Skinner.

The first shock to me, and I later gathered to my father as well who had never experienced boarding schools himself, was to be told by Dr Skinner that I must sit an entrance exam. Father knew my academic skills were very, very basic and so did I! Although I can't claim to remember it clearly, except for being absolutely terrified, I am told that I froze and made no attempt whatsoever to do any of the papers. My father was very angry, my mother was very emotional, and Dr Skinner was either sorry for all of us or very short of pupils, but whichever it was he said he'd take me the next term. I think he might have been short on numbers for although up till then the EAS had housed all its seniors and juniors in one large purpose-built Victorian building in Northgate Avenue, Bury St Edmunds, the school had just acquired a former private residence to hold its juniors, seven-to-nine-year-olds. It was called Hartley House and I became one of its inmates on its opening day. We were looked after by a splendid matron, Miss Corbyn, and a housemaster called Mr Blamey.

I remember the first night away from home at the East Anglian very well. Having handed me over to Mr Blamey my parents left very swiftly – my mother in tears. Pocket money and a book of stamps had been deposited with Mr Blamey and signed for; we were allowed 6d a week. My trunk was unpacked and my clothes stored in Matron's workroom. Overnight cases were stored under the bed beside a 'handless' pot emblazoned with the school crest. Every bed had one as there were only two sit-down lavatories upstairs in Hartley House. Tuck boxes were put in the cellar after Matron had inspected them and approved the contents. Jams, sauces, pickles, tinned beans and sardines were allowed – one little pot or tin per fortnight. One cake or packet of biscuits could be brought at the beginning of term, but no more until half-term. Table games like draughts, chess and snakes-and-ladders were allowed, but no playing cards. Toys were *not* allowed, especially cuddly ones, and if, prior to school, you had been sleeping with a bear or similar toy you soon got out of the habit. That sort of thing was for girls!

Discipline at the East Anglian was strict, but not severe. If you stuck by the rules life was tolerable but if you repeatedly transgressed then you could expect three warnings, followed by loss of privilege in the shape of missing games. I hated organised games anyway so that never bothered me. If you continued to flout the law the punishment was 'lines', copying out so many pages of a little blue spelling book we all had word for word. Strange that I'm not a better speller, for in the end I almost knew the horrid little book by heart. The penultimate punishment was bed with no tea and 'coventry', and the ultimate was six of the best – which hurt. However, you gained quite a lot of prestige if you could show off six clear bruises in the bathroom. Lessons each weekday were at Hartley House, but for special lessons such as singing and art we had to walk up to the main school. Morning prayers and gym also took place in the main building.

There was a strange ritual following morning prayers at the beginning of each new term, when Dr Skinner asked all the new Suffolk and Norfolk boys to come from the body of the assembly hall on to the platform and one by one made them recite the words that I remember only too well. 'Oi loike tew roide moi boike on a foine moonloight Froidy noight boi moi self'. In a way this was cruel as it caused a great deal of embarrassment to the unfortunate boys with the 'roight' sort of accent from the county of their birth, but on looking back one can see why he did it. At the time it was terrifying. However, as term progressed and accents improved – if to lose them was an improvement – it all turned to fun. By the end of the first term we had progressed to singing to the headmaster and the whole school in 'proper' English the folksong 'Cherry Ripe'. I still think it sounds better as 'Cherry Roipe' but I suppose that it's handy to be able to use both versions, particularly these days when to have a regional accent is the 'in' thing. This must rank as one of the first lessons I learned at the EAS.

Sundays were the worst days of all. To start with we all wore Eton suits which consisted of very short black jackets ('bum freezers'), long pin-striped trousers, white shirts and, worst of all, Eton collars. The Eton collar was a 3 inch band of starched white preformed cotton material over a sort of stiff cartridge paper, the whole thing bonded into an unyielding ring and fixed by a metal stud at the front and back of the shirt band. For people like me who had been endowed with very little neck between their ears and their shoulders, it resulted in a permanent feeling of being garrotted. The collars were worn with a silk blue and silver striped school tie, and the Eton collar pulled out over the thick collar of the jacket. It wasn't so bad for the chaps who had long thin necks, but for short thick-set people it caused excruciating discomfort. But worse was to follow as certain traditions went along with collars and ties. Firstly there was 'green tie' Sunday, which was always the third Sunday of term. On this day every new boy, for his first three terms, had to wear a bright green tie. If it had been only to show that he was a new boy I could have accepted it, but it also gave any boy who had been at the school for more than three terms the right to pull the green tie or make it as uncomfortable as possible for the wearer. For instance boys were tied up to radiators or taps, and sometimes three or four green ties, with their wearers, were tied together. I can't remember if I was ever told how the tradition started, but I do remember that it was a very uncomfortable one. 'Flash tie' Sunday, on the other hand, was fun. On the Sunday following 'green ties' any boy who had been there more than three terms could wear as gaudy a tie as he could find and believe me some that were worn, though over fifty years ago, would put today's in the shade.

Although the East Anglian was a Methodist school, religion was optional. 'Step' Sunday, however, was a very strange tradition. The Church of England boys all had to attend Matins each Sunday at the Cathedral, which was situated about one-and-a-half miles from the school on the other side of town. The Methodist Chapel was quite near the Cathedral so we were all lined up two-by-two in a crocodile – Methodists in front and Church of England behind. At the front of each denomination the new boys in each case were followed by a senior boy. The crocodile was preceded by the School Captain or Head Boy who would, at any time to suit himself, change step without giving any warning. As soon as this happened the pair of new boys behind him had to do likewise, by missing a step or giving a little skip. If they were not alert or paying attention then the older boy following them would give one or both a boot up the rear to jog their memory. This strange procession wound its way through Bury St Edmunds constantly skipping and trying to get 'in step' to avoid the boot. When I was about twelve I changed from Church of England to Methodist, having convinced my parents that it was after deep thought and studied conviction. The real reason was that occasionally the Methodist boys were invited out to lunch and sometimes tea as well by the kind people in the congregation of the chapel. Besides it wasn't quite so far to walk, and the hymns were more jolly and easy to sing. When the school moved from Bury St Edmunds to Culford in 1933 I changed back to Church of England because the church boys were taken to Bury Cathedral by bus which I liked, or they could attend the church in the Park which was also very pleasant. Moving the school out to Culford Hall, former home of the Earl of Cadogan, alas, put an end to those chapel teas. But one other tradition which may still go on, I don't know, was that each boy about to leave could choose his favourite hymn to be sung on the last (or if there were too many, the last but one) Sunday night service. I remember I chose 'O Come, O Come, Emmanuel', and when the 'Rejoice! Rejoice!' part came up at the end of each verse, the whole school ignored the 're's' and roared 'Joice! Joice!' etc. After Evensong on Sundays, when we had handed in our letters home, we were all given one toffee – apparently because a dear old lady had once left a sum of money to the school for toffees for the boys. This worked out at one toffee per boy per week. What happened when the numbers increased I don't know, but it was always fun trying to get an extra one by one subterfuge or another.

Talking about toffees reminds me that our pocket money (mine was 6d per week when I first went there in 1929 and rose by steady, very steady, increments to 2s 0d per week when I left in 1937) could be and was spent in the small tuck shop run by a charming old gentleman called Pop Lock – a sort of Mr Chips, except that he was not on the academic staff. Pop Lock looked after the tuck shop, the Scouts, and the needs – except nursing – of chaps in the sick room. He was a general confidant and had a sympathetic ear for anyone who needed it, and believe me we all did from time to time . . . boys and staff alike. He was a sort of 'fringe' staff confessor. Talking of 'fringe' staff, another person I was very fond of was Mr Abbott – or Pa Abbott as he was affectionately known. He was in charge of 'manual training'. When I first went to the EAS this was called carpentry, and I always think that it was pure snobbery that changed the title. Most of us practical boys, and a lot were farmers' sons like me and not very bright at ordinary subjects, slid into woodwork, handicraft and other more physical activities to make it look better on the end-of-term report. We all loved Pa Abbott and since I left I have thought many times about the things he taught me. When he was not taking a class Mr A was usually found fitting a new sash cord to a window, mending a door, making sets for the end-of-term plays, or taking care of the seemingly endless task of repairing desk lids. I asked him about this once and remember his reply to this day. He said. 'It's all very well learning history and geography, but first you need a good desk to sit at and to keep your books in'.

The dormitories were huge at the East Anglian – at least two of them were. I think the south and west each held fifty beds, but the top dormitory was smaller. Each dormitory had a sort of fenced-off piece in the corner

Family Group 1934.
Father Me Betty Jack Mother

where a master slept. What a rotten job he had with fifty potential problems each night varying from sickness and incontinence, to coughing and snoring. He also had to see to it that his charges were reasonably clean and well turned out each day. In the top dormitory of the EAS there was a long lead sink with four cold taps, and each night and morning you took a tin bowl and made the best of it. Sometimes in the winter the taps were frozen – a god-send for you went to bed a bit grubby and got up the next day just the same! Each boy had to take at least one bath per week and lists were put up on the notice-board with the timetable to ensure that nobody forgot. The sickroom was a good place to be if you weren't too ill. The standard of meals was better than downstairs and although Miss Hand, the senior matron, kept an eagle eye on you, with the help of Pop Lock and your chums on the outside, life could be more tolerable than school and you automatically got out of organised games. Incidentally I always felt that the term 'organised games' was a misnomer, as games always seemed thoroughly disorganised to me except for House Matches which were refereed by a member of staff. On other occasions teams picked their own referees for matches and these were usually a complete shambles, as the ref was always someone like me who didn't like playing and had no idea of the rules anyway.

On reflection I realise what opportunities I missed at Culford. The highly qualified staff, under Dr Skinner, were very good teachers of high academic standard, but in me I fear they met their match. My failure as a pupil was not their fault. I was simply not interested in learning most of the subjects they taught and could not, or would not, accept that it was necessary to become qualified in even the basic subjects. I now know that I am and always have been dyslexic, a word that we had never heard of in those days. In my near-seventies certain letters still come out in reverse order, and some words I simply cannot spell. However, I've managed by spelling phonetically (and given half a chance I'd spell that with an 'f'), and usually have a dictionary to hand or, better still, wives or secretaries who are good spellers. Still, I always have to double check when taking down telephone numbers as the last two digits, five times out of ten, come out in reverse order.

The staff at Culford persevered but they never got me as far as school certificate standard. In fact, I never even sat for the mock exams. They never quite gave up as there were a dozen boys in the same bracket – all farmers' sons and all about twelve or thirteen years old. Dr Skinner's solution was to take us out of the main-stream curriculum and put us in a form called, appropriately enough, the 'Remove'. Three specialist teachers came twice a week and taught us farming, basic accountancy and simple engineering. We had a token amount of English, history and geography with some chemistry, physics and biology – the latter I didn't do too badly at. It was a far-sighted thing to do, and I wish now I had made more use of the opportunities it offered. But, although the extra subjects were far more tolerable, my mind was at home on the farm. In my penultimate report, when I was fifteen, Dr Skinner wrote a note to my father saying that his son was wasting too much of his (father's) money and too much of the school's time, and that I had told him that my only ambition was to be a tractor driver. My father, bless him, replied that his son would make a very good tractor driver and he would like him to leave at the end of term.

After I left Culford Dr Skinner and I became firm friends and occasionally he came and stay at my home. He once told me that he always knew there was something I wanted to do that they could help me with, but they just couldn't find out what it was. This was only partly true for something Dr Skinner and his staff did recognise was that, together with half-a-dozen other farmers' sons I had a natural engineering 'bent' that could be developed. So he arranged for an acquaintance of his, a Mr Allen who owned a garage at Bury St Edmunds, to come to Culford two afternoons each week and teach us 'basic engineering'. For our use, six vices were attached to a crude bench on the wall in a building which had been part of the estate workshop before Culford was converted into a school.

We expected Mr Allen to arrive with all sorts of engines and tools and general engineering paraphernalia, but no such luck. When he arrived all he had in the back of his car were half-a-dozen old hacksaw frames, with a good supply of new blades, files, and a new set square. He spent the first lesson explaining the importance of angles and how every budding engineer must learn how to saw and file metal to fine tolerances and get angles exactly right. This he demonstrated on flat pieces of metal. At the next lesson he gave us each a used cylinder head from an old Model T Ford (I discovered later these were renowned for their hardness), and told us to cut out a piece exactly 2 inches square from one corner. This may sound and look a simple thing to do, but believe me it wasn't. The cast-iron, which had been repeatedly heated and cooled when it was part of a car engine, was very, very hard. It took each of us hours and hours and many hacksaw blades to achieve a square, only to be told by Mr Allen, 'It isn't exactly square, or smooth. Do it again using one of the other corners. You've got three more to go at.' It took most of us all the term – over twenty afternoons – to get just one piece accurate. But it taught me how to hacksaw and file, and the importance of accuracy when working with metal or any other material. Many years later when designing and building machines and farm implements I thought of Mr Allen and remembered the occasion when my father asked me why there was a charge for hacksaw blades on his end-of-term school bill. I didn't realise how valuable Mr Allen's disciplined training was then, but I do now. Those blades were worth every penny.

Several years after I had left the EAS I went back to an Old Boys' reunion, and one of my nephews who had just recently been sent to Culford told me that on his first day, when he was exploring and finding out where everything was, he noticed the boards on the walls of the dining hall full of names of people who had gained honours, going back to the early days when the school was founded in Bury St Edmunds. He was going laboriously through the names when the door opened and in walked the Headmaster, who apparently said, 'Ah, young Joice . . . are you looking for your uncle's name on the honours board, because if so you are wasting your time for you won't find it there. I don't think he ever passed an exam during the whole of the time he was here. However, I have to admit that since he left the cricket pitches haven't looked quite so well – neither have the tennis courts been marked out with such precision!' So, although my academic accomplishments were precious few, it consoles me to know that some of my more practical achievements didn't go entirely unappreciated.

CHAPTER FOUR

Testerton: First Impressions and Family Life

Although I was not quite four years old at the time, I can distinctly remember the move from Bridge Farm, Ryburgh to Testerton. Both farms belonged to Mr (later Sir) Thomas Cook and formed part of his estate. By exchanging Bridge Farm for Testerton, Father more than doubled the land he farmed since Testerton comprised 900 acres. A couple of years later his holding was further increased to 1200 acres by the addition of the adjoining Westwood Farm. The road through the long straggling Ryburgh village to Testerton due west of Bridge Farm had not yet been tarred and was very dusty. Although tree-lined, it had broken down gates and high unkept hedges with badly neglected ditches alongside them – the result of the current farming depression. The previous tenants had had a very rough time and the farms were in a very sad state but the potential was there to bring them back to a high state of fertility. At Testerton the main premises were enormous and there were three smaller sets of bullock boxes on the perimeter as well. When the Westwood farm was added, it also had a large set of premises and a very big house, walled garden and seven cottages. In his agreement with the estate, Father negotiated permission to sublet the Westwood farm house and garden.

To a child's eye the biggest difference at Testerton was the house itself. Until this moment in my life we had lived in a house which was no larger than two small cottages, but Testerton Hall was a hall in the true sense. It was a large red brick house built in 1802, with a very fine Welsh blue slate roof, and later additions had made the accommodation even more spacious. On the ground floor there was a large dining room, a drawing room, a breakfast room, two back sculleries, an enormous kitchen, with two pantries, a large butler's pantry with servants' hall, kitchen and pantry, and a small downstairs washplace and cloakroom. Upstairs there were nine bedrooms and one enormous bathroom, probably converted from one of the bedrooms, and four attics. The bathroom had two lavatories and a large cast-iron bath, which was fed with hot water from the kitchen range below. The range doubled as a two-oven cooking stove with a back boiler and just about gave sufficient hot water for bathing. The Hall was described in the Deeds as 'a gentleman's residence', and it had certainly been built for a farming family used to a much more lavish standard of living than that to which we were accustomed.

On the actual day of the move every stick of furniture at Bridge Farm and all the other ancillary effects were loaded on to horse-and-carts and moved out in convoy to Testerton. Father's Model T had all the smaller personal things stacked on or tied to it, with my brother and me squashed into what was left of the front passenger compartment. My mother rode her bike. The most potent memory I have was my first sighting of the new house, The car must have hit a large pot-hole in the gateway of the drive for I distinctly remember that everything in the Model T seemed to rise up, including us, and when it all settled down again a large bowl of dripping and jelly had inverted on top of my head. I arrived at the front door soaked in the most delicious tasting consommé, and I have never lost my taste for it since.

After my clean-up came the great exploration. Getting lost in completely new territory is not funny for an almost-four-year-old, but my brother Jack seemed to delight in taking me to the far ends of this new terrain and then disappearing. A splendid walled garden covering about two acres surrounded the house and it contained all the features that go with a Victorian gentleman's garden, a greenhouse, potting shed, apple store, etc. It was all very impressive and intimidating. The garden itself was beautifully laid out with a criss-cross of gravel paths bordered by small, 3 foot high, box hedges. Box is a very slow-growing shrub and these must have been at least a hundred years old. In more affluent times they had been kept beautifully trimmed, but by 1924 farming was into a depression and the hedges had got out of hand. My father soon had a pair of horses there and pulled up the box borders. Then, having got into the tidying up mood, he harnessed the Suffolk pair with a long wagon rope to the top of the age-old Virginia creeper that covered the Hall, and with a swish on the horses' backsides with a twig and a 'giddup' he stripped the beautiful creeper off the walls as easily as peeling a banana: and pulled out half the mortar between the bricks at the same time! I suppose it did save the trimming costs in the garden and round the house, but the house itself lost its lovely green mantle, which had turned a glorious red in the autumn when the leaves changes. The original trunks of the Virginia creeper were a good 4 inches in diameter so like the box it must have been there for many decades. Father cut them off and the roots were dug out, and it took my mother twenty-four years to grow replacements. Father's excuse in later years for taking the creeper off was that it kept the house damp. In fact, until the whole place was re-pointed it was a lot wetter without it, and my mother made certain that he never forgot his misplaced zeal! Many years later when the sore point of the demise of the creeper came up in discussion

Father admitted that he had been hasty, but said it had done him good at the time because he felt that he had made a start on the new farm.

The move soon revealed serious shortcomings in the size and quantity of our furnishings. These had been quite adequate for our needs at Bridge Farm, but they seemed to shrink to less than meagre proportions when transposed to their new setting at the Hall. So for the first few years we lived in the huge dining room, with its enormous open wood fire. This is where we had all our meals and family evenings. The room was lit by a very big ornate brass paraffin lamp hanging from the centre of the ceiling over the table, and with two small hand paraffin lamps and sundry Wee Willie Winkie-type candles in holders on the sideboard. We all took one of these with us on journeys made to other parts of the house after dark. There was also a hurricane lantern which Father used when checking the cattle or sheep last thing each night. There was no other lighting, although in 1937 my father did put in a limited calor gas installation serving three rooms and the stairs. The rest of the house was still paraffin lamp or candle-lit, and there was no electricity at Testerton until after the end of the war in 1945. I am sure on reflection that the small amount of furniture in relation to the size of the house worried my father. Over the next forty years a great deal of his spare time and money was spent furnishing all those huge rooms. In fact, when my parents moved to the smaller house they built for their retirement in Fakenham, the furniture sale alone lasted two long days. My mother used to say towards the end of their time at Testerton that if Father bought another chair there would be no room left to sit on them.

Mother's regime for the family was just the same at Testerton as it had been at Bridge Farm. Friday night was bath night and the rest of the week you did your best from a hand basin, washing up as far as possible and down as far as possible whilst standing on a towel in front of a wash-stand complete with a bowl filled from a brass water-can carried up from downstairs. I missed the nice warm kitchen at Ryburgh and didn't like being stripped down in this very large and not very warm (in fact, come to think of it, not warm at all) bathroom with its cold lino floor.

The water pumping system at Testerton was basic but it was quite advanced for its time. There were, in fact, three separate systems. For the house, all the down-pipes from the roof led to a brick underground tank, quite large, about 15ft x 15ft x 15ft. This water wasn't used for drinking, though, as occasionally the odd starling or sparrow would float down in it, and quite a lot of caterpillars from the various roses and creepers that Mother constantly tended. The tank was quite close to the house and one of the cowmen was paid 6d a week extra to pump the water from it up into another tank in the roof with a long-handled lead pump attached to the wall near the back door. This water, too, had to be strained and one of my mother's lyle stockings attached to the outlet from the pump into the tank served this purpose. The stocking was changed when extraneous matter appeared in the bath! The rain water was very soft compared with the piped supply from the well, which was diverted into the tank in the house at times of drought. There was also a small tank of hard water feeding one tap in the kitchen, and this was for drinking.

There were two other systems for the farm premises and all the animals. One was a ram, which was a hydraulic pump and extremely simple. But it used about nine-tenths of the water from an open ditch in the valley to lift one-tenth of the water into large tanks in the barn. The water had to be piped from the ram to the farm premises, a matter of half a mile, and rose about 50ft on the way. However, the machine was very, very simple and required no power other than the weight of the water to make it work, and apart from the inlet being subject to blockage by frogs it was very successful.

Quite close to where the ram was located near a stream was a large well – 10ft in diameter and about 120ft deep. This had an iron-framed windmill on top which drove a plunger pump halfway down the well itself. I remember the windmill being built soon after we arrived at the farm. It was very successful if there was a good breeze, but on still days it obviously didn't work. After it was installed Father soon got very fed up with being told, 'You will have to get the plumber because there's no wind and there's a frog in the ram!' But I learned a great deal from Dick Blackburn, who was the plumber. Although he lived at North Elmham about ten to twelve miles away, he cycled to work with an enormous box of tools and often a few lengths of pipe strapped to his bike. A very easy-going man, nothing seemed to bother him. We were having lunch one day when the cowman frantically banged on the kitchen window, shouting that Dick Blackburn had been repairing the pump down the well, but had disappeared. We all rushed out of the house and to the bottom of the pasture where the windmill and well were. My father shouted through the open door which was part of the lid of the well, 'Are you all right, Dick?' and from the bottom, 120ft down, came the answer 'No – my fags are wet!' Apparently he had slipped off the bearers which held the pump halfway down at about 60ft, and had dropped the remaining 60ft straight into the water at the bottom. In later years we always chaffed Father about this incident because apparently he then said, 'Well don't go away,' (as if Dick could) 'we'll get a rope!' I can see Dick now being hauled out of the well with a very badly damaged leg. My father loaded him and his bike and tools (which he insisted on taking with him) into the Model T and off they went to Dereham hospital. Dick Blackburn was a very humorous man, but talking about the accident more seriously at a later date he said that it was a good job he fell down the second half of the well for there were pieces of wood and stretchers as far down as the pump. From the pump bearers onwards though there were no obstructions until you hit the water. The upshot of this incident was that Father installed a small American single cylinder petrol engine at the top of the well which drove a new pump. In fact, by the time I was twelve I knew the best way down to the pumps myself and often went down for a lark or to pack the glands of the pumps with Russian tallow – that is until Mother found out and from then on the well was not only out of bounds but locked.

During the early days at Testerton the only domestic help my mother had in her large new home was a lady called Mrs Fenn, who lived in the village and walked the two-and-a-half miles to and from work morning and night. She used only very basic tools, a pail, scrubbing brush and dwile (floor cloth), dustpan-and-brush and dusters. There was no such thing for us as a vacuum cleaner, not even a Ewbank carpet sweeper. But in any case the only carpet we had was in front of the fire in the living room. On the rest of the floors, apart from the drawing room which was boarded, we had Norfolk Pammets. These were scrubbed regularly by Mrs Fenn and always seemed to be, and indeed were, damp. A year after moving my mother issued an ultimatum. She had to have more help in a house of that size and two fifteen-year-old girls from the village were moved in as maids. Mother's notebook shows that they were paid a half-a-crown (2s 6d or 12½p) per week each. They were provided with two morning dresses and a blue overall, one afternoon dress, two aprons, two caps and a pair of shoes, together with their keep. They had to buy their underclothes and stockings and other private purchases out of their 2s 6d. Every morning the girls were called from their beds by my mother at 6.30 a.m. One got the fires going and did the living room, stairs, bedrooms etc., and the other saw to the kitchen range, washed and packed the previous night's egg collection and scrubbed the sculleries and washhouse, which was annexed to the back kitchen. That was where Mrs Fenn did the washing on Mondays and where my mother dressed poultry and prepared anything else that was going to market. The girls' afternoon work was dusting – a never ending job in a house with open fires, smoky oil lamps and dusty brick floors. My mother still did all the cooking in the same way as she had at Great Ryburgh, and also the ironing, although the girls had to put all the linen sheets and pillow cases through the wringers.

The farm buildings at Testerton were vast compared with those at Great Ryburgh. The cowhouse held a hundred cows and hand milking was still the order of the day. The barn and granary were large enough to seat 300 people, and I remember seeing it used for this purpose on the occasion of my brother's twenty-first birthday. As a small child I found the granary one of the most exciting places of all. After the corn had been threshed in the stackyard, the sacks of wheat, oats or barley were winched up through the trap-door in the floor using a hand-operated chain winch, or sometimes carried up the close-stepped stairs across the shoulders of the men. Most of them were big strong chaps who had the strength to carry up to 20-stone sacks on their backs. The less well-built ones relied on the knack of getting the loads exactly balanced and keeping moving. They hoisted the strong coarse jute bags from the back of a cart and with short quick steps climbed the granary stairs and crossed to the slowly growing heap of grain. Then with a little jump they let go the mouth of the sack, which they had held tight with the right hand, and the corn ran out on to the heap. They made it look so easy and graceful, almost like dancers; but, believe me, it wasn't. It needed fitness, strength and skill. I learned to appreciate this later in my twenties when I had to help load up sacks of grain. The dust was unimaginable, clogging eyebrows, nose and mouth, so a sack with the corners reversed and punched in was worn like a Father Christmas hood. This helped to save chafing on the back as a thin shirt gave no protection, and shoulders soon became raw and itched like mad during the night.

The Testerton stables, too, were very extensive, big enough to house and service six teams of horses. They each had their individual standings annexed to which was a loose box for foaling, and each team had a harness room and chaff house. There were lofts above the stables, surmounted by a dovecot permanently full of pigeons. In the spring they laid their eggs in the hundreds of little nesting boxes – and what a terrible smell went with that.

Although Father started at Testerton with six teams of eight horses, it wasn't long before he realised that the future lay with tractors and in 1925 he bought his first tractor, a Rushton. The tractor did away with the need for three teams of horses, and for several men on the labour book – and it released for growing cash crops the land previously needed to feed and keep the horses. The day the tractor arrived I felt that I was in heaven. I had been with Father when he went to a demonstration on the showground of the Norfolk County Show, which was held that year at Fakenham. It was absolute bliss to think that we actually had one that I could go and watch, and ride on. It was always warm sitting facing the driver, squeezed in between the rear mudguard and steering column, and the flock of seagulls that followed the plough searching for worms provided a constant and ever-changing show. I often used to take my lunch and sit with Charlie Howe, father's tractor driver, and can remember many of his stories. Charlie was comparatively well off, for on top of his statutory 12s 0d per week he got 6d a day extra for tractor maintenance. For this sum he had to ensure that the tractor was kept going until five o'clock in the evening, and then he was obliged to fill it up with fuel and 'grease-up' for the next day in his own time.

Charlie also did three nights' work per week in the village on the 'honey cart', paid for by the local council. Father owned the cart and lent him a horse, for several of the cottage pail toilets on the farm were emptied by Charlie, as well as those in the rest of the village. Mother used to tell me not to get too close to Charlie as his night soil operation was a sticky and smelly business! I remember years later I tackled him on the subject and asked him whether his night soil job was worthwhile. I shall always remember his reply. 'People think that's a messy job going up and down garden paths with pails of other people's shit, but if the shit stink, the money don't.' I don't know how much he got for the job, but, with the exception of one or two houses in the parish, the necessary amenity was down the garden and Charlie visited them all at least once a week. The operation couldn't be divided equally between the three nights, for some houses with more occupants required visits more often than the newly-wed couple for instance.

Lavatories were much more interesting in the days before the advent of manufactured toilet paper like 'Bronco'. Most people used squares of newspaper tied on a string, but the upper-crust had Gamages or some other smart catalogue cut up. Many of the privies were twin, or occasionally, three seaters and all were situated some distance from the house or cottage. There was always a smell, but if the operation was properly conducted with a sprinkling of quick lime, it wasn't too bad. Even so most people trailed honeysuckle and roses over and round the door of the hut, and there were always heart-shaped holes in the doors for ventilation. A favourite trick on Bonfire Night for the more rowdy elements in the parish was to wait for the occupants of a house to visit the privy last thing at night and then drop a firecracker at an appropriate, or rather inappropriate, time at the back. Even without these seasonal hazards a visit to the privy could obviously be quite alarming and uncomfortable on your own at dead of night or if the weather was bad, so it often became a sort of family excursion, led by father with a lantern.

At Testerton of course, we had edged up the social ladder, at least in this respect, and the mahogany-seated water-closet next to the vast bathroom at Testerton was a rather plush, if splashy, affair, actuated by a brass ornamental handle which was lifted as the user stood up. Even so, it could still be a hazard for a five-year-old, as it was necessary to stand on the seat in order to raise the handle high enough for a good flush, and at night it was still a candle-lit affair.

My father hardly ever used the car when we lived at Ryburgh, but it was in constant use at Testerton and he always went to Fakenham market on Thursdays, and Norwich market and the Corn Hall on Saturdays. Now and again he went to other markets if he needed to buy any horses, cattle, sheep or pigs, and this meant an occasional trip to Burnham, Dereham or Kings Lynn. We were coming back from a trip to East Dereham one day when he decided to call on Fred Rivett, a farmer friend of his, with a view to buying some sheep. Whilst he was looking over the sheep my mother and I went indoors to see Mrs Rivett, and the family's latest status symbol – the wireless set. It was a plain black box with dials on the front and a glass accumulator attached to the back, together with a heavy square high-tension battery and a small grid-bias battery. Two wires disappeared from behind the set through the window frame; one, about fifty yards long, went to the nearest tree for the aerial, and the other to a copper peg in the ground – the earth. Both wires had enormous switches which were in the 'on' position when the set was working, but were turned off at night or when the weather looked stormy in case of lightning. There was no loudspeaker but two single earphones, each on a stick. Mrs Rivett pressed one of these to my ear and lo and behold music was playing. My father, who had seen wireless in action as a theatre turn in Winnipeg, had often told us about this 'miracle' but I didn't believe him until I actually heard it for myself. It was another five years before we had a wireless set for ourselves at Testerton, and then we were only allowed to have it on for an hour or so in the evening when Father listened to the news. The low tension batteries, or accumulators, had to be taken to a garage in the local town to be charged and they only had about a six-hour life between charges.

That other miracle of invention, the telephone, came in 1926 – four years before the wireless. The new Exchange was at Fakenham and in order to get 'connected' Father had to supply the labour to dig the holes for the posts. I think I watched every one of those posts put in over the 4 miles from Fakenham to Testerton. The telephone number we were given was Fakenham 63 and, in fact, my father kept this number, with the addition of a few digits when telephones became automatic, until he died. In those days, of course, one lifted the receiver and an operator would immediately ask you what number you wanted to ring. In a small exchange like Fakenham the operator would know everybody, and indeed a lot of the people you were going to speak to. Consequently you would often be told, 'It's no good ringing them – they've gone to . . .'. There were two operators at Fakenham, one full-time and one part-time who did the evening shift. The part-time operator was George Edwards: the man who was also involved in the formation of the National Union of Agricultural Workers and later became a member of Parliament. Indeed he was the first Labour member to be knighted. In later years he would get quite 'stroppy' with people who knew him well if they called him *Sir* George, but with people he didn't know he would always insist on the title.

Animals played a large part in the life and work of all farms during these years, and Testerton was no exception. We were encouraged as children to have as much contact with animals as possible. Cats, although to a certain extent treated as pets, were definitely farm cats and had to earn their living. They lived in and around the farm premises helping to keep down vermin and the only food given to them each day was at the dairy door. This consisted of all the pail and churn drainings and rinsings. After each cow was milked, the pails were stood on a frame to drain while the cowman entered the milk yield on a sheet against the appropriate cow's name. Hygiene was not as strict as it is today. The Milk Recorder came once a month and watched the milking operation, and checked to see that there was no obvious variation which might indicate that the figures were not correct. He also took a small sample from each churn which was sent away to be tested for butter fat or adulteration by added water. Before the days of the Milk Marketing Board this service was run by the County Council in conjunction with the county analyst and was wide open to abuse, through carelessness if not deliberate fraud. The milk from several cows would be combined in each seventeen gallon churn and if the Recorder didn't mix that churn thoroughly with a plunger it could result in a very misleading reading. Anyway the cats always looked very well fed on the churn drainings. The dogs were all working dogs and mostly lived outdoors in kennels, each attached by a chain to a long taut wire which enabled the dog about fifty yards freedom to run up and down for exercise and also deal with intruders at night.

We children had rabbits and guinea pigs and looked after the ferrets, and also had the use of the shepherd's pony. I once had a pet fox which my father brought home as a cub one day after the foxhounds had hunted over the land. It must have been about a week old and I expect its mother had been killed. After a lot of persuasion it took milk from a fountain pen filler, then from a baby's bottle and teat and finally got on to minced meat. The smell from a fox is very strong so it lived in the barn and became quite tame. Eventually it had to be given away because it was a vixen, and one night about forty of mother's growing pullets were massacred. 'Foxey' got the blame for luring one of her wild chums to see her. She was heard baying at the moon, it was spring and she was obviously in season, so in the end she went to a good home with the local grocer. He had a large garden and no poultry. Later her scent glands were removed, which reduced her personal odour and she lived on in the lap of luxury, even going with the grocer to the 'local' each night. She didn't like the beer but milk was provided for her on the bar counter.

A certain amount of dealing always went on between various members of the family. My Uncle George, with his butcher's shop at Melton Constable, bought fat bullocks, pigs and sheep from my father and was always prepared to take a casualty in the shape of an animal (cow, bullock or pig) that had a broken leg, or even the odd 'unthrifty' one. Although Grandfather Bailey was a recognised dealer (indeed a lot of his time was spent visiting other farms and markets together with the odd pub – after all his pony had to be fed, watered and rested as well as himself), my paternal Grandfather Joice was also, in a small way, a dealer. He used to deal more with the smallholders and people who had allotments, all of whom had a pig, often a sow. If this was the case then every so often there was a litter, or a part-litter of pigs to be disposed of. He would go round with a small pig float, buy what pigs were for sale, bring them to his farm and sort them into convenient lots to match orders from interested large farmers. Sows in those days usually brought up litters numbering between seven to eleven piglets. The first-born being first out was usually the strongest and therefore got to a forward teat which had the best supply of milk. Nearly every litter had a weakling or runt who usually attached himself to a back teat. If he survived at all he remained the smallest. However, with very careful nursing and lots of attention these little chaps could survive and some, whilst not fully catching up with their brothers and sisters, could even make reasonable animals. My grandfather used to give these 'peppermints', as they were called, to his grandsons. Two came my brother's way and were, I suppose, the start of Jack's farming enterprise. I envied him and developed an ambition to own a couple of pigs to go with the rest of my personal menagerie.

One day when I was about seven years old I was in Fakenham market watching the pigs being sold – there were hundreds. Mr Long, the auctioneer, came to a pen containing two poor little 'peppermints'. They had obviously been taken from two litters because, being so much smaller, they would detract from the value of the rest. Mr Long walked along the rows asking for bids and no one spoke. He didn't stop, he just said, 'No bid', and carried on. When the sale was over I found Mr Long and asked him if I could buy the two little pigs, but he said I had better ask the owner, who turned out to be my Grandfather Bailey. I went over to Grandfather and said, 'Will you sell me those two little pigs – I've got a shilling.' The deal was struck – two pigs for a shilling. They were very small and weak, but I put them in a wooden box and tied them on the back of my bike, and off I went home. When pigs from different litters are put together they will invariably fight and a favourite old trick is to pour a couple of pints of molasses or black treacle over them: by the time they have licked the sticky treacle off each other they all smell the same so they don't know which is one from another litter. When I got home I took a tin of treacle from my mother's larder and twice each day smeared a spoonful of her best golden syrup over my precious little pigs. When Grandfather Bailey visited us a few weeks later I took him to see them. 'Well' he said, 'you've done very well. I thought you would have lost them,' and gave me the shilling back. At least it proved that little pigs do thrive on golden syrup, a fact I was to recall later in my pig-keeping career. Not long after the pigs I bought a goose with the same shilling and brought it home from Fakenham market tied down in the box on the back of my bike, the goose facing backwards! Now I had also started keeping poultry.

I suppose it was those two little pigs and the goose that started off my first small farming enterprise, and it was almost a secret to me alone as my parents were far too busy to check up on what went on in a small disused building called 'the dungeon', complete with a little bullock yard, situated out of the way at the back of the stables. I think that these buildings were the original ones that serviced the Testerton farm several decades before it became a much larger farm, and they were superseded by much larger premises. It was a marvellous set up: one loose box for my pigs and in the open yard my goose, a clutch of chickens, and eventually a couple of Aylesbury ducks and a wild mallard, which I caught because it had a broken wing. The mallard conveniently laid and hatched out a clutch of eggs. Soon I was able to take the ducklings to Fakenham market in the box on the back of my bicycle. I only got a few pence for them but I also managed to cadge a couple of turkey poults from my grandmother, who had quite a large flock of turkeys and was well-known in the area for her skill in dressing poultry. She was a perfectionist in the art. Every incision made in the birds for evisceration purposes was carefully sewn up with white cotton and invisible to the eye. At Christmas her birds were packed in hampers and sent by train to a butcher in Norwich, each with a sprig of holly on the breast.

Every morning before school, my first job was to feed the animals and birds in the dungeon, then muck out and litter down with straw. In time the two 'peppermint' pigs weighed about eight stone each and had to go to the bacon factory with my father's. It was a sad day, but with the money they made I was able to buy an in-pig gilt. I bought her from a farmer in the next village who told me that she was due to pig in about a month. I walked her home, a very slow job that took all day as she was fairly heavy with pig. Father's pigman, Chris Futter, told me that I shouldn't have walked her all that way as it might have caused her to abort and, what was worse, to eat her newly born pigs. He advised that I watch her very carefully. I did. She must have been the most watched pig in all of Norfolk! I sat with her almost day and night. It was summer-time, nights were short, and I dozed in the straw with my beloved sow. Eventually she farrowed and after I had sat with her virtually day and night for ten days she popped the first six piglets out when I was having my breakfast. However, I saw the last five born, and I think it was the greatest thrill of my young life to actually own a sow and a litter of eleven. Although good mothers, sows are notorious for rolling on their offspring as they lie down to expose their teats to their young. But I was lucky, she was a very good mother and brought up all eleven, and in doing so taught me more about pigs than I would have learned any other way for during the first couple of weeks until the piglets were old enough to scamper away, we were inseparable. It was a great reward, until the sad day six months later when they all had to go to the bacon factory; but by that time my sow was well on the way to having another litter to soften the blow. I think it must have been at this point that my father woke up to the fact that I had been steadily carrying small sacks of pig meal, poultry meal and corn for the chickens and ducks out of the granary. After that I had to pay for what I used, but nothing was ever weighed so they were always pretty big sacks for a small price.

Although the Large White pig was generally recognised by pig breeders as

Father and me with Middle White sow.

the most economical pig to fatten, when it was crossed with a Large Black the progeny showed blue and white marked pigs. These were favoured by the butchers, but as a boy I always had a hankering for the pug-snouted Middle Whites. I was able to buy a couple of pure-bred sows, but the problem was getting them in-pig to a pure-bred boar. It wasn't worth owning a boar to serve just two sows, so it meant that every time mating came round I either had to take my sow to the boar or bring the boar to the sow. Luckily when my enterprise began there was a farmer living in the next parish some three miles away who had a Middle White boar and I was able to walk my sow sedately across country to her nuptials. The problem was that if she wasn't absolutely in season or was just past it, there might be a wasted journey or, at best, a long wait or an overnight stay for her. One of these journeys nearly ended in disaster. It was a Saturday and I had set off with the sow directly after breakfast in reasonable weather, but by eleven o'clock, when we were barely half-way there, it turned very, very hot. Luckily there was a pond on the way where I normally stopped for the 'old girl' to have a drink and a rest, but on this occasion she lay down in the soft mud at the edge of the pond and refused to budge again. Most of the afternoon I pushed and pulled but to no avail. I shuttled to and from home to let my mother know where I was, but as it began to get dark the 'old lady' was still in her mud bath. Eventually my father – under protest – brought four hurdles, two men, a set of pulley blocks and a cart rope and physically winched her on to the side of the pond. We left her there quietly munching some barley meal, apparently quite content to stay the night.

Next morning, soon after daylight, I was back to continue the journey only to find that the sow had uprooted the hurdles with her short stubby snout and disappeared. I searched for some time without success, and finally heard a strange muffled snorting and clumping sound a few hundred yards away. It came from the bottom of a pit where rubbish had been tipped. There was the sow, sitting on her backside like a dog, and on her snout was an empty Tate and Lyle golden syrup tin. Obviously the small amount of treacle that was left in the bottom of the tin had encouraged her to push the hard ring of flesh which all pigs have at the end of their snouts into the lip of the tin, where it had become firmly fixed. Driving pigs is always a problem as they are very wilful but trying to walk a sow with a treacle tin stuck on her snout is even more difficult, if not impossible! Although she could breathe through her mouth, pigs normally breathe through their nostrils, and she went all ways trying to get the tin off. She would stand with her head down for a little while and then make a strange muffled screeching noise and literally gallop off in whichever direction she happened to be pointing. She must have weighed about fifteen stone, as far as I remember, and a pig this weight moving at speed takes some stopping. Luckily she turned for home in the end, and by anticipating her bursts of speed I was able to guide her back to the farm.

The next problem was, how to remove the tin? Every time she banged her head on the ground or a tree or wall – or me – the tighter it became wedged. And by this time her snout had swollen inside the tin making it impossible to remove without taking drastic measures. Chris Futter's helpful contribution was, 'Cut her head off – it'll come off easy then!' But eventually, with the help of the blacksmith, the cowman, the foreman (thank goodness Father had gone to market) and others, the sow was tied up, the blacksmith solemnly sawed through the treacle tin and she was freed of the painful addition to her snout. There was blood everywhere, but very little harm had come to her. Pigs' snouts are notoriously tough – given time they can even root up concrete. Steel rings used to be inserted into their snouts to stop them rooting but my sow had never had one of these fixed. At the end of the day she was completely exhausted and so was I! Although she had recovered by the next morning she had, understandably, gone off season and she had a month in which to get over her adventure before going on the long walk again. It certainly taught me a couple of lessons about pig-keeping. First of all that it's unwise to try and drive pigs long distances, especially in hot weather and, secondly, to make certain there are no empty treacle tins around.

The early years at Testerton were very busy and hardworking ones for my parents. There was little time or energy for entertaining, and they seldom invited friends to lunch or supper. The only people who came for a meal occasionally were those who had come to see Father on business and they would sometimes be asked to stay for lunch. There was also a seemingly endless procession of aunts, uncles and cousins who came to Sunday afternoon high tea. They always came in the early afternoon, looked round the farm, inspected the garden, and had tea: home-baked ham, salad and hard-boiled eggs, and as a special treat, tinned pineapple and cream or strawberries in season. Then it was a quick load-up with cuttings, plants, seeds and other garden and farm produce and often an exchange of clothes with cousins who had outgrown theirs, or who had grown into those that my brother and I had grown out of. I hated this and usually contrived to disappear as soon as the pineapple was finished, as I was more than used to hand-me-downs having a brother seven years my senior.

There are only a few occasions when I can remember going away to stay, until I went to boarding school. I once spent a weekend with a cousin, and twice stayed for a short time with my maternal grandparents: the first occasion was when my sister Betty was born, and another time was when my father had all his teeth out, at home. The dentist and the doctor came out to Testerton and the operation was done in the kitchen. From subsequent accounts it appears to have been a very messy business. They took all his teeth out in one go using a local anaesthetic, and he didn't get his new false ones until his gums receded. He could have had a temporary set, but wouldn't run to the expense. False teeth were obviously an expensive commodity and they featured in one of my most memorable experiences with Grandfather Bailey. Grandfather Bailey was a dealer as well as a farmer and went every Friday to King's Lynn market. He always kept a strong cob in a very smart gig and drove either to Lynn on Tuesday or Friday, Burnham Market on Monday, Fakenham on Thursday, or Dereham on Friday (Norwich was a special market he occasionally visited by train). He made calls on the way at various farms which sometimes resulted in buying some calves, pigs or bullocks. The latter would be taken by a drover and his dog to their new homes a few days later, after Grandfather had had time to arrange it all. He also took eggs and butter and dressed chickens to a stallholder in the market at Lynn. One day he and I had a disaster in the High Street.

Grandfather was walking ahead of me carrying two baskets of eggs, and I was carrying the butter, when suddenly the old gentleman did a violent sneeze! Out flew both his upper and lower sets of teeth. We stood helpless, as we watched his teeth crash on to the pavement and shatter into dozens of pieces. He didn't drop the eggs and we picked up all the pieces, put them in his handkerchief and took them along to the dentist and asked him to make a new set. I'd never seen a gum impression taken before – it was very interesting. When we got home and told Grandma her remark was, 'There goes the profit on the eggs and butter for several weeks. We would have been better off if you had dropped the eggs and caught your teeth!' To which Grandfather replied, 'It's easier to pick up broken teeth than broken eggs!'

Chapter Five

Testerton: The Farm

The first people to arrive for work in the mornings at Testerton were the cowmen and team-men. The cowmen could be heard at half-past-five calling 'ho, ho, ho' (a sort of in between word, not 'ho' and not 'how'). The cows recognised it and would immediately go to the gate and follow each other in their pecking order into the conventional two-bay standings in the cowhouse, where the grub was waiting to eat while they were being milked. There were no milking machines at that time – they came a few years later – but the cows all had piped water in small bowls in front of them. They stayed out on the pastures night and day unless there was an extremely sharp frost or snow, in which case after the night's milking they stayed inside and were given an extra feed last thing. There was no weather forecast on the radio in those days and in any case we didn't have a radio. Farmers and farmworkers seemed to know far more about what the local weather was likely to do than they do today. Mostly they took their signs from the animals themselves and, of course, from the birds and the elements, and many of the countryman's sayings like 'Red sky at night, shepherd's deloght' originated in this way.

At Ryburgh, each cowman had been expected to milk and look after forty cows, and it was the same at Testerton. Some of the 'old dears' were easier than others to milk, indeed you seldom found two alike. It was the kickers and tail-swishers that I didn't like. The milk was carted by bucket into the dairy next door where it was run over a cooler, a larger edition of the Ryburgh cooler. This was not mechanical, but simply a sort of water jacket through which cold water constantly poured. The milk flowed over the corrugations and was cooled from blood heat to the temperature of the water, which varied with the day temperature. After cascading over the cooler the milk went through a round filter like a bottomless bucket which was put in the top of each milk churn, and this in turn had two wire gauzes with a round fine cotton disc wedged in between them which caught the pieces. Today the health authorities would have a fit. Certainly they would if they had seen the filter discs at the end of the evening or morning milking, for as well as the grit and dust there were always a lot of short cow-type hairs caught in the strainer. The water flowed constantly through the cooler whilst the cooling operation took place, and ended up in a very large tank at ground level. It was subsequently used for washing-down and rinsing the floor of the dairy. There was no pressure hosepipe for this job, just buckets of water out of the tank and a stiff broom.

After a couple of years Father decided to convert to mechanical milking. I went with him to other farms and various Shows to see the different types of milking machines available. In fact, the whole family went as it was a big step to take. He chose to invest in a Fullwood machine which comprised a small vacuum pump driven by a 1½ hp Lister petrol engine. The vacuum pipe from the pump ran above the cow stalls with a little brass tap over each cow. The milkers took the buckets to the right-hand side of each of the 'old ladies' in turn and connected the four teat liners to their udders. As soon as the small brass tap on the vacuum line was switched on, the milk was drawn out of the cows' udders into the pails by the pulses controlled by a pulsator on the top of each pail. A man came from the factory and lived in the house with us while installing the machine, and I 'lived' with him during the whole of the two weeks that he was there.

On the first evening that the installation was ready for work the fun started. The cows had always been used to hand milking – I suppose few of them had ever heard a petrol engine running. They certainly didn't like the four rubber tubes sucking at their teats. Each one in turn tried every possible antic to get rid of this claw-like affair which was very different from the gentle squeeze-pull, squeeze-pull of their human friends. They kicked and twisted, pulled and reared and refused to let their milk go. The total yield that night was as little as a quarter of normal. The next morning the 'old ladies' walked diffidently into the cowhouse, extremely suspicious, with bulging udders. As far as I remember this went on for several morning and evening milkings, until gradually they got it into their furry heads that relief came with this sudden intrusion into their privacy if only they would stand still. Matters were not helped by the attitude of the cowmen who knew from the start that the new-fangled gadget wouldn't work! However, they too gradually cottoned-on to the fact that they could milk two or three cows at once and all in all they were much better off: not so likely to get a hoof in the side of the face, or be splashed with 'poop'. Incidentally, that is the way a cow has of registering its objection or demonstrating its nervousness. They either kick you or drop one beside you and when you get a shed full of fifty or so objecting at the same time it can be dangerous, noisy, smelly and mucky. However, at the end of the first week things were much more settled . . . the milk was cleaner in a vacuum-sealed pail and the milking time reduced to about a third of what it used to be. The nice, patient man from Fullwoods, was able to depart for his factory.

At about the same time as the cowmen arrived each morning to get the cows in, the team-men came to give the horses their bait (breakfast) and prepare them for the day's work. Unlike the cows the horses stayed in most winter nights from November through to March. On arrival at the stable the team-man would first of all give each horse its breakfast, consisting of chaff, shredded mangolds or swedes in season, crushed oats and hay. Whilst the animals munched through their breakfast they would be groomed, and any muck delivered during the night barrowed out to the muck heap. At 6.30 a.m. the team-men would have their breakfast; if they lived in a cottage near the farm they would go home, if not they would have it in the stable. At seven o'clock the horses would be harnessed up ready for the day's work, coinciding with the arrival of the other farm-workers, some of whom would be required to use them. A good team-man, knowing his horses and by arrangement with the foreman, would allocate his team out according to the experience, knowledge and skill with horses of the other men. If you were ambitious to get on then your goal was to become a team-man. After leaving school the boys usually started as drivers (leaders) or at harvest-time as 'holla-holgie' boys. This meant that they would sit astride the horse pulling the waggon when sheaves of corn were being carted, and scream 'holgie' (hold-you) before moving the horse from stook (eight to twelve sheaves) to stook. When the waggons were full a mid-term or rising horseman, usually in his early twenties, would bring a trace horse with an empty waggon which was left in the field to be filled. He would then hitch the trace horse to the front of the full waggon so that the two horses took it back to the stack. The empty waggon was left in the charge of the 'holla-holgie' boy and the two pitchers and two loaders to be refilled.

It is difficult to imagine now what an important part the horse played in farming up to the time that the internal combustion engine arrived. About ten to fifteen per cent of the farm was devoted to maintaining the horse, in the shape of pasture and quite a lot of arable land for growing oats and hay to feed in the winter. The horses had to do all the work – ploughing, cultivating, harrowing, rolling and the drilling of the seed – and the mares had to reproduce themselves by having foals. The foals were sold if there happened to be a surplus, or kept for replacement. The gestation period for a horse is near enough a year and mares would be worked normally through seven or eight months of the pregnancy, but given an easier time towards the end. They also worked after foaling, given a reasonable time to give their offspring a good start, but land had to be provided for a year or two for the foals until they were either sold or put to work.

If the farm was big enough to warrant a resident stallion (say, four or five teams of eight horses) then it wasn't necessary to use the travelling stallion; but usually one of the larger breeders would have one or two, and in some cases more, stallions on the road in the spring visiting farms to serve mares. The handlers, who travelled on foot, or at best on a bike, got to know not only where the mares for service were, but when they were likely to come in season. It was a big event when the handler arrived with a stallion, and whereas today many parents would probably be too squeamish to allow their children to see what took place, in those days no one had a thought about it – we all watched. The farm team-man would bring his mare out and lead her up to one side of an ordinary five-barred gate, and the stallion's handler would lead the stallion up to the mare's head with the gate in between. It very soon became apparent if the mare was in season and therefore receptive. If she wasn't she would quickly make her feelings plain, either by biting the stallion or by rearing up and trying to pummel him with her front hooves. The gate was there to prevent this as, were it not, damage could be done to one or both horses. If the mare was 'ready' then they would be brought together and the service would take place. If for some reason it didn't hold then she would be tried again at the next visit of the stallion – usually after one month.

A stallion brought me my first real contact with death. Growing up on a mixed farm I had seen animals die, but a memory which will always be with me goes back to about 1925 not long after we moved to Testerton. Here, with six teams of horses on the farm, Father decided there were enough horses to justify keeping his own stallion. He always kept Suffolks and he went to the best breeder of Suffolks that he knew and bought a stallion called *Emperor Roxburgh.* The horse was bought somewhere down in Suffolk, so it warranted being brought home to Testerton by rail. For this purpose a specially padded horse box was hired from the railway company and on the appointed day my father announced that we would all go to Ryburgh Station to see the arrival. I cannot remember why we didn't go by car, but instead all piled into the pony trap. When we got to the station, there in the siding was the special horse box and *Emperor Roxburgh* could be heard whinnying inside and talking to the pony in the trap. Eventually he was unloaded and what a splendid chap he was, weighing 15cwt to a ton, his coat shining like polished walnut. Father had bought a new special leather halter with brass fittings, the girth (known in Norfolk and Suffolk as the belly 'gatt') that went round his middle and a double rope halter for safety. Whether or not he was expecting trouble I don't know but two team-men were with us and they walked proudly one on either side of the horse leading him behind the pony trap back to the farm.

It wasn't long before the *Emperor* was at work with the number of mares available. He did a good job in his first season and Father travelled him around other farms, wherever he could get customers, provided the mares were known to be in good condition and clean. However, towards the end of his first year he went off colour and there was obviously something more than overwork amiss with him. Various opinions from old horsemen were given and eventually the vet was called. He couldn't diagnose any chronic illness but there was something very seriously wrong. After trying various tonics and purgatives, because the loss of weight and condition were obvious, the vet and my father came to the conclusion that there was nothing for it but that the stallion would have to be 'put down'. I remember the seriousness with which my mother and father discussed this, and the terrible decision to ask the knacker to come and shoot the *Emperor*. It was typical of my father that he allowed my brother and me to be present saying that we would have to get used to death, as that was coming to all of us one day.

I remember vividly what happened that day and the postmortem that followed. The vet was to hand and the evisceration showed immediately what was wrong: in the *Emperor*'s stomach they found a large hard ball, about half the size of a football and known as a hair-ball. These balls result when animals continually lick themselves or their mates and swallow the hair. The hair gets mixed with the stomach juices and perhaps the calcium from the drinking water, turns into a solid ball, and when churned round in the stomach becomes completely spherical and as hard as granite. Today, if the horse was valuable enough, it would probably be taken to an X-ray unit to identify the problem and the offending article could be removed. *Emperor*'s hair-ball spent the next forty years on the mantlepiece of my father's study and is now an exhibit in the Bygones Collection at Holkham Hall in Norfolk.

Sheep always played a large part in my father's system of farming – largely because he used them as scavengers on his vegetable crops so that if there was no trade for cabbages and Brussels sprouts at least he could turn the crops into sheep meat and wool. Sugar-beet tops, too, were a great source of fodder for the sheep. At the same time as eating the residue of these crops the sheep naturally dumped their fertile droppings on the land. Father liked to lamb early, in January and February, in order that the old ewes would naturally produce a good flow of milk immediately after lambing, which would continue until the fresh grass in the spring boosted another flow of milk. This would take the lambs through until approximately June when they would go for slaughter. It was about this time in the year that the old ewes would give up their coats. The sheep-shearing was done by a gang of four men who went around from farm to farm shearing with hand clippers. It wasn't until about 1933–4 that, instead of four men arriving to do the job, two came with a petrol driven set of clippers.

The shearing was always done in a barn, and the sheep were penned under cover in cart sheds, bullock sheds, or anywhere that would keep the rain off them from the night before clipping until they went out minus their fleeces. The job I didn't like took place several days before sheep-shearing when every sheep that was to be shorn had to be caught, turned on its back, and 'clagged'. This involved clipping off any blobs of dried excreta adhering to their rear ends and removing any extraneous matter like small pieces of bramble or burdocks which would automatically decrease the value of the fleeces. There was a special way of folding up a fleece after shearing which involved spreading it out on the floor – it covers as much space as the top of a grand piano. The fleece was then carefully folded into a neat ball. The amount of wool from each sheep varies considerably according to the breed and the type of fleece that the individual sheep grows. A good long staple fleece will yield five to six pounds. The only fun I got out of shearing (for it was a very smelly, messy business) was taking the fleeces to the tannery at Fakenham and seeing them packed into large hessian sacks and weighed. My mother used to make us change our clothes and footwear after a day with the sheep. This was done in the wash-house outside, although I always thought that the smell of the grease (lanolin) from the wool was not unpleasant. It certainly softened the hands.

The other great event in the sheep calendar is really where it all starts – the lambing. A special stack of wheat was earmarked at harvest time. It had to be one where the straw was very clean with no thistles or cleavers (sweethearts) in it. The stack was threshed around Christmas-time and bunched, using a special machine on the back of the threshing drum. This produced flat bales which were used, under the supervision of the shepherd, to build lambing yards. I have an old plan of the recommended size of a lambing yard for twenty-two score (240) ewes. It shows that it should be 36yd long and 34yd wide, and that it should contain fifty individual lambing pens and two small hardening-off yards. A hand-written note on the plan says 'This gives fifty pens, each with small hod for feeding. Don't keep ewes in pens too long – harden them in small yard before turning out. Always have lumps of mineral salt to increase milk flow in each yard.' The lambing yards, of course, were made to the size required by the flock in each case. With five hundred ewes a yard would be about the size of four tennis courts.

The sheep pens were made by putting wooden hurdles round the outside first, and then tying the special bales of wheat-straw to them. Then ash liggers (poles) were used as purlins and rafters for the roof, which was thatched with more wheat-straw. Each ewe then had her own little roofed pen to produce her lamb in which she was snug and warm. Next to the actual lambing yard was an unroofed collecting pen which ewes and lambs were turned into after they had had two to four days, according to the strength of the lamb, in the yard itself. In their lambing pens the 'old ladies' had a small feeding trough, in which they had sliced mangolds, turnips or swedes fed with concentrates in the form of ground barley and oats, and imported foods such as soya bean meal and cotton or linseed cake and minerals. There was also a hay-rack in the corner. The food was always fed in long troughs in the collecting yard, but each day the sheep were turned out on to whatever crop, in the shape of cabbages or swedes, was available. As sheep become older the gnawing teeth at the front of their bottom jaws tend to drop out, which prevents them from biting turnips, swedes or mangolds. It was the job of us boys to go along the rows of growing roots with a special cruciform type of implement, chopping them into four. In this way the older sheep could nibble the corners of the chunks whereas they couldn't tackle a globe.

The shepherd knew every one of his lambs and which ewe had produced them. The target was one-and-a-half lambs per ewe, meaning that he would have anything up to eight hundred lambs and their mothers in his charge. This with the help of one assistant and a boy or two now and again! The boys usually had the job of setting the nets which, with a crowbar, was not an easy job. The wire nets were unyielding and the land often difficult to get the posts into at this time of year. Not only was the shepherd expected to be with his sheep all day, but he also had a four-wheeled hut in the corner of the field where he slept at night. Usually his wife brought him his meals and there was always a kettle brewing on the tiny coal stove in the corner of the hut. With a flock of that size he had two dogs – they slept outside the door of the hut in beer barrels with the tops cut out. Father's shepherd used to say that he didn't take his clothes off from the time he started sleeping out with his sheep until they finished lambing – usually 6 weeks.

Sheep-dipping in the spring or early summer was an event which to me as a child seemed to revolve around a keg of ale and the arrival of a strange looking cart-type vehicle. This contraption turned out to be a mobile sheep-dip, owned by the local chemist. The system which operated was that provided a farmer bought his Cooper's dipping paste from a particular chemist he could have the use of the cart free of charge, so long as he fetched it with a horse from the farm where it had been used previously. We would hear from our chemist that such and such a farmer, usually next door or fairly near, was having the cart on a certain day and arrangements would be made for a boy to be there with a horse to bring it home to us for dipping the following day. The dipping machine was unloaded near a stream or river, a shallow hole dug for the tank, which was wedge-shaped, and hurdles placed round it to contain the sheep. The tank itself held about 250 gallons of water and the yellow sulphur and arsenic dip was thoroughly mixed in. The sheep were seized one at a time by the shepherd and his assistant, and held down and immersed in the bath for a short time with only their mouths, eyes and nostrils above the liquid level. A minute was about enough time for the liquid to soak into the wool. When they were released they scrambled out at the sloping end of the tank and 'drained' on a platform which allowed much of the liquid to run back into the tank for re-use. The art of the dipper was to completely submerge the sheep but cover their mouth and nostrils with one hand so that they didn't swallow any of the lethal mixture. I suppose that still applies today. The tank had to be kept topped up with pails of water from the stream. A well-fleeced sheep retains about two gallons of water in the fleece, and there is no doubt that they were far more susceptible to diseases like scab and attacks of fly-blown maggots and lice if they weren't dipped.

I don't know at what date sheep-dipping became compulsory, but it was before my time: when we were sheep-dipping the local police constable always had to be there to see that the job was properly done. The dipping liquid made the sheep change colour and for some time after the event they had a yellowish tinge to them, so did the dippers. It was another unpleasant job and the police constable stood well back from the yellow splashes. I always thought this must be the reason why the barrel of beer was placed near the point where the sheep went in. The dipping crew certainly deserved the beer, and I suppose it was also an incentive to the policeman to be present at what must have been a tedious task – slowly counting the sheep through the bath.

Galvanised sheep netting was used for folding the sheep. The nets were high and held up by 3in diameter larch poles with two simple staples, one at ground level pointing down and one at the top pointing up. The method used to erect them was to roll out the net or drag it, unrolled, from its previous site, lay out the posts every 10yd and with a crowbar make a hole about 4 or 5in deep and knock the posts in about a foot so that the bottom hook was at ground level. The net could then be hooked on the bottom and stood up and the top staple, pointing upwards, held it in position. It wasn't a bad job if the ground was wet and soft, but when the ground was hard it could be very tough going. The system with nets was always to make a pen forward of the ewes and lambs. For five hundred ewes the pen would have to be about 200yd square. In this way the grazing could be completely controlled and the sheep were not allowed to wander forward and taint the uneaten beet tops, kale, cabbage, swedes or turnips or whatever they were being folded on. In this way too the whole of the ground got an even amount of sheep's droppings – in other words the muck would be naturally and evenly spread by those who were carrying it!

Another practice achieving the same end was to use wheeled iron hurdles. Each hurdle was 24ft long with a pair of small cast-iron wheels on a 3ft wide axle, so that there was virtually a wheel at each corner. They were always much quicker to move than nets for up to six or eight hurdles could be pulled by a horse. It was a simple and easy way of making big pens as long as the hurdles could be kept in straight lines when towing, as there was no method of steering other than walking back along the line and moving each hurdle in turn in order to negotiate the corner. If careful attention was not paid and a row of hurdles did pull over then each chain connecting the hurdle to the next had to be undone, and all the hurdles stood up and re-connected before the operation could proceed. Like everything else there was a skill in doing this because you had to keep your eyes forward when guiding the horse, but you needed eyes in the back of your head to see what was happening to the row of hurdles.

On cold days, in wet and frosty conditions, one would wish to be anywhere else other than with the sheep. On one such day, when I was about fourteen or fifteen years old, I was righting a row of hurdles that I had allowed the horse to pull over when I crushed my thumb and the nail immediately started to turn black. It was general practice when this happened to cut a small hole in the nail to let the blood out from underneath in order to decrease the pressure and lessen the pain. Also, if the hole was kept free until the wound healed under the nail there was a fair chance that the nail wouldn't rot and come off but would grow out. On this occasion the shepherd got his hoof knife out and cut a hole in the nail, put a great blob of Stockholm tar used for the sheep's feet on it, and wound a piece of not too clean rag around my thumb. That evening when Mother saw it she wasn't too pleased. Many years later there was a sequel to this incident, when the same shepherd's son was working with me clearing a drain under the road. He was one side screwing on the draining rods and pushing them through the drain. I was on the other side of the road waiting for the unblocking tool to appear. I was lying on my stomach with my hand in the water feeling for the end as it came through. I shouted to him, 'Push it really hard – you're not quite there.' He did and trapped my finger in between the steel end of the draining rods and the edge of the pipe. It was obvious on inspection that the end of the finger was damaged and bleeding under the nail so I said to Sid, 'Give me your knife. I'll have to cut a hole in it like your father did to the finger next to it some twenty years ago.' I was standing there patiently cutting tiny pieces of the nail away when there was a splash behind me. Sid, who I hadn't realised was that squeamish, had passed out and fallen into the flooded drain. It wasn't deep enough to do him any harm but he got very wet!

In 1912 a very up-to-date piggery had been built by the landlord for the previous tenant at Testerton. It consisted of a row of low pig sties, each with its own little concrete exercise yard surrounded by a small paling fence with a gate. There were twenty of these sties, in two rows, with a feeding and mucking-out roadway up the middle. The sows Father kept were Large Blacks, and they were crossed with a Large White boar. This crossing produced blue and white piglets. They were very sturdy and the food conversion figures (the weight increase of the pig in relation to the amount of food they ate) were the best for the popular breeds at that time. The piglets were suckled by their mothers for eight weeks. Then she was turned back to the boar for the next litter. The litter she had produced was sometimes yarded in with the bullocks, but if the bullocks were out to grass the pigs would occupy the whole of the bullock yard. The sows in the meantime were put out to grass for about fourteen of the sixteen week gestation period, and although they had rings in their noses they still managed to root up the damper places on the meadows and left an awful mess. These 'pig patches' were re-cultivated from time to time and some fresh grass seed thrown on to them and rolled in.

When the pigs were ready for market they were either sold in small batches, in threes or fours, to local butchers or sold to the bacon factory at Elmswell in Suffolk, which meant a train journey. It was quite a business driving a batch of up to fifty 10–12 stone pigs to the station, and although most roads were properly fenced and every cottage, farm and field gated, halfway to the station for no reason at all one pig would often suddenly turn back and bolt for home, smartly followed by the rest of the batch. I always had an uneasy feeling that they knew, or sensed, where they were eventually going to end up. All the young people, men and girls, connected with the farm were ordered to be on parade for these pig drives. The only animals you could say with any certainty were going to get there without rushing back were the Large Blacks. They had very big floppy ears over their eyes and couldn't see which way they were going, so even if there were some with pricked ears amongst them, you knew they wouldn't all bolt for home. It is amazing how far and fast a pig can run. I have known them run until they dropped dead, particularly on hot days. If this happened my father would quickly cut the throat of the dead pig so that it could be bled. It would then be humped on to a cart and dropped off at the butcher's, which was conveniently near the station.

One of the funniest sights I ever saw happened on a pig drive to the station. A Brigadier-General Brayne had arranged with my father to bring forty Indian students through the Boy Scout organisation to stay on the Testerton farm for two weeks. The Brigadier had been working in India, educating village populations to use more modern farming techniques. The Scouts were billeted in tents and, although there were members of most of the religious sects among them, they all lived and ate together in a large barn. It caused a great problem with diets, but if there were any disputes the Brigadier solved them by putting the two lads who couldn't agree into a boxing ring and letting them fight it out! The first boy to draw blood immediately had to clean up his opponent with a sponge.

During the scouts' stay at Testerton Father had one of his bigger pig drives, and these forty lads in their khaki scout uniforms were recruited to help. Exactly what we expected to happen did. We were all ambling down the road from the farm towards the station and had gone about a mile when suddenly the leading pig turned and bolted back towards home. The Indian scouts, following the example of their patrol leader, did exactly the same thing and soon they were all in full flight and also in full cry, followed by upwards of fifty pigs! The Brigadier had to sort out the ensuing argument as many of the scouts refused to have anything more to do with the drives because of their religious principles. I don't think that until then they had realised that the pigs were going for eventual slaughter.

Father and the Brigadier had the same trouble when the scouts were taken to see rabbiting with ferrets in progress. The sight of the ferrets, which to them were mongooses, being put down the holes intrigued them but they didn't realise that when the rabbits bolted they would be shot. A few of them, I don't know which sect, began walking around, arms extended to heaven and chanting: we were told that they were appealing to their god to save the rabbits.

I always thought the pig unit at Testerton was very smart and ultra efficient, but in 1934 or 5, when I was away at school I was shocked to receive a letter from my mother telling me that following an outbreak of swine fever, the Ministry of Agriculture had ordered the pigs to be shot and buried. Father didn't keep pigs again at Testerton after that: but he did on other farms.

During the twenties Grandfather Bailey went to Holland with a party of Norfolk farmers to study the technique of growing sugar-beet. The trip was sponsored by the sugar-beet company with headquarters at King's Lynn. I was very young, but I remember it clearly because we received a postcard from him, posted in Amsterdam, showing a windmill and a man in clogs. I simply couldn't understand how anybody could wear wooden shoes. He also brought back a present for my Grandmother. It was a little brooch consisting of a tiny pair of silver clogs, and we children were each given a pair of little wooden clogs to mark Grandfather's voyage. Influenced by what he had been told about sugar-beet growing by my Grandfather, Father decided to launch into the crop in a big way at Testerton. Years later he pointed out to me the advantage of growing virtually two cash crops on the same piece of land in the same year. There was a crop of sugar-beet to sell to the Sugar Beet Corporation for processing into sugar, and there were the sugar-beet tops, (as good as another crop) to feed cattle and sheep, particularly the cows who liked the tops and milked well on them. There were many other advantages, not the least of which was sugar-beet pulp. This was a by-product left after the sugar was extracted at the factory. It could be bought at a cheaper rate by those who had a contract, and was a very good and palatable animal fodder and another incentive to grow beet.

Another excellent reason for growing sugar-beet was that you knew what price you were going to get before you actually sowed the seed, and provided you grew a reasonable crop you received the money for it within a month of the beet being delivered to the factory. The crop also had benefits for the farm-workers as the sugar-beet was sown in rows about eighteen inches apart and, with no selective weedkillers available, had to be hand-hoed to keep the weeds down. The beet then had to be chopped out, which meant bunching them with hand hoes at about eight inches apart. After that came scoring, or singling, which meant going through each bunch and singling out the 'cock' or largest plants, which were left to mature. In other words in the spring there was a lot more work for more people, and most of it was done on contract according to a deal struck by the 'lord' of the gang and the farmer.

There was plenty of work in the autumn, too, as the beet were all lifted by hand. I never remember it happening at Testerton but apparently in the early twenties the beet were dug with a two-tine fork. My early memories are of the horses ploughing the beet out. When they had dug, or ploughed out, a certain number of rows the gang would go over them again, pulling out beet with left and right hands, banging them together to knock the soil off and laying them very neatly in rows all pointing the same way. Once again they would be gone over, this time with a beet-hook which was like a hand reap-hook but with a point at the end. Each beet was picked up in turn, the top chopped off and left for the animals, and then thrown into heaps about five yards apart. But that isn't where it finished. Using one-horse tumbrils and one or two trace horses, depending on how heavy the land was, the beet would then have to be carted off and haled beside the road or, provided that the fields were reasonably close by, taken straight to the railway station. Alternatively they would be haled near the road and taken to the factory by lorry. The beet were manhandled at every stage, from the moment they were taken off the ground after topping until, using only sugar-beet forks, they were loaded into the tumbrils. After this they were unloaded onto a hale and, with forks, piled up to about six to eight feet high or thrown from the carts into the railway trucks – all by hand. I don't remember seeing a mechanical loader until the forties. The disadvantage of growing beet, particularly on heavy land, was the amount of rutting caused by the wheels of the carts and churning up by the horses' feet. If the weather was bad and conditions became very, very wet the whole field would become a mud puddle and the soil structure was affected, even after ploughing and frosts, to the point where it diminished the following year's barley yield. However, when the autumn was fairly open and weather conditions were good there is no doubt that the spring hoeing which helped to clean the land, and the sheep or cattle feeding off the tops, increased the yield of barley or whichever crop followed in the subsequent year.

When sugar-beet first came into the country in the twenties there was so much repetitious back-breaking hand-work that the men resisted it. In fact, on some farms they actually refused to do it. That situation was cured by gangs of Irish labourers who came over and worked almost all the hours that they could see, and lived very rough. Grandfathers, fathers and sons, would arrive and be boarded in almost any building that was dry and in which temporary bedding and cooking facilities could be installed. Those that worked for my father asked him to send some of the money they earned by wire from the bank or post office to their women in Ireland, but they would keep back enough for food and a visit to the local on Saturday nights. These could be quite boisterous and wild evenings and they certainly gave the poor old village bobby and the local gamekeeper a hard time of it, and, in some cases, the magistrates too. But their labour was important to the farmers, as they only got paid for the work they did and, provided that was satisfactory and the damage to the pheasants not too great, the arrangement appeared to suit everyone.

All game, pheasants, snipe, partridge and woodcock, belonged by right to the landlord: the farmer was responsible for keeping down the vermin, rabbits, pigeons, rats and mice. The farmer was also responsible for controlling the hares. It was expected that a balance of hares would be strictly kept at a tolerable level so that they would not be allowed to proliferate to the point where they devoured too much of the growing crops like kale, turnips and swedes, but that enough would be left to be shot on official shooting days by the landlord and his guests. Pigeons, together with the rabbits, were the real pests but no game or rabbits were a perquisite of the workers. It was only at harvest-time that the farm-worker (if the farmer felt so inclined, and my father always did) legally got his share. In the days before myxomatosis, a good breeding season for the rabbits, which required an early spring and not too many frosts by harvest-time, meant they could become a great problem. A doe rabbit might have up to four litters of young in a season.

When harvesting started and the self-binder pulled by three horses (or a tractor, if the farmer had one) went round and round the field, the rabbits, often in their hundreds in a big field and where there was a big infestation of the pests, would be driven gradually into the centre of the field. By the time there was only an acre or so of corn left standing it would be a swarming mass of rabbits from old bucks and does, down to recently bred bunnies. The men working the field setting up the sheaves into stooks or shocks would all gather round, each with a stick, killing the rabbits as they made a last dash for the stubble and freedom. Usually very few of them escaped, particularly if my father and the keeper, perhaps with a couple of friends by invitation, were there with guns when the binder finished. The drill was that everyone would bring the rabbits they had managed to run down and kill and lay them on the platform of the binder. My father would then pick out a brace each for the men who were not involved with the harvest, like the cowmen, pigmen and any men that were working elsewhere. After that each of those present would take a brace, and any left over would go to widows or pensioners connected with the farm. Then if there were still some left Father would take them to the butchers and sell them. In a good year for rabbits I have seen as many as two hundred distributed at the end of a good day's cutting, and anything up to twenty hares.

Pigeons were also a pest, particularly in the winter-time, as it was then that they seemed to band into big flocks. If it was a very, very severe winter with a lot of wind-frost then flocks numbered in thousands would descend on the green crops, particularly of the kale and cabbage variety, demolishing the leaves they ate and contaminating those they didn't. Although scarers were put up in the shape of mawkins (scarecrows) and boys walked about with noisy wooden clappers or old tin cans, beating them with sticks, the pigeons often became so hungry that they would quietly settle in the corner of a field in their thousands and wouldn't move until the scarer was almost upon them. Automatic gas bangers hadn't been invented then, although there was a clockwork timing device that fired a dozen blank twelve-bore cartridges at pre-set intervals. There was another device which was very simple. It was a piece of rope, about 3ft long, soaked in saltpetre, with the blue taper ends of ordinary firework bangers wound into it at about 4in intervals. The rope was hung well above ground from a curved stick and lit. As it smouldered each blue touch-paper lit in turn, making the fireworks go off at intervals. The only problem was that in very foggy weather, or when it rained, the smouldering rope would go out. Boys who were scaring pigeons were always told to work one end of the field and have smouldering rope at the other end. If it rained and the ropes went out they were supposed to take them home, dry them out and re-soak them in saltpetre. Of course, one day the inevitable happened and one of the lads put a rope that he thought had gone out in his pocket. It went off when he was halfway home on his bicycle and not only blew him into the ditch, but spoilt his already very tatty jacket. He was very lucky to get away without severe burns. I can remember someone making a dummy fire extinguisher after that and tying it to his cross bar.

Harvest has always been the high point of the farming year, and although it was almost completely mechanised by the mid-twenties it was still the most labour-intensive operation on the farm. The team-men, of course, played a vital part in the harvest fields but many other skills were needed too. The men with the long forks who pitched the sheaves were called the pitchers, and they were usually the tallest and strongest. The loaders who packed the sheaves onto the carts were often the youngest and least ambitious. The stacker was the really important man at harvest-time for the provision of dry corn in the winter depended on the way he built the stack. My father would set out the stack, usually 11yd x 6yd which on settlement became 12yd x 6½yd, and then a thick bed of thorns was covered with a little straw as a base. The secret of building a stack was to have all the sheaves placed so that the ear ends were higher in the middle of the stack than on the outside. To do this a shock of sheaves was built in the middle and then the stacker would go round and round, always placing the ear ends inwards and the stalk ends outwards so that any rain blowing onto the outside would not come in contact with the ear at all.

At harvest time the sheaves would be unloaded from the waggons and thrown to the men on the stack. When the stack had reached the height of an empty waggon the elevator would be brought into use. This was a large open-framed affair, big and tall enough for a horse to walk round and round underneath the elevator trough itself. As the horse walked round it drove the mechanism which consisted of two endless chains connected by slats, which carried the sheaves up onto the stack. The trough could be raised and lowered so that, starting at the height of an empty waggon, it could be raised until the delivery end was some 20ft above the ground and would therefore take the sheaves up to the stacker. These machines were so high even in their lowest position that the troughs were hinged in the middle so that the top half hung down and would not catch in the trees when being transported from field to field. At about 12ft high, the stacker would start bringing his roof in so that when he reached the middle he had a good slope. When it rained the water would trickle down from stalk to stalk and finish up at the eaves before falling to the ground. He had three men serving him from the elevator to the outside of the stack. They worked in unison, round and round the stack, with the centre man of the three filling in.

When harvest was over or when time and weather permitted, for instance on wet days, the stacker became the thatcher. A good load of the best wheat-straw would be set down against each stack and a water-cart load – about 200 gallons – in a three-wheel water-cart would be left there together with broaches of split hazel about 3ft long, and a ball of string. The system was very simple. The heap of straw would be dampened by throwing pails of water on it and then the thatcher's server, usually one of the lads, would pull the straw out by hand so that it all laid in one direction. When he had pulled as much as he could carry and fastened it with a wooden clamp called a worrel he carted it up the thatching ladder to the thatcher. Thatching ladders were very special pieces of equipment and were made the opposite way to a builder's ladder. The builder's or tiler's ladder was a long larch pole, split down the middle with wedged staves with the curves outside. a thatcher's ladder was made with the curves inside so that as the thatcher moved along the roof he always had a flat surface to butt his thatch up to. The broaches were the pegs which he pushed into the stack to hold the string and the thatch tightly down. There would be no wastage of corn at all in a well-built and properly thatched stack.

According to the location of a particular field the barley, wheat and oats would be stacked usually at the corner of the field near a convenient gate or road. A certain number of stacks would be built in the stack-yard adjoining the farm premises, so that after threshing the straw would be handy for littering cows, horses, bullocks and pigs. Bullocks would eat a lot of the barley straw uncut, but the oat straw would often be cut up as chaff for the horses. Oat and wheat flites (hucks) were also kept in the chaff houses and

Cutting with horse-drawn McCormick binders.

Stacking with two-horse sweep and elevator.

fed to the horses during the winter. The barley awms were the only things that were burnt, although sometimes these too were used for bullocks. But this could occasionally be a problem as the small prickly pieces sometimes got into the animal's eyes. All the corn was carted to the granary. If it was of malting or seed potential, the men would winnow it through a dressing machine on wet days in the winter-time. This was hard and dirty work for the machine was hand-turned and the corn dusty. However, dressing it up, which meant taking out the dross, dust and small pieces of straw, would often bring it into a higher price bracket. Everything else went for animal feed. It was either ground, if it was barley or wheat, or crushed,if it was oats, for the horses. This, together with mangolds, swedes, sugar-beet pulp, bought-in linseed, and cotton-cake and minerals, made up the rations for the cows, bullocks, sheep and pigs. The skill lay in knowing what proportions of the various ingredients to feed.

Just prior to harvest a swath about 8 or 9ft wide was always mown around every field and the corn hand-tied, often by the women, into sheaves so that the horses pulling the binder should not trample it down. During the cutting with the machine one or two men were stationed permanently at the corners of the field with scythes to keep the uncut crop from running to a point, which would make it difficult for the unwieldy binder and its three horses pulling to turn. One of these men, too, was responsible for sharpening knives. These long serrated knives with four sharp blades per foot were fixed to sharpening stools and whoever was responsible sharpened each of the triangular-shaped blades with a file or carborundum. It was a hazardous job and we seldom got through a harvest without a few hands having to be stitched up by the doctor. Indeed the equipment that went with the sharpening stool, file and carborundum, was a bandage, a bottle of Lysol and a tiny bottle of iodine: and there was often a report to Father in the evening, 'Fred went to the doctor again today for a stitch!'

Father's first harvest at Testerton was in 1925 and it was the last occasion that he paid the harvest wages in gold sovereigns. That year harvest began on August 25th and finished on September 22nd. The full men got £1 6s 6d per week and the boys got 5s 0d. There was no overtime, but if harvest was completed within the month each person received £1 10s 0d extra. The insurance stamps came to 2s 10d. The night that the last load was brought in, leaving the final stack with its corn dolly cross on the top – some people say it was of pagan origin to keep away the devil – the men all assembled outside the front door of the Hall. Inside my father sat at his study desk with my mother paying out each person and making up the books. Everyone was given their wages, together with the harvest bonus of £1 10s 0d for finishing inside the month; and it was all paid out in gold, silver, half-crowns, florins, shillings, sixpences, threepenny-pieces, copper, pennies, half-penny-pieces and farthings. I can still see them all standing in line with their caps respectfully under their arms. Every man was given a pint of beer, sausage rolls and cake; the boys had lemonade and a sausage roll and boiled sweets. The last one to be paid was Jack Green, who was a few years older than me. My mother asked him what he was going to do with the money and he said, 'Take it home to mother'. She told him to turn out his pockets and every single one had a large hole in it, or perhaps more accurately no bottom to it. My mother obviously thought that he might lose the money on the way home and said, 'Well take off your boot and we will put it in the toe.' Jack did, only to find that his socks, too, were full of holes and the boot had a hole big enough for the coins to drop through. Mother, therefore, wrapped the money first in cardboard and then in paper and pushed it into the toe of Jack's boot (they were two sizes too big and obviously hand-me-downs) and off he hobbled. When everyone had gone, my father said, 'I think I'll get the car out and run that boy home. If not his mother will be down here tomorrow saying that he lost his wages, and it will cost us more in the long run!' The Greens lived two miles away so the chances were my father was right.

Years later Jack Green rose to the dizzy heights of becoming a bicycle owner. He was also a great leg puller. One day when the men were all busy hoeing sugar-beet at the far end of a field he changed all their lunches round in their frail baskets. He forgot to change his own, however, so it was immediately obvious who had done it. Apart from the others giving him a playful thick ear nothing happened for a few days, but then, mysteriously, whilst everyone or nearly everyone was at work his bicycle disappeared. When leaving-off time came and everybody went for their bikes Jack's wasn't there and couldn't be seen anywhere. Then somebody said, 'What's that in the top of that elm tree?' It was, of course, Jack's bicycle some 50 or 60ft above the ground and no one present had any idea how it got there. Jack was left alone to sort out the problem. It was still there the next morning and rumour had it that Jack had slept under the tree all night for, although it was second-hand, it was new to him and very precious. It wasn't until after work the following day that he was able to bribe one of his chums to walk with a thatching ladder from the farm to get it down.

I loved the harvest, riding on the backs of the horses, jolting up and down in the waggons, sitting down to dinner in the field at midday, and waiting for the men's wives and Mother to bring the 'fourses' (tea), but I also loved the autumn, perhaps because there was still quite a lot of the eight-week summer holiday from school left for 'messing about' on the farm.

The autumn meant ploughing and, although we had a tractor at Testerton and it ploughed all the daylight hours, a great deal of the land was still ploughed by horses. The fields, particularly those with any degree of slope on them, were always ploughed up and down to help with drainage and the ploughman took great care to set the fields out exactly and to keep the

The stacker's craft: eight cap-ended wheat stacks.

furrows dead straight. In fact a recognised pastime on Sundays was to walk to other parishes and see how the work was being done by other ploughmen on neighbouring farms. The men often finished up in the pub in the village of whatever locality they had visited and, if they had seen any bad workmanship in the shape of wriggling furrows and they found the culprit, they would collect a pint. It also gave those who were likely to be taking part an idea of the skills of a particular person who might have entered the autumn ploughing match, on which there would always be a certain amount of betting.

The setting of the ploughs was a very important and highly skilled job, particularly when opening the furrows. If any of the land was left uncut or not turned over properly it would show in the subsequent crops. For this reason when tractor ploughs first came in and the men hadn't got the knack of them the fields were always set out with horses. Most of the ploughing would then be done with a tractor, and the furrows closed and the fields finished again with a pair of horses and a plough. I think perhaps this was a natural resistance to change and many farmers hung on till the last minute before economics forced them into getting rid of their horses in favour of the tractors. It was said for all sorts of reasons that the tractors wouldn't last; that the weight of them on the land would ruin the soil texture; that the speed at which the soil was inverted would cause the land not to breathe or drain properly. But when it was seen that a man and a tractor could do upwards of ten times the work of a man and a pair of horses in the same time, it was recognised that the tractor was here to stay. I remember hearing an argument between a horseman and a tractor-man. The latter pointed out that horses were eating when they weren't doing anything and you only had to fuel a tractor when it was running, but the horseman replied, 'Well your old tractor is drinking fuel all the time thass going and that don't breed, and there's nothing come out of it to put goodness back into the land!'

Perhaps it was the drilling of the seed which earned the biggest bouquets for accuracy. It really did require a lot of skill to drive a pair of horses absolutely dead straight up and down a field. The early drills had a boy leading the horse and a man driving with reins from the back. He had a steering mechanism and could straighten out any slight kinks, but it was still a job requiring the maximum concentration. It is impossible once the seed has dribbled down the thirteen coulters (rows) into the ground to get it out again to cover any mistakes.

The most unpleasant job on the farm in the autumn was carting the muck on to the ollands, which were the fields that had yielded the hay crop. This was a labour intensive job as there were no mechanical loaders and it all had to be done with forks. If there hadn't been time to cart the muck out of the yards where the bullocks had been before the harvest it had to be dug out then, or, if there had been time to clear the yards, it meant transporting it from a muck heap by tumbril onto the fields. Using a four-tine fork a man would be expected to load twenty tumbrils a day: then, with one horse in the shafts and a trace horse this would be taken to the field where it would be half-tipped and dumped off the back of the cart by a man pulling at the muck with a 'crome' as the horses walked forward. These small muck heaps would be dotted along in straight lines, about 12yd apart in the rows, and from row to row. Like getting their furrows straight when ploughing, it was a matter of pride with the men to have the dung heaps in serried rows. The next operation, again entirely by hand, was to fling the muck off the heaps and spread it uniformly over the land. This was another reason for getting almost exactly the same amount of muck in each heap.

Another autumn and winter job that was extremely time consuming and required a great deal of stamina was hedging, ditching and draining. The trimming of hedges, which was done with a hook rather like a reaper's hook on a long handle, was quite easy. But laying hedges, which required using axes and bill hooks and half cutting through the blackthorn, bending it over and lacing it in, was extremely hard work. Bottoming (in Norfolk known as 'bottom-fying') ditches with a draining shovel was another tedious job, particularly if the ditches round the outside of most of the fields were about 5 or 6ft deep as everything had to be thrown from the bottom up to land level. But I think one of the worst jobs was under-draining. The whole field was marked out in a herring-bone pattern. The drains were dug to the required width (wide enough for a man to work in) and then tiled drain-pipes were placed end to end in the bottom. The bottom level of the drain had to be very accurately dug out in order to give just enough slope to the tiles or pipes to allow the water to run to the edge of the field and out into the open ditch. It was difficult enough on land made up of a similar consistency all over, but it got extremely difficult where the land varied from sandy soil through marl and chalk to clay. Generations before my time the draining was done by placing large stones, thorns and brushwood in the bottom of the trench. Often these stones, thorns and brushwood can still be seen when the ditches are dug today, and indeed in some cases still work. Nowadays of course it is all done by one machine with plastic pipes, and the depth controlled with laser beams. One man can do as much as a hundred used to do.

OLD CURES AND REMEDIES

Rheumatism

a. Carry a potato for 40 days in the pocket
b. Secure some squeezes of oil from the Church bell
c. Sit as nakedly as decency will allow and get well stung by bees

After applying any of these remedies the complaint will disappear.

Chapter Six

Testerton: The Steam-men and the Keepers

Slowly, but inexorably, in the twenties the mechanisation of farming crept on: and with the new machines there emerged new generations of men who used and cherished them. They used to say that the veins of the old steam-men and engine drivers were full of soot. Horsemen and cowmen were supposed to have veins full of a far more messy substance. I loved the animals on the farm, but from the time George Cushing gave me my 'baptism of fire' by putting me – still in white clothes and unable to walk – in the coal bunker of his steamroller, my real love has been steam. It was another engine-man from Thursford, Harry Bushell, who made certain that this love was to last the whole of my life. Harry not only knew all about engines, but found the time to pass his passion on to us youngsters.

One of my first memories of Harry Bushell was when my father bought his first new threshing tackle, engine and drum in 1925 or 1926. The engine was a Marshall, sent from the factory where they were made at Gainsborough to Fakenham station. Father asked Harry if he would go and steam the engine off the railway truck and drive it to a field just outside the town where the Norfolk Agricultural Show was to be held. The elevator which completed the outfit had been made at the Bushell works at Thursford, where for many decades Harry's family had made threshing drums and elevators, and it came from Harry's yard pulled by a horse in shafts. The main body (boiler) of the engine was in maroon livery with fire-engine-red wheels and a black chimney, and it was lined out in black and gold. The oilers, boiler banding and whistle were polished brass and the chimney ferrule copper; a magnificent combination of decor and colour. The drum and elevator were painted in salmon pink with red wheels. The steel hand levers, cranks and steering wheel were purposely left unpainted but were protected from rust by a film of oil, and elbow grease. It was a picture I shall never forget. I understand that the whole lot cost under £600, but the worth and value of the workmanship that went into their creation by the craftsmen involved is almost beyond monetary value.

The journey from the station through the town, with Harry driving and my father as steersman, was like a carnival parade. I was allowed to sit in the coal tender and can plainly remember all the people from the shops, pubs and houses coming out to see us go by. My brother rode ahead on a bicycle with the wheels decorated with red, white and blue ribbons, and my mother brought up the rear in the bull-nosed Morris. The next two days were absolute bliss. The weather was perfect and I didn't leave the threshing outfit for one moment, and cannot remember anything else that was at the Show.

My father, too, was very proud of his latest possession. The threshing at Testerton before the arrival of this new machine had been done by a Farmers' Foundry engine and Bushell drum which the previous tenant of the farm had had for many years, and which Father had taken over. This was the portable engine described in an earlier chapter. It had four iron wheels and was pulled from site to site on the farm by four or more horses, two in the shafts and two ahead in trace harness. The drum and the elevator were moved from place to place in the same way. The advent of traction engines using steam power to drive the machinery to move them, was a great technical breakthrough. Until then, moving an enormous top-heavy machine weighing up to seven tons with four horses and no system of braking except the two shaft horses 'hanging back', as the saying went, was not an easy manoeuvre and relied a great deal on the skill of the horseman. Luckily our farm was not hilly, but even on the slightest incline a couple of men always walked beside the engine carrying two large blocks of wood to throw under the wheels if things began to get out of hand. The old engine and drum weren't in very good order when my father bought them, so the purchase of new machinery was only a matter of time. The old tackle stood in the yard until many years later when it went for scrap, but not before I had threshed scores and scores of imaginary coombs of wheat with it and in the process come to know every nut and bolt and all the complicated bits and pieces that make up an engine and threshing machine.

The corn stacks to be threshed were built in multiples of two and often a dozen would be set out in a carefully measured row. The new machinery would be hauled by the engine and manoeuvred in between each pair of stacks, and the threshing took place from alternate sides of the drum on each successive day. When the drum and elevator had been hauled into position, the engine would then be turned around to face the drum for the actual threshing process, power being transmitted from the engine flywheel to the drum and subsequently to the elevator by flat balata belts. The weather was of critical importance. If the engine was standing up-wind the smoke was carried away, but if it was down-wind everybody working on the stacks or around the machine was 'kippered' by the smoke. Even when the wind was carrying the smoke away, though, the muck coming out of the drum was blown back to the working areas, so you always got it one way or t'other!

Although threshing was a mucky job I liked it because of the smell of the mixture of hot steam and oil. The men tolerated it because of the extra money, as threshing was worth 6d a day more; and Father liked it because of the income from the corn. There were three men in a threshing gang pitching the sheaves of corn from the stack on to the threshing machine. The server made certain that each sheaf was pointing in the right direction across the drum, handing them or pitching them to the bond cutter who grabbed each sheaf in his left hand, catching it with the blade of a serrated knife. The knife was strapped to his wrist so that if he dropped it, it didn't fall into the machinery. Then with a little jerk he would cut the string, which left him holding the twine in his left hand ready to be used again for tying up the sacks of corn. The sheaves were threshed instantly in the drum by the beater bars which knocked the corn out of the straw. The straw was then carried back on 'straw walkers' to the far end of the drum, where it fell on to the elevator which took it up on to the stack. The corn (grain) having been beaten hard fell through the concaves and sieves inside the drum, passing through blasts of air from fans which blew away the chaff and cholder husks. When it reached the lowest point at almost ground level, an elevator took it up to the top of the drum again and it went through another cleaning process and finished up on the opposite end of the drum to the straw. After it had passed through a rotary separator, one of the men sacked it off into very heavy cotton sacks. The weight of these sacks varied according to the bushel weight of the crop. Peas were the heaviest and weighed 20 stone (2½cwt or 280lb); wheat was 10 stone (2¼cwt or 252lb); barley 16 stone (2cwt or 224lb); and oats 12 stone (1½cwt or 168lb). I can't remember what clover seed weighed, but it was heavier than peas and much too heavy for any two people to lift except by using a lifting pole grasped in the left hand by one person, and the right hand of another, the weight being distributed between the pole and the lifter's arms.

As long as the wind was not too strong, the people on the straw stack receiving the threshed straw from the elevator had a nice job. The threshed and moderately dust-free straw cascaded down to them and, using an ordinary two-tined fork, they pulled it into a more or less cube-shaped stack. As the day wore on they gradually pulled it to the centre so that it finished up with eaves and a sloping roof. The chap who had a horrible job was the chaff and cholder man. All the muck from the fans had to be sacked off into very large hessian bags, which he then had to drag out between the stack that was threshed and the elevator taking the threshed straw on to the straw stack. The only face mask available in those days was either a handkerchief or a square of coarse linen. Eye goggles were provided; not made of glass but very fine perforated zinc. Strangely enough there always seemed to be one man who would tackle the job, and he would boast about it. Whether it was from sheer bravado or because the others hated it so much that they would usually buy him a pint at the end of the week I never knew, but I reckon that in today's terms, if it were allowed at all, it would be at treble rate!

The engine driver was in overall charge of the threshing and had to arrive a good hour before anyone else in order to get up steam. He was responsible not only for the running and maintenance of the engine, drum and elevator, but for the quality of the sample. His choice of size and adjustments to various sieves and wind settings could make or mar a sample. A stack with a base size of 12ft x 7ft was reckoned to be a fair day's work. Obviously it was the engine driver's responsibility to keep the wheels turning and to get the best out of the helpers, but it was also in his interest to do so, for his day included the move to the next stack and preparation for another day. Almost every job depended on many other factors, like the condition of the corn at harvest-time, the way that it was stacked from floor to apex in order to keep the water out, the efficiency of the thresher, the vagaries of the weather (in particular the wind) and the back-up and support of the team each to the other. One man on the stack who wasn't pulling his weight could make it all a great deal harder for the rest.

Rats and mice abounded in the corn stacks and although it was great fun killing them it didn't do to think about it, for they had been living in and feeding on what was finally intended for human consumption. Everyone wore 'yorks', a narrow leather strap tied round the leg below the knee, to prevent rats or mice ascending, and in a year of excessive infestation I have seen anything up to a hundred rats killed by boys with sticks and terrier dogs. In the thirties a law was brought in making it illegal to thresh without a wire netting surround to ensure that as few as possible of the rats could escape.

At harvest-time, in order to get a certain amount of cash coming in, some of the corn was threshed directly off the stook ('shock' in Norfolk), and the rest was built into stacks in the corners of the field and threshed during the winter when labour was available. I loved it when the engine and threshing turn-out were working, but my appetite for steam was never satisfied. It helped considerably when Father decided to hire a Fowler steam ploughing tackle from Shackcloth Brothers at Great Snoring. The Fowler engines used for this purpose worked in pairs, and were much larger than those used for threshing. They had enormous horizontal drums, with 800yd of wire rope attached under their bellies. The two engines took up their positions at opposite sides or ends of the field and the plough or cultivator was pulled backwards and forwards across the field between them; then the engines moved on the width of the plough or cultivator for the next bout. Compared with the engines used for threshing, these were huge. They were 16 hp and weighed over twenty tons. The wheels were larger and wider to prevent them from sinking into the ground, but like the threshing engines they needed a supply of coal and water.

The complete outfit used to arrive at the farm from the previous location

Steam ploughing engine with balance plough.

by road. There were two engines, one towing the plough and cultivator and sometimes a mole drainer, and the other towing the coal cart, the water cart and a living van. The latter was necessary because the principal operators of the outfit lived on site during the week going home at weekends. The team consisted of two drivers, a steersman for the plough or cultivator, and one extra as a relief so that they could work non-stop throughout the day; plus a boy who did the cooking and cleaning of the hut and acted as general dogsbody, often getting sworn at in the process. On occasions a wife or girlfriend might also come along to make sure the hut was clean. The farmer was required to provide a man or boy to cart the coal, and to see that the engines had a good supply of water, using the water cart belonging to the contractors. Well in advance of the arrival of the outfit a truck or trucks of coal would have been delivered to the local railway station, carted by horse and tumbril to the fields that were to be ploughed, and dumped in heaps on the headland. Often the heaps were not in exactly the right place so the coal would have to be picked up again by shovel, in order to keep up with the engines. The actual operation was usually very smooth. The drivers used their whistles to signal to each other. Often on large fields and in misty conditions they could barely, if at all, see each other. The plough would be pulled smoothly and almost in silence across the field and only the swish (it was a lovely sound) of the earth being turned would be audible. After the plough had been pulled across the field to the headland, the driver of the engine that had done the pulling would give one toot on his whistle, signalling to the driver at the other side of the field to move up the width of the plough and start pulling the plough back. Two toots meant that he needed water, and three toots meant bring coal as well. As the engine took up the strain the plough would automatically tilt so that its other five furrows would plough their way back across the field.

The official description of the plough was a 'one-way counter-balanced plough', meaning that when it was being pulled from one end five furrows were in the ground turning the soil to the left, and when ploughing was going the other way across the field the other five furrows were turning the soil to the right. The whole thing was a brilliant concept and the forerunner of the modern tractor-drawn one-way reversible plough. The cultivator worked on the same principle except that it didn't tilt but had an ingenious system of turning round as each engine took up the slack on the cable. According to soil conditions the engines pulled the plough or cultivator across the field at what seemed to me to be an unbelievably fast rate; certainly faster than comfortable walking speed as I know – I used to have to run to keep up. Father always hung precariously on the back by his hands. The reason he put in a great number of appearances when the machines were working was to check that they were ploughing at the right depth. His walking stick was always marked off in inches so that he could ride so far, hop off, push his walking stick in and make certain that they were ploughing at the agreed depth. Father used the Shackcloth ploughing outfit for several years, and when it came up for sale he decided that he would buy it. A few years later when the acreage of land that he farmed reached around 2,000 acres he bought another outfit. Ploughing was now being done so speedily that the ever-increasing team of tractors could take care of the rolling, harrowing and sowing, and vast acreages of cereals were drilled with very few men and even fewer horses.

My mother must have had one of the most sensitive noses ever. She always knew when I had been on the tractor with Charlie Howe after his night-time escapades with the 'honey cart', and seemed to have a good idea where any of us had been at any time. She knew, for instance, if we had been in the blacksmith's shop from the smell of burnt hoof and red lead paint. She didn't take exception to that, but she did object to the smell we gave off after we had been mucking out the pigs. The smells from the cows and the dairy were all right except when, once a week, butter-making was in progress. She so disliked that smell that she would only eat 'shop' butter or margarine. I loved butter-milk and drank gallons of the stuff. We always heard about it when we went sheep dipping, for the smell of Jeyes Fluid and sulphur was definitely 'out'. Horses were 'in', and so was anything to do with the garden, except when shoddy was being dug in. Wet sugar-beet pulp was also deemed to be 'no go', but, thank goodness, she would put up with the smell of coal dust and oil from the hot engines. This also applied to the ploughing engines, but the ploughmen's living van eventually became a 'no go' area. She always said that the men didn't wash – but I knew they did. At the end of every day they would bring a couple of pailfuls of hot water in from the steam engines. You can't have steam without boiling water, so there was no shortage of that. They would then do their ablutions at the van. They had two enamel bowls on a stand at the back, one to get the worst of the grease and grime off and the other to rinse in and shave with, perhaps once a week. I expect they occasionally had a bath when they got home, but that wasn't very often. I think that what Mother objected to was perhaps the general 'lived-in' smell that built up inside the van, and came home with me. Most of the ploughmen smoked 'darky' shag or chewed twist and they were past-masters at spitting out through the half-door. It could be hazardous if you were coming up the steps! Often, too, there was a pungent smell of wet clothes from the socks and vests hanging from the roof of the van. The bedclothes on the five or six bunks were just grey blankets as they didn't have sheets, and they all slept in their underwear, including their socks.

The heating for the van was enough, and sometimes too much: it came from a small tortoise stove with a tin oven on the top. This was sometimes swapped for a large cauldron which bubbled away making stew from anything that was available, including the occasional sheep's head. Usually one or more members of the team were adept at catching game: not to be wondered at, for all day they were able to observe where hares, rabbits, pheasants and partridges were on the fields. Indeed they constantly disturbed the game as they ploughed their way from side to side. The steersman on the plough or cultivator always had a stick, and would often jump off and kill a squatting hare on its set. They used snares for hares or rabbits and also a special homemade snare on the end of a stick to catch roosting pheasants in trees on moonlit nights. The keepers hated the steam ploughs because of the upset to their game. They reckoned horses were bad enough, but at least ploughing with horses was a slow job compared with the 'monsters' which could plough up to forty acres a day.

There was always bad blood between the keepers and the engine-men, especially after turning-out time from the pub on a Saturday night when things usually came to a head and often ended up in a scrap. My Father had a favourite story about the keeper reporting some of the ploughmen to the local bobby for poaching. The policeman kept a watch one night and, when he thought they had caught a pheasant, plucked it and put in in the pot, he climbed the ladder into the van and accused them of having pheasant for supper. They, of course, denied it and offered him a taste, saying that it was chicken. They produced some on a plate for his inspection and he had to agree that it certainly was chicken. He said that if they had plenty he wouldn't mind a meal. The story went that they gave him a plateful with potatoes and turnips which he thoroughly enjoyed, and it wasn't until some time later that the truth came out. They had stolen one of Father's cockerels, some potatoes from the foreman's garden and turnips from the hale where they were being stored for the winter. The big question was, did the bobby know that he had become an accessory after the fact? After all Father was a magistrate!

The village constables were usually very helpful to the keepers. Practically every village of any size had a resident constable living in the police house, which was located as near to the centre of the parish as possible and always had a telephone. The constables were able to be helpful to the keepers because the policing system required them to keep their 'points' with the constables in adjoining parishes. They shared any news of local events, including poachers and poaching activities, passing it on by word-of-mouth when they met at prearranged times at these points. The points were usually a crossroads, church or plantation in the country where the parish boundaries met and each meeting was always at a different time of day or night. it meant that the poor old bobbies had a lot of cycling to do, but on the other hand they were far more likely to surprise a criminal – particularly a poacher – especially on moonlit nights when they often travelled in the near-dark to save paraffin in their lamps. As far as I can remember one heard very little of house-breaking and entry, or robbery with violence; law breaking mostly seemed to be concerned with stealing food in the shape of farm produce and game.

The constable also checked that the dogs in the parish were licenced and that people like farmers and shepherds, who had exemptions for working dogs, had the necessary certificates. Gun licences and firearm certificates had to be inspected by the constable every so often, and it was his job to see that special licences granted by the Bench for social events were adhered to. He also had to ensure that the special constables (worthy law-abiding citizens appointed by the Chief Constable on a voluntary basis for duty to help the force whenever necessary) were kept up to the mark and informed of any new police regulations. One of the most important jobs was to see that publicans closed and opened their pubs on time. Mind you most of the policemen I knew were not averse to getting to the pub a little early to make certain that the publican complied with the law, and that the beer was worth drinking! There is no doubt that the policemen knew their parishes and the people so well that they saved many a man from a drunk and disorderly charge by tapping him on the shoulder an hour before closing time and telling him he had had enough. And in Great Ryburgh it was well known that some wives would ask the policeman to visit the pub, particularly on pay nights, to tell some of the husbands to get home before the wages had all changed hands. Because there was a telephone in the police house our constable received and relayed messages for parishioners, although it was against all the constabulary rules!

One of my father's great delights was shooting, but as he didn't have shooting rights his sport was confined to an occasional invitation to shoot on an official shooting day when the landlord brought his friends. Mother was not overly pleased about this as in return the whole party of about ten people would descend on her for lunch and often return for tea. But Father also took a great deal of pleasure walking the hedgerows on his own with his gun and his two dogs, a labrador and a terrier. The dogs worked ahead scaring the rabbits, hares and pigeons, and Father picked off those that bolted out. He also enjoyed stalking without the dogs on summer evenings. He often came home with half-a-dozen or so rabbits in the game bag he carried on his shoulder. These he would immediately 'hulk' by taking out their guts, and 'hurdle', which meant putting one hind leg through a slit in the other so that they could be hung up. The rabbits were then hung in an outdoor game larder. This was an outhouse, with perforated zinc windows to keep out the flies and give a through draught.

The Sennowe Estate was large enough to warrant a company of keepers – usually five – one of whom was permanently based at Testerton. The first duty of the senior keeper and his assistants, under the head keeper, was rearing game in the spring and summer so that there was a good show of birds for the landlord's organised shoots in the autumn and winter. In the winter-time the keepers were responsible for making certain that the game predators – foxes, stoats and weasels – were kept down, but there had to be some foxes left in order to make a chase for the foxhounds. Most of the members of the hunting fraternity were friends of the landlord; farmers and landowners, and other well-to-do local people. The keepers knew exactly where pheasants and partridges would feed and roost and would patrol these areas on most nights when weather conditions were suitable for poaching. The birds were at risk not only from the poacher who poached for a bit of fun and money, but very often from the father of a large family who simply hadn't enough money to feed his family properly.

There was a good deal of netting of partridges: two or more poachers would drag very fine nets over the stubble field to capture coveys of partridges when they were huddled together for the night. Unlike pheasants, which roost in trees or bushes, partridges spend their nights on the ground in the open huddled together. For this reason, before cultivation of the stubble took place, the keepers would be very busy sticking sprigs of blackthorn or brambles about 2ft high at random over the fields, making it difficult for the poachers to drag their nets across without entangling them. The netting of rabbits was another favourite poaching method. The poacher ran a 30in high fine net along the edge of the field where rabbits were known to come out from the banks at night to feed, then a dog, often a lurcher, was sent in to work out in the field. The scared rabbits would run full pelt into the nets where they remained entangled until the poacher could extricate them and break their necks. The poacher could only work when weather conditions were right and when the wind was blowing off the field he was working, it was less easy for the rabbits to scent him and his dogs. Rabbit skins, if properly treated, were an added bonus from poaching. It was only necessary for the person who skinned the rabbit to stretch it and tack it on to a flat board, or the back door of the house or privy, after first smearing it with paraffin, saltpetre and ordinary salt, and then leave it to dry. A good rabbit pelt, well treated, would be worth 2d or 3d at the most, but it was worth the trouble and the risk as the economics of the countryside were harsh.

The rag-and-bone man (he should really have been called the rag-skin-bone-and-feather-man) was a regular visitor in the parish wherever he thought there might be sellers from whom he could purchase skins and feathers, etc. These would be sorted and taken to the larger town-based dealers, fell-mongers or tannery. The local rag-and-bone men that I remember either carried their wares as a pack on their backs or on their bicycles, which they pushed when loaded with broaches hung with partially-cured rabbit skins. If the weather was hot they were always followed by swarms of flies. Most small towns and some larger villages, if there was a good supply of water, had a tannery where the fleeces, skins and hides finished up for curing. The feathers from poultry or game went to the mattress-makers, who bought them for making the feather-beds which went on top of the hair mattresses. Bolsters, pillows and eiderdowns were also made locally. Because of the bulkiness of the feathers only small quantities in large sacks could be carried on a bicycle and then only as far as the railway station, to go the rest of the way by train.

One of the keepers employed by Father's landlord, lived in a cottage in the wood on the boundary of the Testerton farm. He was a person with whom I spent a great deal of my time as a boy. His name was Cecil Collins and he must then have been in his forties. His cottage was in the middle of Highfield wood and an area of about two acres had been cleared for him to rear pheasants. He was a strong, quiet man, although he had a fine sense of humour once you got to know him. He certainly had a way of making almost any subject interesting to me, and at the same time getting me to do willingly some of the nastier jobs which came within his province.

One of the more onerous tasks was hulking rabbits. After a day's ferreting there could be anything up to fifty rabbits on his long rabbiting staff to be carried home and then hulked. I really hated this, but because he always maintained that he could hulk rabbits quicker than anybody else, I was constantly hulking against the clock trying to come up to his standard. To hulk a rabbit you have to take the rabbit in the left hand with its belly facing upwards, make a quick incision the length of the under belly, transfer the rabbit to your knee, place the index finger of each hand in the centre of the slit and pull it open, exposing the whole of the entrails from the rib cage to the pelvis. The right hand is then used to pull out all the entrails together, including the lungs, liver and heart, from gullet to rectum. If done with the knack that Collins had it all came out cleanly in one piece – but unskilled hands could result in some of the contents of the lower gut being squeezed out, leaving an awful mess in the carcass. Hulking rabbits when they had been badly shot was the worst job, as the innards were a ghastly bloody mess. Cecil would never allow water to be used, as he said that water spoiled the pelt. After hulking, the badly shot ones and the baby bunnies were skinned and kept to feed the ferrets. They were not fed the night before a day's rabbiting for, as Cecil always said, 'Full ferrets won't work so keep 'em hungry'. This could be a two-edged precept though, as if they were really hungry they would go to ground and when they cornered a rabbit in a burrow they would kill it and eat it. The whole operation had to stop if the ferret's position underground prevented it from being retrieved by pulling the line attached to its neck collar. It might then have to be dug out, and a lot of sweat could be lost if the digging was in a bank where there were tree roots and large stones. Using a ferret without a line and relying on the rabbit bolting before it was killed was the alternative, in which case very light nets were placed over the burrows to catch the rabbits as they came out. The reason for this was that burrows in banks or large warrens were so interconnected it was difficult to cover all exits. When working very large warrens and burrows Cecil would stand, with his gun, wherever he though the rabbits might escape near the places not covered properly with nets and shoot them as they bolted out. Cecil's twelve-bore must have been one of the most unsafe shooting pieces around for the right-hand barrel had had so much wear during its long life that the trigger catch had gone, so he normally only put a cartridge in the left breech. However, on the few occasions where he felt that he might need a second barrel to have two shots at whatever it was he was aiming at, he kept the external hammer (which wouldn't hold back because it was so worn) in position with a piece of elastic. The gun was held to the shoulder with both hands and after taking aim he would let go of the stock with the right hand (in which he had his always-razor-sharp shut knife) and touch the extended elastic which severed, letting the hammer forward and firing the cartridge.

Cecil, like many other keepers, knew a great deal about vermin, including rabbits. He knew when rabbits were 'on the move', although I never fathomed out what the secret was. Every so often he would say, 'Them rabbits down on the low meadow are going to move into the gravel pit next.' Sure enough after a few days the fresh workings would prove that he was absolutely right. He also knew where foxes were and sensed when they moved from their various earths. My father always said that Cecil really controlled the fox hunting because if there was a Meet the fox would always mysteriously be scented in a convenient spinney or covert and followed by the hounds.

He also had dummy earths all over the place where he caught them, and I once saw him pedalling off on his old bicycle with a fox in a sack on his back. When I asked him why he did it he said it was worth a bottle of whisky from the Hunt Master, and it got rid of a whole lot of posh people on horses who would have disturbed his pheasants. How he managed to have the hares in the right places on coursing days I never did find out! One of the most important jobs for the gamekeeper was to keep the population of stoats and weasels down at hatching time as an old stoat will take eggs from under a sitting hen without the 'old lady' realising it. Cecil knew where all the stoat and vermin tracks across country were. Another problem for the keepers was rats. They were a problem too, on the farm premises and my father always paid the men a bonus to kill them. The price was 6d a dozen – a ha'penny each – and their tails had to be brought to my father's study as proof of execution. Father would then take charge of them, and they ended up in the earth closet so that they wouldn't be re-presented!

Cecil was responsible not only for the ground game, but also the crows, jackdaws, pigeons, jays, magpies, owls and hawks. They all came within his sphere and although his job involved killing he always said, 'Never kill the last one of anything because it might be needed tomorrow'. I hate to think what his reaction would have been to myxomatosis, but I guess he would have thought that the introduction of the virus into the rabbit world was unsporting.

I think the most enjoyable time I used to spend with Cecil Collins was the nesting season when every pheasant's nest had to be found and recorded with a cross on maps in his notebook. The nests had to be visited every day to check the number of eggs, but at the same time Cecil insisted that the birds were not to be disturbed. The inspection, therefore, had to take place when they were off feeding – a nigh-on impossible task which kept me moving round like a lunatic from nest to nest, and reporting back to him. These were the birds that were allowed free range but the ones that were in a netted compound were given chalk eggs to encourage them to lay and branches of fir trees under which they built their nests. A pheasant's nest is not a complicated affair in a tree like some other birds' nests, but just a shallow hollow lined with grass or leaves at ground level. When he sent me out to collect a few eggs from each nest every other day, he would tell me not to wash my hands as the birds could detect the scent of soap. I should always leave my hands dirty, taking care not to handle anything with a strong smell like creosoted posts. When sufficient eggs had been collected they were put on shallow trays for a few days and turned every few hours. The reason for this was that if they were left untouched, the yolks would sink down in the white within the shell, and if the yolks touched the shell they probably wouldn't hatch – the yolk must always be held in suspension. He told me, and it was true, that if you watched any bird long enough you would see that every now and again it would stand up and, by gentle manoeuvres with its feet, turn the eggs. When there were enough eggs in the trays they were put under old hens or bantams to hatch. For this reason broody hens were at a premium, as it is only when they are brooding that they will sit tight on the eggs. If Cecil heard of anyone in the village who had a few broody hens he would go and see them with a crate and either offer them a few pence per hen per week, or payment in kind, perhaps a brace of pheasants at Christmas. The owners had their hens back when they had done their hatching stint so no-one was the loser, but it did result in an awful lot of hen-carting up and down the parish. About that time paraffin-fuelled incubators were beginning to take the place of broody hens but Cecil didn't hold with these newfangled gadgets saying, 'An old hen might go off the "set" and spoil fifteen or sixteen eggs, but if the light went out on one of them new incubators you could lose a hundred and fifty!' So the brand new Gloster Gleaven incubator bought for him to use went back at the end of the season untried.

I learned a great deal from Cecil, most of which was valuable information and absolutely true, but he was a great leg-puller. I can remember when I was very young he swore that because the tenants on the Testerton farm built circular corn stacks he was going to make a gun with curved barrels so that he could shoot round corners. At first I believed him but after a time, when I became suspicious about it, he said he thought perhaps he had better not for the shots might continue round the stack and shoot him in the backside!

One branch of my mother's family, the Baileys, were molecatchers. Uncle Robert would contract with the farmer on an acreage basis to keep the moles on the farm down. My father, along with a great many other farmers, was one of his customers, and he always said that if there wasn't a smattering of moles on the farm Uncle Robert would always see that there was, otherwise he would be out of a job. He travelled by pony-and-cart and his method of tackling a large infestation was firstly to go over the farm and catch as many as possible in spring or tube traps. The moles were then collected and skinned, and the pelts dried and sold. If that didn't solve the problem he used worms. Worming was quicker and more effective than traps, but wasteful because the moles were poisoned and could not be retrieved as they died underground. To do this Uncle Robert had to have a good supply of worms, and he and his two sons used to walk behind the ploughmen and pick them up from the freshly turned earth as they appeared – and before the seagulls got them. Once eased out of the ground, the worms – the bigger and juicier the better – could be dropped into a glass jar in the pocket and taken home and kept in a pail of peat ready for when they were needed. The method used to inject strychnine into the worms was simple. A reel of cotton was soaked in a very small diluted solution of strychnine and then the worms were threaded with a needle on to the cotton. The worms, of course, died instantly. The string was hung up and snipped with scissors in between each worm so that every worm had a tiny piece of strychnine-soaked cotton through it. This was always done very early in the morning. Then, while the worms were fresh and very recently dead the fields would be walked: wherever a mole was working a small hole was made in the mole run and a worm was dropped into it. The mole, paddling along underground, came across the freshly dead worm with the piece of strychnine-soaked cotton through it, gobbled it up and soon he too was dead. The real skill was in identifying the mole's main run.

Uncle Robert was a splendid chap, always smartly turned out and never without a home-made moleskin waistcoat which my mother always said she could scent before he arrived. He always came on Michaelmas Day or soon after to contract the acreage price with my father, arriving at seven o'clock in the morning, stabling his pony, and making certain he was around for eggs and bacon. Mother didn't have breakfast on that day because she couldn't face eating in front of all those dead moles that Uncle Robert was wearing. I was very fond of him and intrigued by the care with which he used his worms. It wasn't until later in life that I realised that strychnine is pretty potent stuff: indeed he eventually told me that the tiny bottle he used to buy from the chemist, only about half-an-inch high, contained enough of the poison to kill everyone in Fakenham! Both my cousins are molecatchers to this day – and very good ones too.

Chapter Seven

Testerton: Change and Uncertainty

My father wasn't a betting man; in fact, in all his life I only ever remember him having one bet, and that was on a greyhound. Coursing was quite a popular pastime in North Norfolk and the Swaffham Coursing Club held meetings at various places, usually at groups of farms like Testerton and Highfield. The annual meeting would be held in the autumn by arrangement with the landowners and farmers. On the chosen day the hares would be gently and skilfully 'rounded up'. This meant that they would be persuaded to go towards a certain part of the farm, usually an olland. There, with luck, the hares would rest quietly until they were needed for the chase. Only one hare was coursed at a time by two greyhounds. The great skill required by the Clerk of the Course and the organisers was to bring forward one hare at a time from where they were resting, on to the adjoining field where the chase was to take place. An official 'slipper' released the dogs, which were held on a special leash terminating in two leather collars. Each collar had a spring-released catch which was actuated through the hollow leash by a cable with a toggle attached. As soon as the hare was seen by the greyhound the 'slipper' pulled the toggle, both collars opened together, and the chase was on. The hare, of course, took off at full speed followed by the dogs. After the initial spurt, or as soon as the dogs got near the hare, it would turn and twist and take any evasive action it could to avoid being caught. Sometimes if it was lucky it would dodge through a hole in the fence and escape, but more often than not it was caught and killed. A coursing meeting was a real day out, rather like a miniature point-to-point or steeplechase as 'bookies' were there to take bets, and there were beer tents and so on. On one occasion when Father was owed some money by one of the greyhound breeders he agreed to take a puppy in settlement of the debt. It lived with the other dogs on the farm and grew into a very attractive bitch, so much so that the local butcher, who bred and trained greyhounds, offered to take and train it for Father. Eventually she was taken to a few coursing meetings and did quite well, and the butcher asked if he could race her at the Boundary Park Greyhound Stadium in Norwich. Again she did well and won some races. Up till then she had been called 'Spot' because she had a strange spot on her forehead, but then one day when the back door was left open Spot strolled in and stole a joint of cold beef from the kitchen table. Her new name became 'Cold Joint' and it was under this name that she was entered for a race at the White City in London. The butcher and my father took her to London by train, placed a bet on her, and she won! They sold her there and then, and came home on the night train very well pleased. Father boasted that Cold Joint had covered the bad debt and made a little profit as well, but he advised us never to put money on dogs or horses as many people had to lose for a few to win. He reckoned he was one of the lucky ones. I was sorry we didn't see Cold Joint again.

Although he advised *us* never to gamble, my father did gamble in a big way with his farming enterprise. These were the years when farming was experiencing the worst ever depression in living memory. Bets with bookies he may not have placed, but he certainly bet on farming, and at a time when the odds were very much loaded against the industry. Starting as he did in 1912 on 400 rented acres and all the capital borrowed, it was an extraordinary achievement that by 1938 he was farming almost 5,000 acres, all tenanted, on eleven farms in different parishes as far apart as nine miles. Although I well remember that every other year or so we were taken to see yet another farm that Father was to become tenant of, I wasn't experienced enough to understand how it was actually being done. Years later when I asked him how he managed for capital at this time he told me that he always asked himself how much he could afford to spend on a crop in order to leave a profit, and not what was the maximum yield he could grow. This meant that he had to look very carefully at costs. Mechanisation was just getting underway and a man and a tractor could plough up to ten times the area ploughed by a man and a pair of horses in the same time, so as he took on each additional farm the only labour taken on for that farm was the bare minimum. Labour was moved about between the farms as required, using three old open-topped Ford Model T charabancs that had previously been used to run holiday trips from Norwich to Yarmouth. Each day at harvest-time the seats in these old buses were temporarily removed and the buses were then used to cart sheaves of corn in the fields to the stacks; all stacking was at the field gate and none was brought home to the stack-yard. After the day's work the seats were replaced in the buses, and everybody rode home.

From 1924 to 1938 the number of tractors owned by Father increased from the first Rushton I loved so much to thirty. These were mostly Fordsons, but there were some larger American-made Model L Cases which could pull three-or-four-furrowed ploughs, or very large single- or double-furrowed digger ploughs. These digger ploughs did the land the world of good. They turned up virgin soil that had not seen the light of day before and which yielded up its fertility, and they broke up the plough pan built up by the shallower four-inch deep horse ploughs over many generations. The deep ploughing meant that there was double the depth of aerated soil for the plants to use, and it helped immensely with drainage.

During the time that the tractor population was steadily increasing the horse population was declining and as there was no longer the need to feed upwards of eighty horses, the land that was set aside to grow food, hay, oats, etc., for them was turned over to growing arable cash crops. Roughly fifteen per cent of any farm had been devoted to maintaining horsepower which was now being replaced by tractors, all running on cheap vaporising oil at only a few pence per gallon. The increasing use of steam and petrol power with threshing engines, ploughing engines, gyrotillers and the new tractors (the latter continued to arrive with great regularity as they were needed on the various farms that Father took in hand) marked the demise of the horse and a great reduction in hand and manual labour. Two names I remember that epitomised this revolution were Ford and Ferguson. I think history will compare the impact they made on agriculture to the revolution in farming methods brought about by Townshend and Coke many decades earlier. Henry Ford mass-produced simple tractors with integral solid construction. Their engine, gearbox and transmission-housing were solid blocks of machinery bolted together so that there was no need for the chassis that all tractors had featured up until that time. The Ferguson (originally fitted to the Ford) was a system that had its implement close-coupled to the Ford power unit and was originally actuated by springs. It eventually ended up as the famous Ferguson hydraulic system, which made the tractor and implement (plough, cultivator, harrows and so on) virtually one machine but quickly inter-changeable. It was a real breakthrough. Father had tried one of the spring-loaded ploughs, but I don't think it was a great success for it lay about in a bed of nettles unused for many years. However, the first time I saw the Ferguson hydraulic system will stay in my memory for ever.

I think the year must have been 1930 or perhaps 1931. I should have been away at school, but had come home for the day because it was my birthday. I was told that there was to be a secret demonstration of a new tractor and plough – so secret that it would take place on a remote part of the farm and no one except those involved were to know anything about it and was sworn to secrecy on pain of being returned to school before the event took place. I remember it as if it were yesterday. In the middle of a field of quite heavy land, a small area (I think it was about an acre – approximately 70yd x 70yd) was roped off ready for the demonstration. A box van arrived and when the back-doors were opened, out came a new Ford tractor and attached to the rear of it was a two-furrow plough connected by links to the axle housing, but looking very much like the Ferguson spring-loaded plough which had already been tried and discarded. Not long after, three gentlemen arrived in a Bentley. I had been told who was coming and couldn't contain my excitement. They were Tim Birkin, later Sir Henry Birkin, the famous racing motorist, Harry Ferguson and another gentleman who made cars. He was William Morris, later Lord Nuffield. The purpose behind it all was to give William Morris a demonstration of the Ferguson system, with a view to persuading him to manufacture the tractor. It was a beautiful day and my brother Jack, then in his late teens, was to drive the tractor after Ferguson himself had given a convincing demonstration. This all happened. After the roped-off area was ploughed the cultivator was attached and the same area cultivated; then a set of harrows left the one acre plot ready to be seeded in a fraction of the time it would have taken to do the same job with horses. To a ten-year-old it all seemed nothing short of miraculous. Then Harry Ferguson said to my Father, 'Has your younger son ever driven a tractor?' My father said, yes, I was familiar with how clutches and gears worked and Harry Ferguson said, 'Well, let him have a go.' So with harrows on the back, I was put on the tractor and told to copy what my brother had just done. I remember it being so easy: I felt convinced that father would get one. He didn't – at least not then. He went on buying the much heavier Case American Model Ls. He, like so many others, thought you had to have weight and power to get traction. In other words, if the going is slippery, hang on another couple of horses for weight and power. The Ferguson system showed that traction could be increased by the configuration of the tractor and the implement and by the use of hydraulics.

After the demonstration my mother arrived in the bull-nosed Morris, with a picnic lunch packed in a laundry basket on the back. Lunch over I was taken reluctantly back to Bury St Edmunds to school. Before we left, Harry Ferguson, Tim Birkin and William Morris solemnly shook hands with me and one of them said, 'Well we had better find a half-crown for the boy.' None of them had a coin, but my father promised to see to it that I got one. For years afterwards I couldn't forgive Father for not buying a Ferguson – or a Bentley. But he never regretted buying the bull-nosed Morris. It gave years of sturdy and reliable service and when, finally, it was on its last legs he had the back of the body cut off which turned it into a two-seater, and he put a light cultivator with five tines on the end of the chassis frame. Chubby, the blacksmith, fitted an extra gear in the transmission to make it run at a very slow pace as the engine constantly over-heated, and a large drum for extra water was put in the place of the passenger seat and connected to the radiator. This strange contraption worked, and cultivated between the rows of thousands of acres of Brussels sprouts and cabbages. It must have been one of the very first examples of mechanical inter-row cultivators.

At the end of the school term, when I returned for the holidays, I asked my mother what happened after I was whisked away on the day of the demonstration. She said that everybody had come back to the house and they had sat well into the night discussing proposals for the manufacture of the new tractor. The idea was that the tractor should be built in the

Midlands at Morris and other factories, and the unit parts, engine, gearbox, transmission-housing and wheels be brought by train to a site at Fakenham where the LNER and the M&GN railways crossed. The different components would then be assembled by local labour and either sent off by rail to Kings Lynn docks for shipping abroad, or distributed to other parts of the country. Sadly, nothing ever came of this meeting and I was told that it was because Ferguson wouldn't sign an agreement with Morris relinquishing his right to change the design at any time if he so wished. Morris's point was that once he had tooled up at great expense to meet the requirements of the original design, any changes would lead to heavy additional costs. So, when the design had been finally agreed, he must have the prerogative to veto any additions or alterations. Before his meeting with Morris, Ferguson courted practically everyone in America who manufactured anything in the way of tractors and implements, including Ford.

Eventually Ferguson went back to Ford, and their liaison resulted in one of the biggest lawsuits in history, which Ferguson won. But that is another story. Surprisingly, after being so closely connected with Ferguson, Father stuck to Fords for the lighter cultivation work on the farms, but for the larger tractors used for ploughing he bought the American-made Case Model L. Ferguson was proved to be right in practically every aspect of design, as witnessed by the fact that the modern tractor employs the hydraulic draught control principle invented by him. In the case of the plough, the suction of the implement being pulled through the soil increases the pressure on the back wheels to stop it slipping. As the Ferguson patents ran out, all tractor manufacturers copied or near-copied his design.

An imaginative enterprise started by two brothers at South Creake in Norfolk which completely abandoned the horse for the tractor greatly influenced my father and many others. John and Eric Alley decided that given the right location labour could be cut on arable farms growing a high proportion of barley and wheat and horses done away with altogether. First they found and obtained a block of land. Bluestone Farm had 1313 acres, of which 950 were arable. The rental value was £900 per annum, including shooting rights, and the soil was light loam with gravel subsoil, regarded by the Alley brothers as being ideal for what they hoped to do. The farm belonged to the Townshend family and had been farmed for fifty years previously by one tenant who had adhered strictly to the four-course rotational system developed by 'Turnip' Townshend. Because of the Depression, however, the standard of farming had deteriorated and the land was full of weeds and the yield low. It was absolutely tailor-made for John and Eric. All the fields were over fifty acres (one was a hundred acres), and because of the gravel subsoil there were no drains or ditches. Before the Alley brothers took the farm fifty agricultural labourers and thirty-two horses had been employed to work it. Under their new system all the work was to be done by a foreman who, with a Ford truck, conveyed all the supplies, including fuel, to whichever part of the farm the tractors were working. The only other labour amounted to two tractor drivers and a farm blacksmith.

There was a great deal of scepticism amongst farmers in the area, most of them saying that the land wouldn't stand that sort of treatment and that, being light, it would blow away. In fact, the general opinion was that the whole concept was doomed to failure. The Alley brothers forged on; the average week worked by the tractor drivers was seventy to eighty hours. There were two reasons why the men worked such long hours; one was for the overtime, but secondly there was a tremendous spirit amongst them which fired them with determination to make the system work. The wage bill for the farm was cut from £4,000 a year to £700. The implements were brought over from America and were much bigger than anything that had been seen in Norfolk before. There were two big caterpillar tractors, each of which worked three thousand hours a year. They originally ran on petrol but were converted to paraffin, which when they ran for ten hours saved 17s 6d a day. Instead of ploughing the fields up and down which had been the traditional way with horses, the tractors started in the middle, ploughing on the square and finishing at the headlands, leaving no furrows or unlevel ground.

An article published in *Country Life* in October 1931 summed up the economics of the system.

> In attempting to estimate the economic aspects of this farming venture one has to recognise at the outset that the system was devised at a time when wheat was commanding 40s a quarter. Messrs Alley calculated upon a 4qr crop of wheat per acre and one pound's worth of straw, making the total receipts £9 per acre. Since then wheat has fallen considerably and, naturally, some concern is felt as to the future trend of prices. Full costs are being kept on this farm and it is estimated that ploughing costs under 7s per acre, cultivating under 3s; harrowing costs under 7d, drilling 1s, rolling, 9d and manure distribution, 1s 6d. It can be readily appreciated from these figures that once wheat does command better prices the success of the scheme will be assured. The amazing possibilities of this type of specialised farming, with wheat stabilized at an economic figure, almost makes imagination run riot. Translated into terms of actual fact, it rendered possible from the middle of September to November 6th last year the ploughing and pressing of 370 acres in 19 days, the harrowing of 470 acres in 47 hours, the drilling of 360 acres in 62 hours, the rolling of 160 acres in 20 hours, and the ridge ploughing of 58 acres in 2½ days. All this was done with the services of four men, two tractors, the appropriate implements and without the services of a single horse. In view of these achievements one is not surprised to hear of farmers changing over from horses to tractors, but it must be recognised that not all farms are

> so conveniently placed or laid out for this type of farming as the one which Messrs Alley have been fortunate enough to discover. Here everything is organised as in a factory. Sentiment has no place in the farming policy. Expediency and profit-earning capacities govern the methods employed. Horses are not used, because they are too expensive. Cattle and sheep are not kept, because manurial reserves in the soil can be maintained by artificial fertilizers at a cheaper cost. One is impressed most of all by the thoroughness of this undertaking. The two partners have worked out every detail of their practice beforehand – even to acquiring an interest in the local mill as a means of finding a ready market for their grain. Good judgement, ability, capital and enthusiasm are evenly yoked in this venture, and Bluestone Farm promises to become a centre to which all progressive arable farmers will turn for enlightenment.

Mr Robinson, who wrote the article for *Country Life*, doesn't tell the end of the story. The Alley brothers went on to open a factory in Creake for making a breakfast cereal called 'Farmers Glory', very similar to the maize flakes that Kelloggs were making in America, but using wheat. Unfortunately Kelloggs were able to reduce the price of their product by marketing it through the Woolworths chain and the Alleys were forced to pack up.

In 1936 the first combine harvester arrived at Testerton. It was an International Model 31 T with a 12ft cut. It needed three operators, four if you count the tractor driver. One operator sat on top like a ship's captain in the bridge and controlled the height of cut. Another two men worked on a platform on the side of the machine bagging up the corn. The harvester arrived at Fakenham Station in four large packing cases and took two men and a boy (me) three days to assemble. I think I saw every part of this giant jig-saw put in place. It was a monster, with a large six-cylinder petrol engine on the front. The driver of the caterpillar tractor that pulled the machine made up the total team of four men. The output varied with field conditions and the weather, but I would estimate that on reasonably good going these four men did the work of about thirty men and a dozen horses using the old methods and equipment. After the first year's results Father bought two more machines of a similar type the next year, together with a vast dryer fuelled by a coke furnace to bring the moisture content of the grain down to the level where it would keep. The dryer was static, and occupied one end of a large barn.

Mechanical harvesting, on the scale that the Alley brothers introduced at Creake, coincided with my leaving school, and during the four to six weeks of harvest that year I lived with the whirling mass of chains and belts and sieves and cranks which drove the combines in those days. Occasionally I was allowed to drive the tractor pulling the combine, but mostly I sat up-front with the captain on the bridge. From this position I operated the levers that raised and lowered the platform with its reciprocating knife and whirring sails to push the cut corn onto the canvas taking it into the machine. Two men bagged up the grain from the combine into 2–2½cwt sacks and slid them down a chute onto the ground. The sacks were then picked up again by hand and loaded onto a lorry or tractor and trailer and carted to the farm premises, where they were emptied into the dryer pit. The dryer was built by Ransomes of Ipswich. A 40ft long by 10ft wide slatted conveyor slowly inched its way over a perforated zinc tray carrying a stream of fresh barley or wheat at a constant depth of about three inches: small turners on the way ensured that the grain was evenly dried by warm air heated and blown by the nearby coke furnace as it passed. Another fan of similar proportions cooled the grain down to ambient temperature and it was then taken by a cup elevator into the roof of the barn and graduated down through a dressing machine which took out weed seeds and dross before it was sacked-off, weighed and stored. Another job I enjoyed at harvest-time was helping with the pick-up baler which followed the combine. The 12ft width of straw, which had been condensed into about 3ft, was picked up by the baler on its spring fingers, taken into the body of the machine and forcibly rammed by a plunger into square bales. This was in the days before plastic string and the bales then had to be wired up by two men who sat either side of the baler. I liked driving the tractor or standing on the top of the machine and putting in the wire boards. I even liked putting the wires through and twisting them, but what I didn't like was picking up the bales again and loading them onto trailers. Each one weighed about twelve stone and, particularly with wheat-straw, they were not pleasant to handle.

Although by today's standards the amount of capital required for the tractors, ploughs, combines and dryer was small, it was an immense amount of money in an agricultural depression. In Father's case it all came from Barclays Bank, and he always boasted that he never bought anything on hire purchase. Money could be borrowed from the banks at about four per cent interest, and this was the way he preferred to do business. I think that over the years I have fathomed out how it was that my father was able to survive the Depression when so many farmers went bankrupt and many more lost all their capital. I believe it would be true to say that the war coming along in 1939 was the salvation of many of them, but that after weathering the first world war most non-farming people in the country were not concerned with the fate of farmers. Certainly the politicians were not. They preferred to see Britain purchasing food cheaply from abroad (Russian grain, American wheat and maize and Argentinian beef). This was fine for the large industrial conurbations in the Midlands and the North, enabling them to sell more manufactured goods such as knives, forks and railway engines, but it was death to farming. It wasn't until the German U-boat campaign of the second world war started, coupled with the realisation that Britain had only a month's food supply in store, that everyone woke up to the fact that unless they gave farmers a fair chance England would starve.

By 1939 the land Father farmed was on five of the largest North Norfolk estates: the landlords involved were Sir Thomas Cook on the Sennowe Estate with the Testerton and Westwood Farms; Lord Leicester at Holkham with the Mileham Farm and Lord Townshend of Raynham with Hall Farm, Lodge Farm, Uphouse Farm, Paxfield and the Raynham Parks. Then, on Colonel Scott-Chad's Pynkney Estate there were Broomsthorpe Hall Farm, Pynkney Park, and the Tatterford Farm at Sculthorpe; lastly, from the Ecclesiastical Commissioners, he hired the Glebe Farm at West Raynham. The rents that he paid varied from 5s 0d per acre per year down to nothing. The classic case of the latter was the Pynkney land which was very light, had never been very productive and was so run down that Father finally took it as a favour to Colonel Scott-Chad who had not been able to find a tenant at all for two years. The rent was eventually agreed at a penny an acre per year to pay for the seal on the agreement!

As I mentioned earlier, although Father farmed on virtually the same rotational system, he would not concern himself with the absolute maximum he could grow per acre, but would wherever possible ask himself 'What can I afford to spend on growing the crop in order to leave a profit?' With the advent of new technology such as the fertilizer placement (a combine drill that put the fertilizer in the ground very close to the seed) and the new selective weedkillers, it was very easy to increase the cost of input to the point where more was spent on growing the crop than the crop would return. It was a question of compromise; tractors and machinery had to replace horses in order to reduce costs, and dual-purpose crops needed to be grown like vegetables, potatoes, sprouts and cabbages, which could be fed to sheep if there was no trade for human consumption. The horse population was reduced and this made available the land which had fuelled the horses. The increased use of machines meant that the people who had worked the horses had to learn a new trade, which they did remarkably well. The labour force was also decreased by natural wastage and far fewer lads became farm-workers – the ones with initiative and luck migrated to industry. It was amazing how the old boys who had worked with horses all their lives took to tractors, although many of them talked to the new machines just as they had talked to Bonny, Tinker and Flash. I have often heard them, particularly on cold mornings, having a severe word with a recalcitrant Fordson which would not start until it had been sworn at and given a good kick in the trembler coils. The gentlemen concerned always said, 'A good kick in the coils will start anything!'

The railways played a great part in Father's scheme. He made contracts

Grandpa Joice, Grandpa Bailey, Self, Father, Grandma Bailey, Mr Ireland Estate Agent, Mother, Mr Brockbank Bank Manager, Lt Col Scott-Chad Pynkney Estate

Earl of Leicester Holkham Estate, Mrs Gwyneth Cook (Later Lady Cook), Jack Joice My Brother, The Dowager Marchioness Townshend Raynham Estate, Mr Thomas Cook Later Sir T. Cook Sennowe Estate, Betty Joice My Sister

Principal guests at Jack's twenty-first 28th May 1936, representing estates on which Father was a tenant.

with them to transport vegetables – peas, Brussels sprouts, carrots, cabbages, swedes and turnips – to the ever-expanding and highly populated areas of London and the Midlands. Monday to Thursday each week in season a whole train-load of railway wagons would leave the local station in the early evening and be in London or Birmingham when the markets opened the next morning. His contract with the railways specified that the bags of vegetables would be stacked only one deep on the floor of the open railway trucks, which allowed air to circulate and the greens in particular to arrive absolutely fresh. Looking back on those years I think a great deal of Father's time was spent away from home making contracts for the sale of his vegetables, and my mother was constantly on the end of the telephone, either taking messages from him or from the various vegetable merchants that he dealt with about orders and the destinations of the produce. My brother Jack spent a lot of his time either with a lorry or a Ford V8 car and a trailer (which was far too large for the car) carting bags of cabbages, peas or sprouts from whichever field they were grown in to the nearest village railway station. My contribution was cycling with messages from Mother on the phone in Father's study to the fields where the men were cutting and packing the vegetables, with any alterations to the orders and requirements of the vegetable merchants. I wasn't paid for being a messenger-boy, but I earned a new bicycle for my fifteenth birthday in the process. The vegetable story was an interesting one as the reason why London and other cities were looking further afield to Norfolk for their vegetable supplies was because Bedfordshire, which had always been the traditional source of supply, had been overcropped: vegetables had been grown in the rotation too often and diseases like clubroot were rife. Vegetable crops were new to Norfolk and fitted in well, together with sugar-beet, as a break crop. The other big advantage for the farmers was that the residue, in the shape of the stalks of the sprouts and cabbages and other root vegetables, could be used to fold sheep on. The benefits from this were two-fold: the residue provided an extra food supply for the animals, and their droppings benefited the subsequent year's cropping. Following these practices, Father was able to supply the highest quality vegetables for human consumption.

In some cases the railway wagons from the Midlands returned to the local station loaded with shoddy – a residue of the wool factories. Shoddy itself was everything that was left over after the fleeces had been washed and processed in the woollen and garment factories. If left alone for a time after arrival it became very hot and, apart from the smell, was not at all unpleasant to spread on winter days. I quite liked shoddy carting and certainly preferred it to sugar-beet carting as a forkful of shoddy weighed very little compared with a forkful of beet. Shoddy was used to improve the fertility of the land, and you could certainly see its beneficial effect in the subsequent cropping. It was very cheap. Indeed many train loads of it came for just the cost of the transport, as there was no other use for it after the good wool had been treated and the lanolin extracted. Sometimes there were loads of cotton waste as well as wool shoddy, and Father also bought fish meal from the Humber Fish Manure company for the same purpose.

As well as the now comparatively small permanent labour force Father, when necessary, used casual labour in the form of gangs of men and women, and transported them from the villages to the fields, and from field to field as required in the converted Model T charabancs I described earlier. During pea harvesting Charlie Howe, one of the drivers, would drive through the village at the crack of dawn, hanging out of his vehicle and ringing a brass school bell. On his return trip the ladies would be standing outside their houses with their 'docky' bags, and often with their children, ready to be taken to the pea-fields where the pea packing was done entirely by hand. They were usually a very happy bunch but they sometimes gave Charlie a hard time. One of the reasons was that he had to weigh the sacks of peas they brought in from the fields, as they were all on piecework. They always swore blind that he gave them short weight, and he in turn said that they were not averse to putting some stones in the bottom of the sacks.

I wouldn't say Charlie was the best or most careful of drivers, but he always seemed to manage to get his bus-load of ladies to the pea-fields in double quick time; on one occasion almost managing to frighten them to death. The steering wheel of the Model T Ford was held to its shaft by a centre nut and this had been lost on one of the vehicles, so that the wheel could be lifted off. On this particular trip Charlie was driving the vehicle with the missing nut. The ladies had been playing him up even more than usual, pulling his leg, and criticising his fast driving. At the top of a very steep hill, when they were being particularly vociferous, he suddenly removed the steering wheel, turned round, held it out to them and said, 'Here you are then – you drive!' He must have had a lot of faith in the Ackermann steering system on the Fords for they were travelling at about twenty-five miles per hour! Needless to say, it quietened the ladies down.

The landlords of the farms, and Barclays Bank, helped enormously with Father's enthusiastic progress. The landlords were flexible and didn't insist on implementing each tenancy agreement to the letter, particularly over points like the four-course rotation which should have been wheat, roots, barley and hay. In other words they allowed a cash crop for the tenant and root crops in alternate years, the latter grown for cattle and sheep in order to maintain fertility. By allowing a five or even six-year rotation, the landlords enabled Father to grow extra corn crops, which meant extra cash sales. They also sanctioned the use of artificial fertilizers to make up for the shortage of muck. Having said that in praise of landlords, I must add that good tenants were sometimes hard to find. In the case of the banks, many of them at that time had local directors who were estate owners and farmers themselves.

They knew only too well what the position was in the farming industry, and were as helpful as possible about approving overdrafts to farmers. A favourite saying of Father's was: 'If you have got any bad news for your Bank Manager make certain that he hears about it from you!' Although the bank rate at that time was around 4½ per cent, thousands of businesses went bust but not a lot of banks! As an indication of how bad things were during the Depression I quote from the report of a speech my father made – I think to the NFU in London:

> I feel very strongly that if any government viewed the Land from the point of view of the production and maintenance of new wealth, it would be far better for the country generally. I cannot help saying how foolish I think the present system is – sending British capital abroad for foodstuffs for our workless people to eat, while we have the land here capable of growing far more than it is doing at present. And this at a time when we should curtail our imports, if we are incapable of increasing our exports. In my district the average loss to the farmer has been £9 per acre over a period of ten years. My own accountant does the accounts relating to 60,000 acres, which showed losses amounting to £90,000 in 1931, averaging 30s 0d an acre, and he tells me that the average loss will be not less than £2 per acre this year, or £120,000. Say £210,000 lost on 60,000 acres in two years; a simple calculation shows that we must have lost well over a million of money by way of farming capital in that short time, to say nothing of the previous eight years. I have no wish to reduce the labourer's wage, but if arable farming in Norfolk is to continue we must either have economic conditions all round, or artificial prices for our produce, in other words, subsidies.

But even greater changes for farming, and the country, were on the way. In July 1936 Father received a letter from the Air Ministry about the Paxfield farm at West Raynham. It read: 'I hereby send you a plan showing the boundary of the land which it is proposed to acquire under compulsory powers and which you hold under tenancy for the Marquess Townshend. Signed: Rosalind Colman for the Air Ministry at Adastral House, Kingsway, London.' The map showed that the government proposed taking 378 of the 600 acres of the Paxfield farm for an airfield, which was all the very best land on that particular farm. My father was furious, and wrote letters to members of Parliament and everyone else he could think of who might be interested in fighting the proposal, including the Minister of Agriculture. He also wrote to the Prime Minister. But to no avail. Miss Rosalind Colman, on behalf of the Air Ministry, won the short, sharp battle. However, although he had only farmed at Paxfield for a year the compensation paid left him with a reasonable profit on what he had spent on it, and the 'upset' figure, although meagre by modern standards, was generous for the time. Always an opportunist, Father turned the circumstances to his advantage by taking on the contract with the Air Ministry to level the land and sow it down to grass. Grass runways had always been quite satisfactory for the small planes of those days, but this particular area of land was very highly productive and on the heavy side with small fields bounded by drainage ditches. Local people who knew the land well warned that just filling in the dykes and sowing the land with grass would not give them a satisfactory surface on which to land planes and drive vehicles. But the Air Ministry and Office of Works turned a deaf ear. In consequence they found that in winter the whole place became water-logged and unusable, and it took two years to put in a complete system of under-drains to take away the surplus water. (It showed that our forebears knew where to put their drainage ditches to get rid of water). Even after this huge operation, the first lot of aircraft that landed at Paxfield (from then on known as RAF Raynham) proved that the runways would, in any case, have to be concreted. Father and many others locally, were contracted for this work too. The job had to be done quickly as by this time war was imminent.

The requisition of land for Raynham aerodrome was a prelude to almost the same thing happening two years later to the land on the Pynkney Estate, known as Brazen Hall Farm. Father was again notified by the Air Ministry that they proposed to requisition, with compulsory powers, the land occupied by my grandfather at Tattersett, together with some of the Pynkney land farmed by my father. By this time he had become more philosophical, so he accepted the requisition order without a fight and concentrated on ploughing up as much grassland as possible in order to increase production of cereals, which the government was encouraging farmers to do by paying £2 an acre as a ploughing-up grant. The new airfield became known as Sculthorpe.

Whooping cough

a. Chopped up mouse made into shortcake – would also cure nocturnal bed wetting
b. Spider caught alive and hung in the chimney – by the time the spider was dead, the cough was cured
c. A swede chopped and covered in brown sugar to make syrup for the patient

CHAPTER EIGHT

Testerton and Raynham: Work, War and a Wedding

My own working life on the farm started when I left school at Easter 1937. The first few years were fairly carefree, but with pretty strict routines. All farmers are early risers so getting up at six o'clock was not new to me. Ablutions came next and Father insisted that Jack and I shaved immediately he had finished with the bathroom. We each had a pair of cut-throat razors and he taught us how to strop and look after them. The six instruments (all made by Krupps of Germany and recognised as the best in the world) went to Mr Newman, the barber in Fakenham, for professional grinding once every eight weeks, and woe betide either of us if we maltreated them. Father used a cut-throat razor all his life, until rheumatism and poor vision caused him to 'go electric' in his late seventies. I don't think Father was an insomniac, but he certainly seemed to need very little sleep and, like many energetic people, could catnap anywhere at any time that became available. He nearly always had ten minutes after lunch and seldom sat up late. Just before going to bed at night he had an annoying habit of telling everyone what was to happen the next day on the farm. Then he would walk off with the paraffin lamp (or turn off the gas, after that was installed), leaving us all in the dark! It was not surprising that my mother invariably went upstairs first. After Father retired, we followed. He was usually in bed by ten o'clock. He was up with the lark in the mornings and would often come padding down the long corridor at Testerton, night-shirt flapping, to the room where Jack and I slept. We shared a room and Father would appear at any time after five in the morning, perch himself on the end of the bed, and start to re-organise the orders for the day. However sleepy you felt you had to sit up and listen; then he'd say, 'Well there's no point in lying about, let's get on'. Having acquired the early rising habit it has never left me, and most farmers will swear that one hour before midday is worth two after.

As well as tractor driving my job in those days was helping to service the equipment at the Home Farm, Testerton, and keeping the wheels turning. My means of transport was a bicycle, but as Father acquired the tenancy of farms further afield at Mileham, Raynham and Broomsthorpe, a not very new Ford 8 hp Popular with trailer was bought for me: it cost £50. The car had its back seat removed, and this gave space enough for a rudimentary workshop and tools. The trailer was specially built and was exactly the right size to take cans of paraffin, petrol, oil and grease. After the morning shaving ritual Jack took the milk to Fakenham station in a trailer behind his two-seater Ford V8. Sometimes he took the milk all the way to King's Lynn and then came back to Raynham to work, or he went to one of the 'off' farms, Broomsthorpe, Raynham or Mileham. My father would visit each farm at some time during the day, but always at a different time so that no one knew when he would turn up. Jack would usually spend the day carting with the Ford V8 and a much longer trailer than was good for it, loaded (or rather overloaded) with sacks of vegetables, which he delivered to the nearest railway station.

Everyone who worked at Home Farm, except the horsemen, cowmen and other stockmen, who were there an hour earlier, met in the big barn at seven. Jimmy Newton, the foreman, then 'turned out', which meant telling everyone what to do and where to do it. This same ritual was performed by the foremen on the other farms. Besides stockmen there were about twenty labourers, including boys, and the whole plan for the day would have been discussed by Jimmy and my father the night before. Jimmy lived in a cottage a couple of hundred yards from the Hall and nearly always came up and saw Father at about eight o'clock after high tea, and before having a last look at the stock. Often they both went round the animals together. After being given the details of our jobs for the day we went out and got on with it. If we were lucky and working close to home we came in for a quick breakfast; most of the men brought theirs with them in their side bags or frail (wicker) baskets. A break of twenty minutes was allowed for breakfast and half-an-hour for lunch. During harvest-time 'fourses' at four o'clock was a thirty-minute break, and the grub was often brought to the men in the fields by their wives. On normal days work finished at 4.30 p.m. and at 12.30 on Saturdays. A man's wage in 1936 was £1 13s 6d for a fifty hour week. I was paid £1 and my keep, and I also had the money I made on the side from my pig and poultry enterprises in the 'dungeon'. Working on the farm, tinkering with machines and the tractors, and pottering with my animals in the 'dungeon' were work and recreation to me during these years, and left little time for any other interests. Father was a director of Norwich City Football Club, and every alternate Saturday he went to Carrow Road to see them play. He also went to 'away' matches in the bus with the team, or in the special carriage if they went by rail. Jack often accompanied him as he, too, was very interested in the game, but I'm afraid I wasn't. The same applied to Father's other passions, bowls and shooting and cricket, and in these respects I suppose I was a disappointment to him. I didn't like shooting, I didn't play bowls or watch cricket, and I only developed a passing interest in Norwich City Football Club.

The possibility of another war exercised everybody's mind during the twelve months leading up to September 1939. There was a great deal of talk, and some activity. Many of my friends and contemporaries felt, as I did, that it would be a thrill to fly, and a number of them did become pilots. But I failed the RAF medical, and returned home with a result indicating a weak heart. I was told to carry on farming as the industry would play a crucial part in the war effort. Even so, failing that medical was one of the unhappiest days I have ever experienced, and even now I feel a sense of loss at the outcome. Father was well aware of the regret and disappointment I felt throughout the six years of war. On Armistice Day he said, 'You can stop worrying now. You've worked hard . . . and we won anyway!'

At the time, to compensate for the disappointment, I joined the Cadet Norfolk Artillery. Training was a six-month crash course on how to be a good soldier. This entailed several nights a week and most weekends rushing about with a dummy rifle, marching up and down in disused gravel pits, and learning how to read maps. At the end of this training period we were given one pip, and were expected to buy our own uniforms and take a medical, which I always failed. There were five of us budding officers on my course, under a splendid chap called Colonel Crosskill – a distinguished ex-army officer who in civilian life headed the firm of Crosskill Cork Manufacturers in Norwich. The cadets occupied a disused part of a factory and our actual training was in the hands of Sergeant Major Reynolds, who lived at Foulsham and was a retired professional soldier. Your blood ran cold with the sound of his voice. In fact, he was a very kindly man, but dedicated to getting England 'ready' and settling old debts with the Germans and Boers. He had very unpromising material with me though and, like the masters at Culford, was on to a 'loser'. But despite my soldierly shortcomings I stayed with the Cadets until joining the Home Guard in 1942. Early that year I was informed by the authorities that the allocation of petrol which covered the journey I made for Cadet training had to be stopped. I needed about one gallon a month to get to my battery at Aylsham, and the meetings were once a week. It was suggested that I join the Home Guard and that I should see Colonel Jones of Anmer, who was the divisional Home Guard Commander. I did, and he sent me to see my uncle, who was a Second Lieutenant in the Home Guard and in charge at Great Ryburgh, which also covered Testerton. Uncle Arthur told me that he couldn't offer me a pip or three stripes, as he was the Lieutenant and he already had a Sergeant, but his Lance Corporal was moving to another parish, so if I would like one stripe I could have it. I thanked him but refused, as there was a possibility that I would be moving to Raynham within the year. I think by way of consolation, he told me that his section had just been allocated one Tommy gun. It was to be shared between

Great Ryburgh and the next parish and there was no allocation of bullets, but if I would like to be in charge of it, I could be when it was at Ryburgh. This time I accepted his offer and kept the Tommy gun in my car, together with half-a-dozen petrol bombs that we had been taught to make in case we ran into the enemy!

I only once got a chance to fire the Tommy gun, when we were taken down to Brancaster beach and given tuition with it and another gun called a Spigot Mortar Bombard, made incidentally by the Singer Sewing Machine Company. The Spigot was a shell-firing gun with an internal barrel. This meant that the shell was hollow and it slid onto, instead of into, the barrel which was just a straight shaft of steel. Two men were needed to fire it: one lying down on the ground behind the gun with the supports pressed up tight to his shoulders and his finger on the trigger, the other lying close beside him looking through a little sighting device – like an upturned garden rake. The Spigot Mortar Bombard was designed for beach warfare and when fired the shell was supposed to bounce across the flat sand and, if aimed correctly by No. 2, blow up the target. We were trained by the army and on one occasion the target they used was a large white sheet tied to a frame on wheels which was pulled by a lorry. It looked a bit like a land yacht. Once or twice we hit the target, until disaster struck and tuition came to a swift end. We had all been watching as the lorry towed its target across the horizon. No. 2 took sight and shouted, 'Fire'. No. 1 pressed the trigger, the detonator fired, and the shell shot off the spike in the general direction of the target. It soon became obvious that No. 2's aim wasn't too accurate but that, with luck, the dummy shell would pass between the lorry and the target. But our luck was out. The shell hit the lorry amidships, passed through the driver's door panel directly under his seat (which was, in fact, the petrol tank) and came out through the passenger door. The passenger seat was occupied by one of the Sergeant's instructors, and I have never seen two chaps get out of a lorry and run so fast in my life. The lorry, of course, stopped as all its petrol ran out onto the sand, and we had to manhandle it back ahead of the incoming tide. It was then, as we lay panting on the sand, and the Sergeant was still swearing, that someone was heard to say, 'They shouldn't let cross-eyed people aim Spigot Mortar Bombs.'

One of the last Home Guard exercises I remember taking part in was a mock invasion of our village by members of the local RAF regiment, as a change from us invading the RAF station. We were all deployed around the village at strategic sites and managed to ward off the morning attack. We stopped for lunch and all the Home Guard members went to the Greyhound pub where, as part of the exercise, we were fed by members of the local Women's Voluntary Service. They gave us a vegetarian meal, made with vegetables scavenged from the local allotments and cooked in a home-made field kitchen (an old petrol can). Very good it was too, except that the publican entered into the spirit of the thing and emptied a bottle of whisky (a very rare commodity during the war years) into the tea urn. It was a lovely summer's day and after lunch we all lay down on the lawn of the pub. The trouble was that the officer forgot to deploy any of his troops to watch for the enemy, and when the afternoon attack began the whole section was literally caught napping, and captured to a man!

As I remember it, the year between the Munich crisis of 1938 and the declaration of war on 3rd September 1939 was a period of frenzied activity in the country. The territorial army was placed on a war footing, and Air Raid Precaution (ARP) committees were set up and gas-masks distributed. Everybody attended a centre in the towns and villages and was given tuition in how to put the gas-masks on and test them by blocking up the air supply in the front with the flat of the hand. When they were first issued schools began each day with a gas-mask drill and everybody carried their masks in stout cardboard boxes, measuring about 6in square and 4in deep. As time went by people began to make more sophisticated cases to carry the masks in, but even the most refined ladies couldn't disguise them completely. Gas, or the effect of it, seemed to be the thing most people feared because of memories of the 1914–18 war. In Ryburgh there were men who still suffered from the after effects of gas attacks in the trenches in France. Everyone expected that it would be used by the Germans early in the war and the government decreed that all pillar boxes should have their tops painted yellow with a special paint that changed colour if sprayed from the air with mustard gas.

In February 1939, Suffolk farmers organised a protest march to Westminster about prices, and in the same month everyone was advised to dig a slit trench in their garden – or wherever possible – that they could jump into if air raids began. In March, the local authority representatives came round and surveyed properties and made lists of available accommodation which could be used during air raids. Those who wished could also apply for air raid shelters if they felt that a slit trench wouldn't suffice. In May the government announced a £2-an-acre ploughing-up grant on every acre of permanent pasture which was ploughed by the end of September 1939, and in June, the first 200,000 conscripts had to register at the Labour Exchange. Early in August Parliament adjourned for the summer recess but was almost immediately recalled and the Prime Minister, Neville Chamberlain, warned of the imminent peril of war. The British ambassador met Hitler in Berlin and flew back to London to report to the cabinet and Parliament, and it was then that plans for a National Register and the issue of identity cards were announced. On 1st September the mass evacuation of children from the cities started. My mother thought that all the empty rooms at Testerton Hall, which was a large house, would immediately be filled with evacuees, so she cleared the decks for action, even removing all the apples from the attics where they were usually stored on layers of wheat-straw. The evacuees never came because Testerton was too near the east coast, and because of the proximity of the RAF airfields and the dummy ones which were being built to lure the Germans to drop their bombs.

On Sunday 3rd September, war was finally declared. I cannot remember exactly where all the family was at that moment, but my father and I were sitting at the desk in his study doing the farm books and when the shattering news came through on the wireless at 11 a.m. we both solemnly stood up and shook hands. I can still remember his first words after the announcement: 'I have lived through one war and have prayed all my life I wouldn't see another – God willing it won't be as bad as the last one. We've got a very important job to do and from now on we shall work a seven-day week'. Until then he had never allowed Sunday working, with the exception of attending to stock. During the rest of that year many new regulations and laws came into force: ration books were distributed; the Ministry of Supply announced petrol rationing; the Ministry of Agriculture announced central slaughter for cattle.

On 29th September the national registration census was compiled and a few weeks later I received my Identity Card. My number was TSBI 188 3. All the letters and figures meant something and were based on where you were domiciled at that time. I can't remember how it worked, but I do know that the last figure represented your position in the family. By 1939 Jack had moved to Colkirk and my sister, Betty, was at boarding school and therefore registered away, and so the last digit on my number meant that I was third in the family. Identity Cards had to be carried at all times which was often difficult when working out in the fields, particularly in the summer, and by the end of the war I had just about sat through mine in my back pocket. However, it didn't do to be caught without your ID card, particularly if you lived or worked in the coastal fringe anywhere around England and we constantly heard of people who couldn't prove their identity being held in custody until someone could vouch for them. The card also had to be produced if you were working within the confines of an RAF base or military area and, as some of our land at Raynham fell into this category, our tractor drivers had to produce theirs when coming to work. I remember well an enterprising tractor driver who was one of the first people on the scene the morning after a German plane had dropped bombs on Raynham aerodrome. He was locked in a cell in the guard room as, although he was legitimately on site, he was caught picking up pieces of shrapnel from the bomb and said his reason for doing so was because he knew he could sell them in the pub! Until then no bombs had been dropped on Great Britain, except one stick that was dropped across the Outer Hebrides. The bombs that dropped on

Raynham didn't do much damage. At the time we thought the holes were enormous, but compared with what happened later to our cities they were potholes.

January, 1940 was the beginning of a very, very hard winter. Rivers froze, 31.9 degrees of frost were recorded in Norwich, and there was an epidemic of influenza and measles. A lot of activity was taking place off the east coast and lightships and coastal traffic were attacked by German bombers. Very little detail was given, except in cases like the sinking of the German tanker *Altmark* in Norwegian waters. The Royal Navy rescued 299 British prisoners from that tanker. In March, a lot of people voluntarily evacuated the east coast and a system of constant fighter patrols was instituted over the North Sea convoys. In April, Germany invaded Denmark and Norway, and after this there was constant talk and fear that we, too, might be invaded. In order to confuse the Germans if they did land, all signposts were removed and carefully locked away. This didn't worry the local people, but it did cause considerable chaos and difficulty for those not familiar with the area. The local doctor, looking for a remote house he had never been to before, was told by an old man working beside the road, 'Don't you know where you are then? 'Cos if you knew where you were and where the house was you wouldn't be asking me, and if you don't know I shan't tell you!'

In May, Norway surrendered and Germany invaded Holland, Belgium and Luxembourg, and then France. Winston Churchill formed an all-party coalition government and delivered his famous blood, toil, sweat and tears speech. Troops were now posted along the coasts and school children were evacuated inland. Bombers from East Anglian bases were blasting targets in Norway and Denmark and Parliament passed the Emergency Powers Defence bill, which meant that aliens could be taken into custody. Many vessels from the east coast ports and from up to and above Kings Lynn were involved in the Dunkirk evacuation, and many East Anglian regiments were in action in France. On 14th May, Anthony Eden broadcast an appeal for men to join a new force of Local Defence Volunteers – the LDV – which later became the Home Guard. The response was tremendous and over a million men, some in their eighties and many teenagers, had enrolled by July. A great deal of training went on day and night. In June that year Italy declared war on Britain and France and the Germans entered Paris and signed the armistice with France. Visitors were banned from the defence area around the coast and urgent defence work was constantly being done on the beaches.

In July the Battle of Britain began, and we were told that Hitler had ordered preparations for his invasion. Lord Beaverbrook, the Minister for Munitions was having a tremendous production drive and all in all there was a very high level of morale, although I think most people were scared stiff. In August the Germans really hotted up their attack on the east coast and on convoy bases in East Anglia, even laying acoustic mines off the coast, and in September a great blitz began on London that went on for sixty consecutive nights. Although by October 1940, Hitler had apparently suspended his invasion plans, in that month 289 bombs were dropped on Norfolk in a single day, several of which fell on Norwich, resulting in the 'Back of the Inns' fire. The Germans latest trick was to drop a mixture of incendiary and high explosive bombs and in November came the news of the first major raid on an industrial city, Coventry, in which over a thousand people were killed. The Germans were by this time openly flying low and machine-gunning areas, particularly on the coast. Right through December 1940, night raids on industrial cities continued and fire blitz attacks on cities such as London and Norwich. Bombs fell in the precinct of Norwich Cathedral but the cathedral remained intact.

These were difficult and worrying times for everyone, but the war years for me were also a happy and optimistic time which culminated in my first marriage and the start of an independent working life. In February 1938, a couple of days after my seventeenth birthday, I passed my driving test and almost immediately fell in love with a farmer's daughter who was not quite sixteen years old, on the point of leaving school, very pretty, dark and slender and exactly what I had in mind as the sort of girl I hoped to fall in love with. There were other benefits as well, as her father was a threshing proprietor and owned several steam engines! My brother Jack was married in October 1938, and Father was able to obtain the tenancy of Hall Farm, Colkirk (which adjoined the Testerton farm) so Jack went to live and farm there with his wife after their marriage. This was obviously an expensive time for my father as he had to find the necessary capital to start my brother off. Not surprisingly, therefore, he wasn't too keen when in 1939 I announced that I wanted to get engaged to Margaret Dann, who was still only sixteen years old. Father was very angry with us and frequently said so. But the strange thing was that although he and Margaret's father were great friends and always had lunch together on Saturdays in Norwich, as well as playing bowls and shooting together, they both told me years afterwards that neither of them mentioned the subject to the other. It wasn't that Father didn't like Margaret; he just decided that we were too young.

It wasn't until 1941 that our parents at last got it into their heads that Margaret and I meant business and Father suddenly said one day, 'Assuming you two know what you are doing, if you want to become officially engaged and get married next year, you can, and go and live at Hall Farm, East Raynham and manage the Raynham farms. At least it will save petrol!' At that time, of course, petrol was strictly rationed and my courting trips were severely limited!

So at Michaelmas 1942, on 27th October, Margaret and I were married in North Tuddenham church. The guests who didn't live close by travelled courtesy of the Eastern Counties Bus Company, or by rail to the station at Dereham, where they were taken by coach to the church at North Tuddenham. The reception was held at the King's Arms Hotel in Dereham, and afterwards Margaret and I departed for our five-day honeymoon in London. However, we were back in Norfolk two days later as the blitz on London had begun, and we moved straight into our new home at Hall Farm.

The farmhouse at Raynham was large, although originally it had been very much bigger. In 1927 part of it had burned down. The fire started when a paraffin incubator flared up and set fire to one of the bedrooms. Nobody had bothered to rebuild the house afterwards, but had simply blocked up the end where the fire had been. That end, with no cavity wall, was always damp afterwards. Our families were very good to us, particularly in making various bits of furniture available for the house: but except for a double bed, a sideboard, a kitchen table, some chairs and a couple of armchairs we didn't have much in the way of furniture. We spent every spare minute when not working on the farm in painting and decorating. Downstairs the house consisted of a small morning room, a hall, and two staircases running parallel to each other, one for family and the other for the servants who lived there in more affluent times. There was also a very good sitting room, an equally nice dining room, and a sensibly-sized kitchen. We soon got rid of the old range in the kitchen and installed a secondhand Aga, so that we had at least one room that was permanently warm. Then we took out the service stair and built a modern bathroom in its place. The original bathroom was extremely basic and the water (the little that there was) was heated by the back boiler of the cooking range, or rather it wasn't heated but slightly warmed. There wasn't much of it, but it was war-time and we were only supposed to have five inches of water in a bath anyway. The house had never had electricity but because we planned to start a herd of cows at Hall Farm, a spur line for electricity was brought from the mains, which luckily ran across the farm. There was no mains water, but a well was situated under the kitchen floor with a hand pump to pump the water to the storage tank in the roof. Thankfully, after a few months the electricity was connected and an electric pump fitted. Very shortly after that we noticed that the drinking water had a sort of bluish tinge and tasted very slightly of disinfectant. We discovered that the outflow from the bath was making its way through the open drainage system into the well. So, whereas everyone else had cool, clear, tasteless water, ours was far from that, and the well was condemned. We then had to run to the expense of putting in a bore hole, but it also provided water for the dairy and the new herd of cows.

The farm buildings were extensive and adequate for a farm of that size, farmed on the Norfolk four-course rotation. There were two large barns; one was originally used for threshing by hand with flails and one for storage and grinding. Between the two barns were two sets of ten traditional bullock boxes, each designed to house one large or two small bullocks. These acted as a surround for two open (not roofed) bullock yards which held fifteen bullocks each. In the centre of one side of each yard was a turnip and chaff house where the food for the animals was mixed, and above the mixing sheds was a granary, which held grinding fodder such as oats and bought-in imported cotton and linseed cake. The cotton and linseed cakes were fed through a hand-operated cake crusher turned by a strong lad. The machine had a large flywheel which gave it momentum once you got it up to speed, but getting it up to speed required a lot of strength. The chaff cutter and oat roller was driven by a horse walking round and round in a special shed called the round house just outside the granary. Usually the horse was harnessed to a gear mechanism which in turn drove a shaft into the building to cut, roll or grind. Although this machinery was still there when we took the farm over, it was soon replaced by a 5 hp Rushton Hornsby internal combustion engine.

Unlike the tenants of the farm fifty years before us, we grew sugar-beet. The beet themselves gave us a cash crop. The tops were first-class fodder, and the pulp, which we bought back from the factory was mixed with chaff, rolled oats and cake to produce a wonderful ration for sheep, beef cattle or milking cows. So it was decided that the yards and boxes would house beef cattle to fatten as they always had, and that a new cowhouse should be built to accommodate a herd of forty milking black and white Friesian cows. The best of the female calves from the milking cows would be brought in as replacements for the milkers and the bull calves castrated and reared as bullocks to be fattened. The nucleus of the new herd of forty down-calving heifers at Raynham which came from Testerton, were still suffering from the effects of the Red Poll crossing my father had experimented with in the thirties. The herd of Friesian cows that Father took from Ryburgh to Testerton in 1925 ranked quite high in the county milk yield herd average tables. I seem to remember they averaged about 900 gallons per cow, but the butterfat content of the milk was low. The law said that all milk had to be a minimum of 3.5 per cent butterfat and the Testerton cows were only fractionally above this. The only way to increase quality in milk is by breeding, using bulls bred from proven high butterfat yielding cows. Father thought he would go one better and use a Red Poll bull, that breed being known for high butterfat, in the hope that the Friesian cows would produce cross-bred calves with a higher milk yield like their mothers, plus higher butterfat, like their grandmothers on their father's side. The initial result was very satisfactory and the first cross-calves gave lots of milk of high quality, but after that it didn't seem to matter whether a Red Poll bull or a Friesian bull was used on the subsequent generations of calves and the quality and quantity went down. At this point Father gave up milk production, and started to breed for beef alone. The heifer calves I took with me from

Testerton to Raynham were the remaining few from this cross-breeding experiment. Their yield was low, the butterfat was low, and all in all the milk was not up to standard. In spite of buying very good new sires from high-yielding herds the yield and quality of the milkers did not reach the standard expected, and the bullocks did not fatten as quickly as they should. The animals all looked well, but the butcher who bought them didn't like the conformation of the carcass. The solution was to change the breed, which I did as soon as Father handed over the reins and let me take over the farm on 11th October 1946, soon after the war in Europe ended.

In 1942 my position at Hall Farm was that of manager, but my father also expected me to go on servicing his tractors on the other farms. During the war he felt that it wasn't appropriate for me to be farming on my own account as other people's sons were being drafted into the forces. He, therefore, paid me a wage of £4 a week with electricity, vegetables and firewood as perquisites. The cropping on the 700 acre farm at that time was 200 acres of pasture, 300 acres of cereals and fodder crops, 30 acres of vegetables and 70 acres of sugar-beet. The remainder was grazing pasture. We had two tractors, a team of eight horses, and a labour force of about fourteen people. With my brother farming the other Raynham farms for my father I was able, when they were available, to borrow a certain number of implements. Somehow we managed to get all the work done. On moonlit nights we often worked the tractors with no lights because of the black-out, although we did have one tractor with a large acetylene lamp with blackout mask.

Rationing, of course, was in full swing during these years. It began on 8th January 1940, and each person was allocated a ration book which allowed them 12oz sugar, 4oz bacon and 4oz butter. Meat rationing didn't start until 11th March that year and adults were entitled to 1s 10d worth of meat per week. Children under six got half that amount. Everyone had to be registered with a retailer and queues formed because the shop assistants had to stop and cut out the tiny coupons needed for each commodity with scissors. Restaurants were directed to supply one lump of sugar per cup of tea or coffee to their customers and one slice of bread. We were permitted to kill one pig per year, but then had to forego the meat coupons for a specified period. With the shortage of keepers around (many were in the forces and the rest had been directed into farmwork) the incidence of poaching increased considerably. But who wouldn't take a cock pheasant if they had a hungry family? Sparrow and blackbird pie were a delicacy, the sparrows were caught with nets at night around the corn stacks. Pigeons, rooks, rabbits and hares were taken by anyone who could catch them. In fact, if it hadn't been for these extras, together with home-grown vegetables, it would have been very difficult to feed a family. People in towns and factories had the facility of canteens and British restaurants set up by the government, but there were none of these in country areas.

As the war went on petrol rationing got tighter and tighter, but we were allowed a small amount for starting tractors. All tractors, even some diesel-engined models, needed petrol to start them before turning over to Kerosene, or TVO (tractor vaporising oil) as it was called. There was no petrol allowance for things like lawn mowers, and things became so tight that it wasn't possible to squeeze any for lawn cutting from the tractor or lorry allowance. There was quite a large lawn and tennis court, as well as a bowling green, at Hall Farm when we moved in, all of which looked terrible if not cut. So I had the bright idea of fitting our old lawn mower with an electric motor in the place of its gas-guzzling petrol engine. It worked well except that to start cutting under load was a bit of a strain on the 'electrics' as there was no clutch. The motor drove direct onto the blades with a chain so it was necessary to do a lot of pushing and heaving to get going. Still it did a reasonable job, especially if you had someone else there acting as a 'trace horse'. But the idea misfired when some helpful person wrote to the local paper: a small piece appeared in the gossip column implying that it was all right for some farmers who could get petrol for tractors as they could use it illegally in their lawn mowers. Furthermore, one had been seen cutting his grass in the early hours of the morning, presumably to avoid detection! After that we fenced most of the lawn into the adjoining meadow and let the cattle do the grass cutting for us. But this is just one instance of how, during the war years, there was always someone around watching. All the same there was a marvellous community spirit and even people who were not directed joined an official organisation, and usually did voluntary jobs as well. Most women knitted for the forces, often using pulled out wool from old garments. The WVS made tons of jam in season and got a special allocation of sugar to do it, although every pound had to be accounted for. Similarly, farmers got a special allocation of cheese when it was available, to cut up and hand out to every employee engaged on essential heavy duty war work.

During these years the military were to be seen everywhere. On one field on the farm we had the headquarters of the Searchlight Batteries for the area. The site was requisitioned and very quickly laid out with concrete roads and Nissen huts for personnel and stores. The searchlights were dotted about all over the area, it was said about one every four square miles. There were about two hundred personnel operating from the main site at East Raynham, and the RAF were very conspicuous. If you ventured out at night without good reason there was always the possibility that you would be stopped and asked why you were out, either by the police, the LDV or an army patrol, which were usually near searchlight camps or RAF stations. Special Constables were issued with rosters telling them where to meet up with police patrols. Raynham aerodrome was fully operational with satellite landing fields close by at Massingham and Bircham, and Sculthorpe became a main USAF bomber base. Raynham Hall was requisitioned and occupied by the army, who put up Nissen huts all over the park. There was always a great deal of training going on and all the parks had long deep ditches dug all over them – the idea being to stop German aeroplanes landing or to make them crash if an invasion took place. Tree trunks were also dumped around on fields with the same idea in mind, which made the growing of crops even more difficult.

Set in the wooded park about five hundred yards from Raynham Hall is the large early Victorian fruit and vegetable garden complex, of the type you would expect to find supplying the needs of the occupants of the magnificent Hall. The garden is surrounded by a 12ft high brick wall with a door at each corner leading out to orchards and other fruit gardens. The garden is not quite square but wedge-shaped, to trap the sun, with a fine pair of wooden doors in the longest side, leading to a delightful small house for the head gardener. This little house is attached to a vinery complete with heating arrangements and boiler house which also heats the greenhouses. The head gardener lived in the kitchen gardens of the great house, so that he could closely supervise and monitor the supplies of vegetables and fruit sent to the kitchens in and out of season. The long south wall of the Raynham Hall kitchen garden was devoted entirely to soft fruit like peaches, plums and nectarines, which reached up to the full height of the wall. On the west wall there were cucumber frames and on the east wall special mushroom and melon houses and a lot of store houses for apples and even nuts. In its heyday the head gardener had a team of five full-time helpers plus a couple of apprentice boys to produce what was needed for the cook in the Hall, and to send to London when the family was there. The main part of the garden and orchard, some three acres, was devoted to the less exotic vegetables like potatoes, greens and roots. The whole area was attractively laid out with paths and ornamental hedges.

The Townshend family fortunes declined during the Depression of the twenties and thirties and the garden complex became run down. The staff was reduced to a bare minimum, and when it became cheaper to buy fruit and vegetables in the shops the garden began to look sadly run down. Soon after war broke out I met the agent for the estate and he asked me if I could think of any way of making the garden more productive to help with the war effort and to stop it from deteriorating further. I gave it some thought and it was agreed that I would hire the whole garden complex: vinery, greenhouses, cold houses, frames, the gardener's house, gardener and all. My idea was to pull out all the ornamental hedges and box borders and fences, grow tomato plants in the vinery and cold houses, then plant them out in what had been the old vegetable garden and orchard. It seemed like vandalism to tear out shrubs and plants that had been there a lifetime and more, but there was no other way of doing it without a very large labour force, and that we didn't have. Imports of tomatoes from the Channel Islands, the Scillies and France had dried up so there was a demand. The difficulty lay in getting the produce to the markets and we used any method possible. Sometimes the tomatoes were carried in the guard's van of a train if it wasn't full up with a more important cargo of war goods, and sometimes we managed to get a load away with a lorry going back to its base empty. Some we sold within the county, and some greengrocers fetched their own.

The outside planting was done by women and children from the village in the evening and at weekends. When I asked for local girls I was told very firmly by a member of the wartime agricultural committee that tomatoes were a luxury crop, and local girls were to be engaged in producing essential crops, so we had to manage as best we could. I asked our local MP, Sir Thomas Cook, to put a question to the Ministry of Agriculture about it and even went to see Sir Thomas at the House of Commons during the afternoon of the second day of our honeymoon before returning to Norfolk. Sir Thomas did his best but was told very firmly that potatoes and cereals were, in the opinion of the Minister, much more important to the war effort than tomatoes. We carried on for a couple more seasons but were soon faced with another problem, a shortage of boxes to pack the tomatoes in. Eventually we gave in and grew potatoes. Looking back on the project, it was clearly a lot of work with little result. But I learned a great deal about growing tomatoes, and later grew them out on the fields and sold them to the chutney makers. For this purpose they could be sold green and in bulk, and they didn't need special packing.

Transporting produce was always difficult during the war years, and on one occasion we nearly got into trouble over a consignment of tomatoes and strawberries. There was an old strawberry bed in the garden which yielded very succulent strawberries, some of which went to the officers stationed in Raynham Hall. At a chance meeting with the Commanding Officer I mentioned the problem we were having getting both the tomatoes and strawberries to market. 'Well,' he said, 'I've got a one ton truck going to the London Docks shortly. The driver can drop them off at the market for you. Just keep quiet about it and load them yourself.' The factor we didn't allow for was that the driver's home was en route to the docks and being an opportunist he stopped to have an hour with his wife. While this was happening another opportunist cleared the lorry! I got to know the CO very well after this incident. His name was Knight. I can't remember his rank but his nickname was 'Podge'. He was a bachelor and, on the evening before he embarked with his unit for Italy, he asked us to have a drink with him. For two years his billet had been one of the larger, and nicer, rooms in the Hall. When we arrived his luggage was being loaded. As well as all his army gear and clothes there appeared to be a bicycle, a pair of Purdys, a labrador, a Jack Russell, and a box of ferrets. We had a merry evening and wished 'Podge' well. Eight weeks later we heard that as soon as he landed on the beach at Anzio he stepped on a mine and was blown up. Margaret was very close to producing Miriam, our eldest daughter, when 'Podge' left for Italy, and one of the last things he had said was, 'Joice, when that baby is born I shall go to London, stay at my club, and buy the baby a doll.' How he arranged it I don't know, but not long after Miriam was born, and before we knew that 'Podge' was dead, a doll arrived by post with a small card attached saying, 'Best wishes from Podge'.

I am often asked where I learned my engineering skills. I suppose I started with meccano as a lad and spent a lot of time with the blacksmith and in tinkering with the tractors on the farm. Then again, Mr Allen's sound basic engineering tuition at school improved my knowledge, and I have always had an insatiable curiosity about how things work. But it was shortages of parts and machinery during the war that really made engineering innovaters of us all, and one of our first projects when we moved to Raynham was to convert part of the old stable into a workshop. We couldn't do any welding, but we had a forge to heat and bend, a drill, anvil and bench, and a good vice and hand tools. Over the years, as the machinery got more and more sophisticated and complex, and gas and electric welding and power tools were all developed, the workshop became a highly professional area requiring a skilled mechanic. It was in this workshop at Raynham that Reggie White and I adapted many existing farm machines and innovated many more, like our sugar-beet machine. The most labour intensive job on the farm was the handling of sugar-beet. The seed is such that nature puts anything up to five seedlings in a hard husk about half the size of a pea. When this was sown into the ground the seedlings came up in bunches. At that time there was no satisfactory way of singling the plants other than by hand-hoeing, and even this meant individual men going up and down every row twice, first of all chopping out and then, when the plants had grown a little more, singling. A few firms had attempted to mechanise the chopping-out by making a machine with a rotary action, with hoe blades that passed through the braid of plants taking out some of the seedlings. But it was very hit and miss and still required a lot of hand work. In the workshop at Raynham we made a machine, which we dubbed the 'Down-the-Row Thinner'. It was patented and subsequently manufactured by Catchpoles of Bury St Edmunds. We entered the machine in the New Machinery Invention Section at the Norfolk Agricultural Show and it was awarded a silver medal. Hundreds were built and sold – many going abroad, and several to the Middle East. However, the seed breeders put an end to the invention when they managed to bring out a monogerm seed which not only cut the seed rate per acre by 90 per cent but also did away with the chopping out, although singling was still necessary. Obviously what was then needed was a placement drill which could place a seed every 6 to 9in with sufficient

precision. So we turned our attention to making such a drill. This wasn't quite so successful as the 'Down-the-Row Thinner' and it didn't win a medal. Our drill worked, but a large manufacturing firm had already captured the market. So we bought one of theirs and dropped the idea of making our own commercially, although we did use the prototype for many years with great success.

As far as the handling of the mature beet was concerned a lot of the hand-work was being replaced by front-end loaders. The next machine we made was an 'up-and-over front-end loader'. This meant that the tractor didn't have to plough into the heap to get a scoopful and then reverse and turn round to place the beet in a trailer. The machine was simply pushed straight into the heap, backed a few yards to the trailer then the loader with its bucketful went over the top of the tractor and shot the beet into the trailer behind. Alas, the development of hydraulics still had a long way to go and the jerky motion of going over the point of balance with a half-ton of sugar-beet, 15ft off the ground, was a problem we never solved. So, as I wrote in my diary at the time, 'the path of the inventor is both arduous and expensive', and I went out and bought another make!

Stomach trouble
Swallow a live spider – stomach guaranteed to become thoroughly clean.

Anaemia
Gather quantity of rusty iron nails, do not wash but boil for several hours, take half teacup of liquid, sweetened, three times a day.

For septic sore
Rub on live snail or burnt alum to draw poison.

For bleeding or cuts
Cover wound with cobweb or raw tobacco.

From Grandma's *Commonplace Book*.

CHAPTER NINE

Raynham: Family Life, the Farm and Holidays

When we were married in 1942 Margaret and I made a conscious decision to have a family more or less straight away, in the hope that the early restrictions of a young family would be more or less behind us when the war came to an end and things became easier. The three children duly arrived: Miriam, in May 1944; Jennifer, in July 1945; and Carole, in December 1947. Although the war ended in 1945, the shortages certainly didn't. Buying a pram, for instance, was almost impossible. We weren't able to get a new one for Miriam, but were lucky enough to find a secondhand one. Although each child arrived complete with green ration book and extra coupons were allocated for nappies, the shortages caused problems particularly with everyday things for the children. Luckily for us, when the supplier of dairy requisites told us that udder cloths and dairy towels were going to be rationed and in very short supply, I asked him to send us whatever he could spare. He did. Two enormous boxes of Harrington squares and two more of Turkish towelling arrived. The consignment was so large it would have been an embarrassment to send it back. We quickly put the boxes in the attic and steadily worked through them during the next few years on the nether regions of the children.

The three girls had a very free, but disciplined, life. They had the freedom to explore the whole of the farm, the premises, the woods and the water-meadows. The discipline was confined to the proper observance of meal-times and looking after their own pets and bedrooms, usually in that order. At around four-years-old, they each went to a small kindergarten school in Fakenham, which was nearly four miles away, and this created the daily problem of how to get them there and back. The only possible solution was for us to become a two-car family before we could really afford it. One of the reasons for sending the girls to school at that tender age, was that they always seemed to be up to mischief. One memorable escapade happened on the day they went into the workshop and found two tins of hard gloss red paint. The painters had left the pots without their lids on and with the brushes in them whilst they went for lunch. The girls painted each other from head to foot – hair too! When the painters came back after lunch they found three, by now, bright red children and brought them back to the house. We sat them in the sink and carefully, without removing too much skin and with the use of a gallon of turps, got some of the paint off. When we came to their hair, a pair of scissors was the only answer. They got very strange looks from the mistress and their chums at school the next day. On another occasion, when the annual crop of fruit in the garden was still green, they decided to pick all the blackcurrants, redcurrants and gooseberries and put them in neat piles on the sandy garden path. Margaret was able to use most of the fruit after many washings, but the jam that she made that year was, to say the least, rather gritty. This exploit was especially hard on Margaret, for she loved her garden and always did well at the local shows.

When each of the girls turned seven-years-old they were sent as boarders to Riddlesworth Hall Girls School near Thetford: an up-market preparatory school for young ladies where the fathers vied for a place to park their latest status symbol at the front door. Ours went round the back! It was far beyond our financial means, but somehow or other we managed to pay the fees, and as each of our daughters joined the school she seemed to settle down quickly and happily. Then one evening we had a telephone call from the Headmistress, Miss Ridsdale. She was a charming person, who was kindness itself and concerned always to do what was best for those in her care. She said she would like to see us as soon as possible. We went to Riddlesworth the next day and were told in the most diplomatic way that in her opinion, and that of her staff, it would be better for the three girls if they were split up. Apparently they had cottoned-on to the fact that if they stuck closely together, and each supported the other when in trouble, they were foolproof. They had also discovered that passive resistance, bordering on dumb insolence, was the best weapon if a situation developed between one of them and a member of staff. Multiply this attitude by three and they were unassailable. We had to agree with Miss Ridsdale that she was absolutely right and followed her suggestion that two of them at least should be moved on. Miriam went to St Margaret's at Bushey in Hertfordshire, a good middle-of-the-road Rover/Wolseley-type school; Jennifer went to Crofton Grange, near Royston, a no-uniform, 'free-thinking', musically and artistically-orientated establishment; Carole stayed at Riddlesworth for another term or so when she also went to Crofton.

We kept a pony for the girls from the time they were very young and eventually they had one each, but not until they were old enough to look after them. All their time during the school holidays and between leaving school and getting jobs seemed to be taken up with pony club camps, one-day events, trekking and gymkhanas. On leaving school, Miriam took a secretarial course and found herself a job in Norwich, while Jennifer took a job on a local milk round. Leaving home one morning in the little Morris 1000, Miriam, in a hurry as usual, met Jennifer coming home from her early morning milk-round. There was an almighty crash as they collided with each other. I don't think the insurance company ever did believe me when I rang to tell them that my daughters, each driving one of my cars, had run into each other in my own garden! Both cars were written off, but luckily the girls didn't damage each other too much.

In spite of these parental traumas, we were and are proud of all three of our daughters: they were spirited, gifted and capable children and young women. Now, all three are also very good and loving mothers.

The house at Hall Farm, East Raynham, was a very convenient house compared with some farms, and it was just the right size for our family. When we first went there in 1942 we didn't have any resident help, but a succession of ladies living close-by lent a hand. When the children were born various young girls who had just left school came as 'living-in help', some from quite a long way away. Mary, who stayed with us for several years, lived at Burnham Market, some twelve miles from Raynham. She thought nothing of cycling home and back once a week to see her family. One of the many people who helped Margaret in the house during the twenty-plus years we lived there was a lady who lived with her husband very near the farm. Her name was Mona Taney, or Mrs T. She arrived promptly each morning at 8.30 a.m., bustled around till 12.30, stopped for lunch till 1.30, then worked on again until four o'clock, when she went home to look after her Bert. Mona had a sister, Ellen, who was an extremely fine dressmaker. Ellen made clothes for our children as well as many other people. Mrs Ellington (Ellie) also worked at Hall Farm and was a great favourite with all of us, particularly the children, perhaps because she was a most marvellous cook.

Harold and Harriet Curry had lived in the parish for as long as I can remember. They worked for many years for my Uncle George, who farmed in the next village of Toftrees. Harold was a stockman and Harriet worked in the house. When he left my uncle's employment, the Currys moved to a house only a hundred yards or so from ours, and after he retired I often sat and talked to him in his garden. He had been born around the turn of the century and had little or no schooling, but he was well travelled, highly articulate, and had lived a very interesting life. He told me he was one of a large family and, because of the shortage of space in the house and lack of money to buy even bare essentials, at the age of seventeen he had decided to leave home and go to London, a place he had heard a lot about from a man he had once met who said he knew 'orl abut Lunum and them what lives up thar'. In spite of his mother's pleas he set off one morning wearing his brother's trousers, a jacket belonging to another brother and his father's top coat. All he had with him was a half-a-crown, a loaf of bread, a piece of cold bacon, an onion, and a tin whistle: Harold was quite musical. On the first day he walked the twenty-four miles to Brandon, and when it got dark spent the night 'nesting' inside a stack of straw. The next morning when it was light he could see a scare-crow in the next field, so he pinched its hat and continued on towards London. Turnips and swedes taken from fields as he passed were his staple diet for four days, until he reached the outskirts of the city and the common on which Sanger's Circus was set up. The story goes that the lion-tamer's boy assistant had been severely mauled by one of the lions the day before, and when Harold told the circus people that he was experienced with all types of stock he got the job! It seems though that he was soon moved to another job. Sanger's Circus was a very large and well-known one and Harold, in his ill-fitting clothes and scare-crow hat, used to join in with the clowns and was heard one day by the band-master playing his tin whistle. He was obviously a natural musician and was given a position in the band, complete with a bandsman's uniform. He eventually graduated to the euphonium, which he described as 'a great bugle thing what go round your neck about four times and you put it on like a shirt!' Harold stayed with the circus and travelled round Europe playing, as he said, 'before all the heads of Europe and even the Tsar of Russia'. Eventually he came home and settled down with Harriet, and took a job with my uncle. It must have seemed very dull after the circus. Harriet worked in the farmhouse for my aunt.

When, sadly, Harold died it was not long before Harriet arrived at our back-door and informed us firmly that she had always worked for a Joice, so now she had come to work for us. She said that we didn't need to pay her as with her garden, her pension, a few shillings a week, and four hens she could manage very well, but she would like to have lunch. I told her gently that we didn't really need anyone at that moment, but perhaps she could come once a week and clean the brass (we had a large collection of horse-brasses). She could, and did. *Every day* at eleven o'clock she would arrive and, after cleaning and re-cleaning the brasses, would draw her chair up to the kitchen table for lunch at 12.30. We obviously couldn't accept her services without payment, so she went on the pay-roll for what was just a token amount. The enthusiastic, efficient lady who did the wages and PAYE each week gave her a number and paycard to fill in. It came back with the single word 'helper' on it. Harriet was quite old by then, but as she got even older she sometimes forgot about cleaning the brasses. However, she never forgot lunch, or her paycard.

Harold told me many, many stories, some of them repeatable in all company, some doubtful. One in particular about the birth of one of their children went as follows, spoken by Harold in broad Norfolk. 'Coss Harriet is only a littel old gal (she stood a little over 5ft) but she's a good muther an I shel never forgit the day one of 'em was born. Harriet started her pains and told me to trot orf to the village and git the district narse. When we cum back an hour later Harriet hed got the baby. I knew she'd manage 'cos altho she's small she could pass a piana!' Harold didn't relate this story about Harriet in a derogatory sense, it was just his way of saying Harriet had an easy time giving birth.

Harold was not the only colourful personality we encountered during our years at Hall Farm. Lord Townshend had a Spanish butler called Emilio, and he told us one day that he had a young, single brother in Spain who wanted to come and work in England. We decided to take him on, and converted two of the attics into rooms for him. His name was Jesus (pronounced Haysoos) and he looked very Spanish, slightly built and with jet black hair. He couldn't speak much English when he arrived but picked it up amazingly quickly, helped in the early days by frequently telephoning his brother at the Hall, who could speak English fluently. Jesus was a great success with everyone and tried to emulate his brother Emilio, even to the extent of becoming my personal servant, much to the amusement of my daughters. When the television station opened in Norwich and I began to drive each day into the city, he would stand at the front door with my briefcase and hat ready, and would be in the same position when I arrived back in the evening. Presumably he moved during the day. He also served at table when necessary, complete with black tie and cummerbund. One evening when we had some friends to dinner Jesus was on parade, bringing round the food from the serving hatch leading from the kitchen where it had been cooked by Ellie. The first two courses had come and gone uneventfully, and then Ellie placed the sweet, a banana flambé with the brandy well alight, on the serving hatch. Jesus took one look at the flaming bananas, then stripped off his black uniform jacket and used it to douse the flames, at the same time scattering squishy bananas all over the room and some of the guests! There was no more to say but – end of sweet course, bring on the cheese! The incident did have a sequel though, for a few weeks later we again had guests for dinner. Nothing so elaborate as banana flambé was being served this time, but during the meal a quite serious fire broke out in the roof of the house due to an electrical fault. My son-in-law immediately dialled 999. The fire engines arrived quickly, by which time we were all out on the lawn, having first shut all the doors and windows. The captain of the brigade decided to douse the flames which were already licking through the roof with water, and told everyone to stay outside. Apparently Jesus hadn't got the message when we all dispersed into the garden: through the windows we saw him quietly lighting the candles on the dinner table. Possibly, because of the flambé incident a few weeks before, he thought this sort of thing was an old English custom!

The farm, the children and holidays, left only limited time for other activities, but Margaret was a governor of the local village school and put a great deal of energy and effort into raising funds for the lifeboats over the years. She was awarded a silver badge and a gold badge for her work. In my own case, I found time in the early days to be a member of the Walsingham Rural District Council and Parish Council, and Margaret also carried this on in later years. Margaret's other keen interest and pleasure came from the garden and the Horticultural Society. The garden at Raynham was large and we were able to grow virtually all the vegetables needed for the family. In the early days we didn't have a full-time gardener, but hi-jacked someone from the farm whenever there were hands to spare. But eventually Dan Bond, a professional gardener, joined us, and Margaret and he went on to win an embarrassing number of prizes for both produce, flowers and flower arranging at the Shows.

The secret of success for any enterprise lies in the quality and expertise of all the people who are involved in it. There are many that I could name who have helped me in my own career, the Drew family, who hailed from Colkirk, are a fine example. I think there were thirteen of them. It was reputed that Mrs Drew always said that she wanted a football team, but her husband demanded a couple of reserves. Several of the Drews worked for my family: some for my brother, including Father Drew; one or two for my uncle at nearby Toftrees; and Cecil Drew, who was already working for father at Testerton but joined me when I moved to Raynham. Cecil was an extraordinary man and highly skilled in many crafts. He was an expert hedge-layer and would happily tackle a 15ft high and 6ft wide thorn hedge bringing it down to 2ft 6in or 3ft high, according to the height of the bank it was growing on. With his axe he would partially cut through the main stem of ash, hawthorn or hazel at ground level, and then bend each piece over to about twenty degrees, pegging it down and weaving it in with the next. In order to make it stock-proof and secure so that it would all grow together, he would cut short stakes from the surplus material and hammer them in, one almost every foot. The skill was knowing how to make use of the material, and how deep to make the cuts, so that they didn't break off when they were bent and the whole fence when finished was stock-proof. With annual trimming, Cecil's fences would last a lifetime by regenerating themselves. He used to say that the fences were the roadways of the countryside for the birds and small animals. The trouble was that during the Depression many fences were neglected beyond redemption, and it was much cheaper to pull them out and replace them with posts and barbed wire. Some fences also had to go in order to make fields more economic to work with larger modern machinery. However, barbed wire doesn't stop wind and well-laid and maintained live fences are a marvellous shelter for stock in winter.

Cecil was also an expert thatcher of corn and hay stacks. He had a good eye and knew how to lay drains to dry out water-logged fields. He was skilled with horses but didn't like cows. He always said that they didn't like him and that anytime he touched a cow's udder it automatically 'dropped one on him'. Obviously the old cows knew that he didn't take to them, and their nervousness made them defecate. He was an expert warrener; he knew when the rabbits were on the move and where they were going to, and would be ready for them. He was highly skilled with traps and snares, indeed rabbiting was his principal recreation outside his work. Cecil wasn't averse to poaching an old pheasant, especially when the food shortage was at its worst and the keepers on the estates had been called up or directed into essential war-work. However, when he came home with an 'old Sally', as he called them, he always maintained that it had flown into telephone wires or died of old age. I never had reason to suspect that he ever sold one. He only took them for his own pot.

I learned an enormous amount from Cecil. We were friends for life. The very day that we got the tenancy of Hall Farm he asked if there was a house available and, if so, could he have it and move from Colkirk to Raynham. There was; he did; and I was very glad that he did. The little house where he was to spend the rest of his life was attached to the buildings of Hall Farm and only a hundred yards or so from my own back door. Cecil was a great gardener. The garden that went with the house wasn't big enough for him, so we gave him a chunk of the next field so that he could grow all the vegetables he needed. He didn't follow in his parents' footsteps with a large family but had a boy and a girl, Terry and Pat. Pat took after her father and became one of the best and most highly skilled gardeners in the area, and later on she and her husband Jack ran the local horticultural society for many years. After doing very well at school she worked for a time in the laboratory at a local agricultural feed merchants, and Terry, too, did well. He didn't follow his father onto the farm, but went to work for a pharmaceutical firm in Norwich and was very successful. Cecil's wife died as a result of a very unfortunate road accident at East Raynham and Pat took on the job of looking after her father, and also doing the Hall Farm office work – and later the garden.

Before Cecil came to Raynham he hadn't driven a tractor but had always worked with horses. The tractor he learned to drive was a Fordson, a particularly poor starter. In fact, she was called the 'old snot', which was Cecil's description of her after hours of winding the handle. One day, after harvest, I was burning a field of straw and suddenly to my horror saw that Cecil was running like mad to where his tractor stood, which I hadn't noticed when I started the fire. Thankfully he gave the starting handle one pull-up and she started. In the nick of time he jumped on the back and shot forward just as the flames were licking at the wheels. When he was safely out of the way I got across to him saying how sorry I was, but I hadn't realised he had left the tractor there. All he said was, 'At least the "old snot" knew when to go first pull!'

I don't know how we would have managed without Cecil in the first two years at Raynham. Every evening after tea we met, usually in his garden, and discussed what was to happen the next day. He saw to it each morning that everyone knew exactly what they were supposed to do. When we first went to Raynham there were fourteen on the labour book and we had one team of eight horses with at least four people, including Leonard Doy the team-man, working with them. The cows took up two men and a girl, and there was one man as a mechanic on maintenance. There was also a lorry driver, as we had to get the sugar-beet to Kings Lynn and the corn to the station, or the merchants' premises. Cecil saw to all the detail and then fell in and did any job that there was left to do; he was known as 'the Lord' or the headman.

Soon after we started at Raynham, PAYE was introduced and we needed to have time sheets. Up until that time we hadn't used them, and I used to walk round the farm on a Friday afternoon with a small leather bag full of half-crowns, florins, shillings, sixpences and coppers, and a pocket full of pound and ten shilling notes. Each man was paid according to what he had earned, and I noted down the amounts in my day book. PAYE tables and a lot more figures to sort out meant that paying wages became an office job, so we started collecting time sheets on Thursday evenings and paid out on Friday night. Each person wrote on his slip the date and his name, designation and hours worked. Cecil collected them up and checked the figures before the PAYE was collated in the office and the money put into small buff sealed envelopes. When I was doing the envelopes in the first week, I found that the last one in the pile was Cecil's and written on the top was: C. G. Drew – Foreman. This was instantaneous promotion without any discussion! I think Cecil was gently trying to tell me that he should be foreman. It was never mentioned, but for the rest of his life on the farm until he retired thirty years later he was the Hall Farm foreman. The week after he promoted himself, and no doubt assumed that it had been accepted, he put his wages up two shillings a week, again without any discussion, although he did ask me if I thought the sum was fair. It was, in fact, lower than the figure I was going to offer, so I put his wages up another five shillings a month later. Without adding anything he just said, 'Thanks'. The total wage bill for our first week ending 19th October 1947 for the fourteen employed at Hall farm was £69, including National Health and Unemployment Insurance as it was called then.

Being foreman didn't alter Cecil's job one iota. He still continued to fill in wherever there was a need, and he did all the complicated tasks like stoking the grain dryer furnace. The furnace was very temperamental and would go out if the fire wasn't stoked sympathetically, or, worse still, would flare up and if not swiftly controlled cook the grain and ruin germination. It was Cecil who mastered the art of getting it right, although Ben Boggis also acquired the knack after we had a heating and ventilation expert down from London in sheer desperation to try and fix up an automatic furnace control.

This man worked for the firm who were making very complicated ventilation controls in submarines, and his modifications improved the plant slightly. However, after two harvests we decided that we must convert the dryer to oil firing to cut out all the man-hours spent shovelling coke. An even bigger step forward was the conversion of the combine harvester to bulk handling of grain. The man-hours saved were enormous. It brought to an end the old system of filling grain sacks weighing up to 2¼cwt, letting them slide on to the ground, picking them up by hand, loading them on to a trailer, taking them to the farm, tipping them one at a time on to the dryer, and sacking them off again the other end. It didn't end there though as the grain after drying still needed to be loaded on to lorries which took them to the station and thence on to the railway and away, or delivered to the maltings. Bulk handling revolutionised harvest and I'm sure saved a lot of personal ruptures, but it did away with labour and a lot of jobs were lost in the farming industry. Fortunately not those of Cecil and Ben and they and a few more men were with us until we left Raynham twenty-four years later.

It didn't matter what you asked any of the men to do, they would always have a go. Both Cecil and Ben were also very handy in other ways. Ben worked in the garden sometimes and as relief milker. And Cecil even came in one evening when we wanted to go to the pictures and couldn't find a babysitter. Margaret had just put a cake in the oven which needed another hour or so to finish cooking, and she asked Cecil if he would keep an eye on the cake and listen for the children. She explained that he could test to see if the cake was done by plunging one of her steel knitting needles into it. If the needle came out clean, the cake was ready and could come out of the oven. When we got home about three hours later the cake was out, but the top was like a piece of perforated zinc with hundreds of holes in it! It hadn't been clear to Cecil that the oven door had to be kept shut and the cake only tested every now and again. He must have sat all evening opening the oven door and pushing the needle in every few minutes, letting all the heat out of the oven at the same time. Still, the children didn't wake up and although rather flat the cake was as light as a feather.

A few of the farm work-force were in the territorial army and only these men got their papers when the war started. One of them was Dick Lee, who helped with my father's sheep flock at South Raynham. It was in 1939 that the local postman came and found him on the farm, and gave him a telegram which said he had to report to his TA centre as soon as possible. He was away for a few weeks, and then he turned up one day and announced that he was on embarkation leave and was shortly due to go with his regiment, the Norfolks, overseas. After that, apart from seeing him briefly when he was on leave, we heard no more of him until he was posted as missing. There was no more news of him again until we heard that he had been taken prisoner. At the end of the war when he was liberated and demobilised he came straight back to us. He married a local girl and came to live in a house in the parish only a few hundred yards from the farm house. It was necessary for him to be close at hand, as his job was to look after the herd of cows at Hall Farm. Even as a lad, before his army experience, he had always been good with cattle as well as sheep, and he was to excel himself with our new herd of pedigree Jerseys. As our foundation stock of Jerseys came from the island of Jersey we sent Dick over there for a short time to get first-hand information on the blood lines we had bought, and especially on the techniques of showing cattle. He had a natural gift with these pretty little cattle and in 1948, the first year we showed, we won prizes at three of the Shows: first and second at the Newark Show, the Championship at the Norfolk Show, and also at the Royal. The next year also we did well at the Norfolk and the Royal. At the Norfolk Show in 1950 we beat the cow entered from the Sandringham herd of Jerseys into second place. Our cow was 'Coiffure's Design Fern' and his late Majesty King George VI and the Queen (now the Queen Mother) and the two princesses, Elizabeth and Margaret, watched the judging and were there when his Majesty presented the cups. It was a great thrill, especially as my landlord, Lord Townshend, had also won a cup for the best Ayrshire in the show. The two of us went up to receive the cups together from the King.

One of the shows, however, almost ended in personal tragedy for me. It happened at the Royal Agricultural Show, Shrewsbury, in 1949. We were preparing the four cows for judging in the canvas-covered lines, when suddenly there was a hubbub down at the far end, away from the cows and heifers, where a young Jersey bull was kicking up a fuss. The bulls were in separate standings, each with a halter and a leading rein fixed onto their nose rings. There was a double rail to keep each bull in place and a smooth piece of 4ft wide iron plate, standing 8ft high, in front of the animals. For some reason the clip attaching the rope to this particular bull's nose ring had become detached. Thinking I could reach it and put the clip back on whilst the bull was busy feeding I leaned over in front of him, but he took exception to this and threw his head back. Luckily for me one of his horns went between my legs, and they had a sufficient curve on them to accommodate the width of my thigh. As he tossed his head I shot up the iron plate like a jack-in-the-box, and my head struck one of the roof trusses which knocked me out. Albert, a stockman from Thriplow Farms, saw what was happening and rushed in with a two-tined fork, beat the young bull off and pulled me away. I don't remember much about it until I came round and found myself staring straight up at a sea of faces, mostly stockmen and cowmen, and discovered they had taken my trousers off to examine the damage. A doctor arrived and I was taken to the Shrewsbury hospital, but thankfully the damage was only superficial. The bump on the head hurt the worst but of course the press went to town. A typical report was:

Pet bull gores man at Royal

Wary crowds gathered round the Jersey ring at the Royal Show today expecting trouble from one of the bulls, 'Keeper's Fairy Prince'. The bull's owner, Mrs L. Parker, wife of Treasury Solicitor, Mr Parker, stood anxiously watching the judging 'bull staff in hand'. Reason for the excitement: 'Keeper's Fairy Prince' had attacked farmer Richard Joice of Hall Farm, Fakenham, Norfolk and sent him to Shrewsbury hospital with severe lacerations and bruises.

Lives in garden

Farmer Joice, himself a Jersey breeder, was helping Mrs Parker to tie up her bull when he made the mistake of getting in front of its head.

Twin horns flashed and Mr Joice was tossed up against the pen wall, thrown to the ground and gashed across the forehead.

Stockman Albert ran from the next pen and dragged him away. Without his quick help the farmer would have been killed.

Said Mrs Parker: 'It was as if my own husband or child had turned on a friend. I never expected it of "Prinny". He lives in the front garden at home. I did want to lead "Prinny" into the ring myself', said Mrs Parker, 'but now he's too dangerous. I suppose all male animals are a bit treacherous. I'm horrified when I think how easy I've been with him leading him along the lane like a pet dog. Not any more after this.'

It is true to say I learned a lesson about bulls that day, and about the hazards of keeping them as pets. I still have the scars to prove it! I already knew that you should treat all bulls, particularly Jerseys, with respect, and especially the front end of them. But I also learned another important lesson: that the Press will usually exaggerate and sensationalise their news items given half a chance.

One of the pioneers of early mechanical farming techniques was Bill Newcome-Baker of Sedgeford and Holkham in North Norfolk. Although he was a 'no cattle' farmer he maintained and increased fertility on the light soils he farmed by a strict ley system and sugar-beet. His secret was the use of alfalfa, as it was called in the USA, or lucerne as it was known in this country. The Americans had developed strains that would stand the rigours of the Norfolk winters better than ours, so he imported fresh seed from there. However, whereas stock farmers here had grazed their lucerne with sheep he cut his alfalfa and dried it, not as was occasionally done on stock farms for hay, but artificially, using vast oil-fired driers. When sufficient moisture had been taken out of the lush foliage it was ground to a fine powder, then put through another machine that compressed it into nuts or pellets. He sold this in half-hundredweight bags as dried grass, and its dark colour and taste impressed the cattle and their feeders. Sheep, horses and cattle loved it and, when mixed with barley meal which he also grew in generous quantities, it made a very palatable high-protein ration which had all the advantages of easy handling and storage. Lucerne, being also a legume, converted nitrogen from the air and produced a greater bulk than clover and could yield up to three cuts in a season according to rainfall – it also fixed nitrogen in the soil for the following crops.

David Maufe, whose father was in business in a big way in the Midlands, was Bill Baker's partner. He and his wife, Anne, lived on and looked after their large farm at Branthill on the Holkham estate. David, too, was one of the new 'no stock men' and although we used to have heated arguments on this subject we became close friends. He was, and still is, a great sailor and I often crewed for him, but hadn't his nerve in the twelve-metre 'Sharpie' he sailed at Brancaster Staithe harbour and out to sea. The weather there can and does change in minutes and there's an awful lot of sea to get wet in. The friendship also blossomed with the children, as our three girls were more or less the same age as their three girls. His wife ultimately added a son, Tarquin, to their trio and I am afraid he was at the receiving end of a lot of indulgence and 'spoiling' from the six young girls.

We had several successful holidays with the Maufes – the first to Mégève in Switzerland in 1952. At that time the travel allowance abroad was £15 per person and you were allowed to set off with a full tank of petrol from Southampton. There were no 'drive-on' facilities – the cars were hoisted on by crane straight into the ship's hold. We set off from Norfolk in the early hours, the two cars loaded with all the children, who always seemed to want to be in the other car. We had hoped to make the journey from Norfolk to Switzerland in convoy, but this didn't work for many unforeseen reasons. After landing in France we decided to drop the convoy idea and meet in Dijon. I was to go ahead and find a suitable hotel and meet the Maufes at the railway station that evening. My French is very limited, but we made the journey and met up with them later that day. I triumphantly conducted them to the small cheap hotel I had found where I had booked three rooms, eight beds, for the night. Luckily Anne, who spoke fluent French went in to inspect and check that everything was in order. As the rest of us trooped into the lobby she came out, very flustered, followed by an irate 'Madame'. I hadn't noticed the red light over the door, and with my sketchy knowledge of the language had apparently led Madame to believe that I wanted rooms for my men friends and a party of girls! We finished up with a meal at a nearby restaurant and drove on through the night with a load of bewildered children. Luck was with us for the rest of the journey though and we drove into Mégève the following evening, tired and grubby but in good spirits.

The scene in Mégève was one I shall never forget. It had snowed very heavily the night before and everything was covered in a sparkling, white mantle. They had just got the roads open with their mechanical snowblowers, and there were few cars about, but lots of pretty horse-drawn sleighs swishing through the snow, with their bells tinkling. We'd never seen anything like this in Norfolk! Mégève in those days was a very small town and had not long had its ski lift. In fact, I don't remember there being much there other than the ski lift, station, hotel, a handful of shops, the police station and Town Hall, and a few cafés. The sports centre had a gymnasium and a restaurant and, what the children liked most, a patiserie. David was already an experienced skier and had taken his own ski-ing gear on the top of his car, but Anne was expecting Tarquin and couldn't ski. Our biggest difficulty was that we simply didn't have enough money to hire boots and skis for everyone. Several of the children had similar-sized feet, so we hired a couple of pairs and they had to share and make the best of it. But the experience of just being in a completely new environment was sufficiently stimulating to keep them occupied between meals.

The journey home was uneventful except that the carburettor fell off David's Ford Pilot and, after a makeshift repair, Anne decreed that the Maufes would always travel in front so that if it happened again the Joices would be on hand to help. The Ford didn't break down again, but the cases tied on the roof-rack came adrift one at a time and landed in our path, spewing out their contents as they hit the road! It's quite a problem packing up damaged cases and getting them into a car already over-full with children and luggage, whilst the car from which they fell disappears up the road its occupants nonchalantly unaware of the drama unfolding behind. We retrieved two of the Maufes three cases but failed somehow to rescue Anne's small personal holdall; that was left behind. The most frustrating aspect of the holiday was not being able to buy anything but the bare essentials, and therefore not being able to let the children take full advantage of the new experiences. We arrived back in England in the early hours of the morning with literally a few shillings between us, and had to wait for the banks to open to get money for petrol and breakfast in Southampton.

On balance the Swiss holiday was voted a success by all participants and on the strength of it, eighteen months later, we decided to go to Brittany in the spring. It seemed, indeed it turned out to be, a good choice. This time David decided to take a collapsible boat on the top of his car so that he could teach all the children the basic principles of sailing. History repeated itself as once again the luggage came adrift from the roof-rack, together with the collapsible boat, in its folded state of course. The boat wasn't damaged too badly and although the wives were very suspicious and doubtful about its safety David sailed blissfully round the Brittany coast and enjoyed himself immensely, even if every time he went out of sight Anne sent one of us scampering off to see if he was still afloat. Audierne and Concarneau are beautiful little fishing ports and, with fewer financial restrictions this time, (the travel allowance was up to £25 per person), we were able to hire professional fishermen to take us out, so we could all enjoy views of the beautiful Brittany coast from the sea. During this holiday, too, Dr Gervase Woodsend and his wife (who were mutual friends of both families) flew down to Douarnenez with their sons in their light aeroplane and joined us. This was a great success as all the children, a few at a time, were taken up in the aeroplane for trips. It was their first opportunity to see what landscapes and oceans looked like from the air, and was tremendously exciting for the six girls. But I think the flights probably gave their mothers some anxious moments.

The next time Margaret and I took the children abroad we decided to fly by cheap night flight to Milan. We arrived there at four in the morning and picked up a hire car. It was a large Fiat and we drove at a leisurely pace down through Italy to Rome, via Verona and Pisa. I explained to the children beforehand that it was a long journey, and that it would in all probability be very tiring. However, there would be lots to see and, with travel games to play and a whole night's sleep to catch up on, I hoped it would be trouble-free. I had also warned them that if there was any squabbling, sulks, fights or bad temper on the way I would take rigorous action. All went well at first. We took a look at the leaning tower of Pisa and the Coliseum at Verona, stopped for lunch, and made several other stops for ice-cream and drinks. It was very hot and about forty miles or so from Rome, at one of those unscheduled stops dictated by the call of nature, a quarrel broke out between two of the girls. They were arguing about a pair of shoes and it went on for some time in spite of pleas from the front pointing out that there was only another hour or so before we reached the hotel in Rome. But to no avail, the row went on and on as, for the umpteenth time, we wound our way round the bends on the snake-like mountain roads. Finally, I stopped the Fiat on the very edge of a ravine, opened my window and said, 'Pass me those shoes.' I took hold of the shoes, hurled them out of the window, and we all watched them describe a great circle and disappear into the ravine below. There was complete silence from the back as we drove off. I thought my impressive shock tactics must have worked as in my mirror I could see that they were soon all asleep, and peace reigned for the rest of the journey. It wasn't until later, when we arrived at the hotel in Rome and Margaret emerged from the car with bare feet, that I realised that it was *her* shoes that the girls had handed to me and that I'd thrown unceremoniously out of the window! I was not allowed to forget the incident over the next few days. In any case of dispute, without a word, the girls just slipped off their shoes and looked at their feet. In the end they settled for a new pair each in exchange for the promise to forget the whole affair – a promise, incidentally, they didn't keep. However, for over thirty years I have given my children full credit for swift thinking, and still do!

To strengthen the heart
Eat Hawthorn leaves and chew the hips

Toothache

a. A pepper plaster i.e. brown paper soaked in vinegar and liberally sprinkled with pepper
b. A little tobacco soaked in whiskey and placed in the tooth
c. Burned bread pushed into the tooth (also a cure for constipation)

Nettlerash
Boil the blossoms of white nettles and drink the liquid, sweetened to taste

Chilblains
Cut top off onion, dip into salt and rub well into affected parts (paraffin or turpentine could be similarly used)

From Grandma's *Commonplace Book*.

CHAPTER TEN

Raynham: the Enterprises and the People

Before I was married, and when I was still living at Testerton, an incident occurred which was to have far-reaching effects on my life in later years. At about 4.30 a.m. in late September 1941, I was wakened by what I can only describe as a flash of light which passed the window of my bedroom, followed by a dull thud or rumble. As I leapt out of bed I remember thinking that because it was so quiet it must be a light aircraft crash-landing, but I couldn't judge how far away it was. I quickly dressed and woke my parents. They hadn't heard it, but my father suggested that I drive the truck to where I thought it might be. 'Take your gun with you', he advised. As the fields had been harvested it was a simple matter to drive straight across the land without headlights. The field in question was near the house and no more than half-a-mile from our front door. I could see a small fire burning and silhouetted against the early morning sky I made out the shape of the huge bulk of a large plane. There wasn't sufficient light to identify the make, and I immediately thought it might be German. A small fire was still burning in one engine about 20ft from the ground and in crash-landing the starboard wing had been torn off, cocking up the port wing and leaving the fuselage lying on its side. We were all very familiar with the makes of RAF planes, but the aircraft was lying in an unusual position and I couldn't identify it. The thought uppermost in my mind was, perhaps it was German and the invasion had started.

I left the truck, taking the twelve-bore, and as quickly as possible walked round the plane at what I thought was a safe distance, expecting it to blow up. The fire was still gently burning, but there was no other sound. I had walked about half-way round in a large circle when I suddenly heard voices, but couldn't make out what was being said. One sounded foreign and the other not English. Crouching down I listened – one man seemed to be saying that his leg was broken and that his boot was full of blood. By that time it was getting light so I approached them, and pointing my gun at them said, 'I take it you chaps are British?' Of course they were. The one with the broken leg was broad Scots and the other very Welsh. They asked where they were and said that they had limped back from a bombing raid on Germany after being hit by a shell, and that the rest of the crew had baled out. They had lost a lot of fuel: in fact, the plane's tanks were empty, and just as the captain had decided to abandon ship one of the remaining engines had seized up and caught fire before they hit the ground. This must have been the flash of light I had seen from my bedroom window. The two men were the pilot and co-pilot and as soon as the plane came to rest they had climbed out of the door, which was pointing skywards, and jumped, fearing that the whole thing would go up in flames. It was in the fall from the plane that one man's leg was broken, but his boot wasn't full of blood. There had been a heavy dew and his boots were soaked as he stumbled through the sugar-beet away from the plane. With no petrol left in the tanks the fire burnt itself out and we carefully lifted the injured pilot onto the truck and took him back to the house, where my mother put a splint on his leg and we all had breakfast. An hour or so later an ambulance arrived from RAF Bircham and eventually the local policeman, notebook at the ready. The other crew members were picked up later from the villages where they dropped. Fortunately they all landed safely by parachute.

There was a very sad sequel to this crash. An RAF guard was placed on the wreck in the middle of the sugar-beet field, and a couple of days later a team arrived to dismantle it and take it away. A sergeant with a driver came first to remove the machine guns but, with the fuselage lying at such a strange angle, it was not an easy task. Whilst manipulating the gun out of the upper turret, the sergeant was shot in the stomach by a bullet which had somehow got stuck in the breech. I was at home when the driver rushed in and told us what had happened. I went back with him to the plane and found the sergeant in a pretty poor way. The bullet had gone clear through his abdomen, and obviously he had to be got to hospital as soon as possible. We lifted him into the RAF van and took him to the small RAF hospital at Raynham. I drove and the driver nursed the sergeant, making him as comfortable as possible on a bed of corn sacks and straw. It was a terrible journey and the poor chap died the next day.

It was through this unfortunate incident that I got to know the RAF doctor at Raynham. We had a mutual interest in vintage cars, and he was rebuilding a battered well-worn Frazer Nash in the annexe to the morgue on the station. Rumour had it that he had needed to move his car out in a great hurry a couple of times following local tragedies on the base! I often went to see him and occasionally gave him a hand with the Frazer Nash. One day in 1943 he asked me if one or two of the pilots suffering from strain after long night flights could occasionally sleep at our house during the day, as it was almost impossible for them to get a good rest on the base. The men concerned were mostly those stationed at Massingham, which was the satellite base to Raynham. The accommodation there was in ten Nissen huts, which were very noisy. So we set up a couple of sparsely furnished rooms at Hall Farm, which became known as the home for clapped-out aircrew. The squadron based at Massingham was No. 169 and it was equipped with Mosquitoes. They went out as pathfinders, usually in the early evening, to locate the main targets for the heavier bombers by dropping incendiary bombs and causing fires so that the following planes could wreak the maximum amount of damage. If the planes took off in our direction and flew over the house, we would count them out, and then count again when they came back, or not, as fate dictated. A harrowing business, but during those years we constantly lived with the knowledge and talk of death and destruction.

However, quite unwittingly our RAF doctor friend introduced me to a man who had far-reaching effects on my life. One day, because of bad weather conditions, all flying was cancelled and the crews were grounded. The doctor telephoned and asked if he could bring over a bunch of pilots and flying crew plus bread, cheese and pickles and have an impromptu party. I think they were all keen to get out of the mess. As far as I remember Margaret rang a few girl-friends and, helped by the food, beer and the gramophone, we had an amusing time. These parties became a regular event, and on one particular evening the usual crew turned up and announced that they had brought a new member of the 169 Squadron, a not very large chap called Harry Reed, affectionately known as 'Shorty'. He was to become one of our greatest friends. He once said that he came uninvited to a party but never went home, for our home became his. Any moment that he had to spare he was at Hall Farm messing about with his car or helping on the farm. His own home was at Stockton-on-Tees where his father was a local council administrator. Soon after we met he told me he would like to get into farming, or an allied trade, if he survived the war. He did, and after leaving the Air Force with a gratuity of just over £500 and taking courses in various aspects of farming, he returned to Norfolk full of ideas and eager to start.

Harry was keen to start a poultry unit, which was not something I had on the farm, nor did I have any spare capital. However, he was so enthusiastic that eventually in the spring of 1957 we agreed that we would each put £500 into a small company. The company was called Culford Poultry Farms and we bought one thousand White Leghorn pullets and twenty-five fold units to house them in. It was agreed that Harry would be the labour force and I would provide the land. The twenty-five units, each holding forty birds, had to be moved up about the length of a unit each day. As they were pulled forward a fresh patch of grass appeared for the birds to eat so we had, in effect, a controlled free-range system. Each unit also had a built-in water drinker and supplementary feeder attached to the front, and nest boxes in the covered area on the rear. The units were each finely balanced on a pair of wheels in the centre, and could be pulled by one man from the front. The first couple of seasons the birds laid well, the grass grew well, and high protein concentrated food was not too expensive. With great enthusiasm we ploughed the profits into a breeding unit. To save on costs we bought the wood and Harry made ten larger huts this time to hold two thousand birds. He planned to produce hatching eggs for breeding day-old chicks to sell to other commercial egg producers. This project wasn't such a success, and Harry decided to become a specialist breeder.

The hybrid bird was all the rage in the fifties. This was only a new name for a cross between two breeds. If you were lucky enough to choose the right breeds or strains to cross, the resulting bird would be a better commercial proposition than its parents. Careful crossing would produce a bird that matured earlier, was less liable to disease, had a smaller body weight, and therefore consumed less food and laid more of the right size eggs. In later years the eggs had to be brown, the colour preferred by the housewife on the breakfast table! To get a hybrid there obviously had to be two different breeds of poultry. We had White Leghorns and we got our cross by using cockerels bred by a well-known breeder who lived quite close to us, Dick Hill. He was breeding pure-bred Rhode Island Reds so we linked up with him, mated his cockerels with our pullets and got very good results. To know exactly what is happening, the eggs produced by the union of any cockerel with a particular hen must be marked with the number of the dam and sire. The only way to know which hen lays which egg is to trap nest every one, so that when the chicken goes into the nest box to lay she automatically shuts the door of the little cubicle and can't get out until someone comes along, opens the door and writes the number off her leg band onto the egg she has just laid. The houses specially designed and built for this purpose need someone constantly checking each nest box, releasing the hens and recording the eggs. The eggs are then placed in an incubator, each in an egg-sized compartment so that as soon as hatching has taken place the number from the discarded shell can be transferred to the leg of the new chick. The recorded progress of the bird will indicate whether or not she is an improvement on her parents. If she is, her parents are kept to continue to breed. It's a slow and frustrating job, bearing in mind that every other egg produces a male bird that doesn't lay any eggs at all. Harry discovered that at Cornell University in America they were speeding up the whole process by feeding all the information into a computer (not like the modern electronic machines but using punch cards). He went to Cornell armed with all our breeding results and came back with some of their findings, which as far as I could understand told us which strains not to mate, and therefore indicated that if we mated the others we might have a better bird. The upshot of it all was that it worked, and we started breeding our own 'Hygrade Hybrid'. In 1960 we formed a company called Joice and Hill Limited to keep the enterprise separate from our other farming activities. I was Chairman, and Dick Hill and Harry did all the work!

The Americans, with their much bigger units under test and their vast production units, were ahead of us in the poultry field in the fifties and we had planned to buy good parent stock direct from them. But, following the outbreak of 'Newcastle' disease in the States, a complete ban was placed on the import of poultry and poultry products to this country. Two legal ways round this restriction were found, via Ireland and Sweden, where they allowed eggs to be brought in from the States and chickens exported to this country as long as they went to a quarantine station. The law relating to quarantine was very strict. The birds had to be kept inside for the period involved, with no chance of coming into contact even with wild birds. All doors and windows had to have double protection and every person entering had to change his clothes. Even the Ministry inspection vet had to take a disinfecting shower between changes of clothes. In spite of these difficulties Joice and Hill flourished and expanded, eventually starting hatcheries as far afield as Scotland and Malta. I'm out of it now, and Harry Reed has retired. The company under Dick Hill, with other new directors, is now one of the leading European poultry breeding establishments franchising the 'Hisex' bird. But Harry, the pilot who came uninvited to a war-time party, earned the DFC, married a local girl and had three daughters, was for me one of the nicer outcomes of the war.

In 1946 Father decided that, as the war was to all intents and purposes over, the farm could be transferred into my name. When he told me this, I asked him how I was to pay for the growing crops and equipment which were, of course, his. We were sitting in his car beside the Colkirk road which bounded one side of the field I was ploughing when he happened to pass. He pulled an old envelope out of his pocket and jotted down the list of equipment and growing crops on the farm and said that it would cost me, in round figures, £5,000. Then he pulled out his cheque book and handed me a cheque for £5,000 and announced that it was a loan from him to me, interest free. Then he asked me to give him a cheque for the same amount to cover the cost of the growing crops and equipment. He had been very generous for the crops in the fields were sugar-beet, cabbages and sprouts, all of which would be harvested and turned into cash by the next spring. He had charged me the cost to him of growing them, but had not left himself any profit. Just as he was about to drive on he said, 'Oh, by the way, I have been to the bank this morning and guaranteed you to the tune of £5,000 as an overdraft to get you through to next harvest. Here is a new cheque book. Good luck, you are now a farmer in your own right. I have also seen Lord Townshend and put the tenancy of the farm in your name.' Could you have a better start or father?

All I needed now was good weather and a lot of luck. The weather was passable in 1946, but 1947 really put me on my feet for in that year I grew a comparatively large acreage of cabbages and sprouts. The winter of 1947 was hard and long, which put the trade for vegetables up to an all-time high and resulted in prices that we never thought were possible. In the spring of 1947 I had also been lucky enough to be allocated an ex-army caterpillar D4 tractor. This put us right on top of the work and enabled me to sell the few remaining horses. A young friend of mine, Dick Burgis, had also applied for a reconditioned tractor and came and drove the D4 for me until his came through when he went into partnership as a contractor with his brother. When in 1953, because of the pressure from other businesses I had undertaken, I needed a full-time manager for the farms, I asked Dick Burgis if he would join me as a partner. He did and we farmed as a company called Richard Joice Limited. The partnership has lasted in one shape or another for nearly forty years. Dick and his wife live close by now, and we still do many things together.

Early in 1947 I met another dynamic individual who, like Harry Reed, was ex–RAF but had been invalided out following a crash with a Spitfire in the Battle of Britain. When we met he was busy taking over the family farm at Thorpland Hall on the outskirts of Fakenham. This was Berry Savory. His family were stockbrokers in the city and his mother had kept a pedigree herd of Jerseys all through the war, supplying Channel Island milk in and around the town of Fakenham. Another farmer, Mr W. E. Porter, of Pensthorpe, was also supplying milk in the area from his herds of British Friesian and Jersey cows. I had always fancied having a milk round and had considered retailing from my own herd at Raynham. However, it seemed an impossible idea unless one could buy an existing milk round and the goodwill of the customers, as with milk rationing in operation everyone had to be registered with a retailer. So, working on the principle that if you couldn't lick-'em, join-'em, and after a lot of talk and negotiation with Mr Porter and Berry Savory, together with my father we formed a company called The Wensum Dairy Farms Ltd (named after the River Wensum, which ran through the farm). We each had a quarter-share and guaranteed the company at the bank.

We bought the Heath Farm, Fakenham, from Mr Porter and converted the old farm premises into a modern creamery. Milk from Mr Porter's and other neighbouring herds was collected, bottled and distributed from our little creamery. Pasteurisation was not yet known in the area, although it had been introduced in more highly populated areas of Great Britain. The government offered a pasteurising subsidy to approved creameries to give a service to other retailers, so we installed a pasteurising plant and offered a service to other retailers in the district, also to schools under the school milk scheme. We had the services of an ingenious engineer, David McCormick, who, as manager, designed and built much of the complicated bottling and capping machinery.

On the milk production front the price emphasis in the world had begun to lean towards quality milk as opposed to quantity, and so we sold the Friesian herd at Raynham and began a Jersey herd. A reasonable time had elapsed after the liberation of the Channel Islands and the quickest, easiest and cheapest way of getting to Jersey was to drive to Hatfield, the north London airport and at that time the only recognised airport for the city, and fly direct to Jersey. It was comparatively expensive, but a very cheap way of doing it was to get to the airport in the early hours of the morning, and travel with the newspapers which were flown each day in a twin-winged De Havilland Rapide plane to Jersey and Guernsey – they simply took out the seats and we sat amongst the bundles of paper. The day could then be spent visiting small farms looking at and sometimes buying cattle; after a few hours sleep and breakfast, one caught the next plane back to Hatfield. As far as I remember it was never official, as there wasn't a ticket, and it only cost a pound or two each way. I have also travelled in one of these planes, with its two sets of wings and a lot of wire struts, complete with a load of early tomatoes and cucumbers.

John Rondel, the person who organised the shipping of the animals to us, became a very dear friend, and Carlyle Le Galais, the Jersey auctioneer, dealt with all the paperwork. The cattle came across from the port of Jersey as deck cargo in wooden crushes and landed eight hours later at Weymouth. John Rondel is still one of the best judges of Jersey cattle, and has shipped them literally all over the world.

We supplied the creamery at Fakenham with milk from the Raynham Jersey herd, and for a few years things didn't go too badly and we showed a profit. Then in 1953 Berry decided he wanted to emigrate to South Africa to start a grass drying project. We bought him out and soldiered on, but it was obvious that the expense of rural and village delivery was not economic and our biggest rivals, Seamans at Kings Lynn, were finding the same thing. The margins were getting smaller and the running expenses bigger and really it was becoming more than ever necessary to have the dense town rounds to help subsidise the more sparsely populated rural delivery. At this point, David McCormick decided to go and manage a laundry in Bristol. So, again working on the 'if you can't beat-'em etc.' principle, we contacted Seamans and offered them the whole enterprise – pasteurisation, bottling and delivery, the lot. I bought the farm and paid Mr Porter out. Eventually I did the same with my father, adding the acreage to the Raynham farm, making 1,200 acres in all, which Dick Burgis ran very efficiently. After I had sold the dairy and there was no contractual reason any more for supplying Jersey milk I decided to go out of milk production and into beef, and for many years afterwards we kept Hereford cattle.

The years from 1945 onward marked a time of great activity for most people. The war had been fought and won and businesses that had been turned over to war work (and there were few that were not affected by the war effort) had to be brought back and fitted into peace-time conditions. Because of the shortage of supplies and shipping from abroad, maximum effort was still required from the farming industry and this was to remain the case for another twenty-five years. Our own situation was that Dick Burgis was running the farms with unsurpassed efficiency, while Harry Reed and Dick Hill were completely in charge of the poultry.

The forties had undoubtedly been a time of great strain and effort, but the climate at the end of the forties and through the fifties and sixties was one of opportunity and challenge. During the war there had been little chance of developing new ideas unless it was to increase production, certainly not to launch into fresh fields. However, that behind us, the first challenge that came our way was when a friend of mine, knowing of my interest in the subject, suggested that we form a local photographic society. While I was at school my mother had saved up the tea coupons that were attached to every packet of Mazawattee tea, and one day in the grocers we were given a catalogue of what you could get with them. Eventually she allowed me to exchange them for a No. 1 Box Brownie camera which, in spite of its cheapness, produced amazingly good pictures. Indeed, in 1936 I took it to Switzerland and returned with some jolly good snaps. From then on my burning ambition was to get enough money to buy a more sophisticated camera. The formation of the Fakenham Photographic Society was a great incentive as everyone else seemed to have a 'bought' camera and made great fun of my Brownie No. 1. Eventually I acquired a secondhand Rolleiflex and a very cheap enlarger. I bought them from a man who became a great friend of mine, Ernest Swain at Hunstanton. Ernest had a kiosk near the pier, from which he sold cameras and films and also took beach photographs. On Saturday, 12th June 1939, at 6.30 p.m., Hunstanton Pier, with its dance hall at the outer end, caught fire. Ernest grabbed the only camera with a film in it near at hand and rushed out to take some pictures. When the fire was out it was seen that the end of the pier was burnt down. Ernest went home and developed his film, and found that by a million-to-one chance he had photographed a lady jumping off the pier into the sea, lit by the flames from the raging fire. He had the world copyright of the photograph and made enough money from the sales to open and stock a proper photographic shop in Hunstanton. He also started a developing and printing business and ultimately opened another shop in Kings Lynn. About that time I became Chairman of the Fakenham Photographic Society and started taking 16mm movie films, mostly of the family, but also farming activities. Ernest persuaded me to buy a sound projector to put, I am afraid, very amateurish commentaries onto the films. Out of our mutual interest and friendship a partnership in Norfolk Mobile Cinemas was born. We took our equipment and travelled to all the larger villages in the area which had no proper cinema but reasonably-sized village halls. The law at that time was that if a hall had less than two hundred seats the audience was not charged entertainment tax. We hired shows from the main film libraries in London, which consisted of a short cartoon, the news and a main feature. The charge for the two-and-a-half hours entertainment was one shilling for the best seats in the hall, sixpence for the front row and ninepence in between. We made money and were soon able to buy three more projectors, so that we each went out two nights a week with two projectors linked together to give a continuous showing, with no stoppage for changing reels. However, if it was a good house we stopped after the cartoon and news and sold ice-cream, sweets and cigarettes. It really was a case of, stop the film, run to the front of the hall, walk round with the tray selling the goods, and then back to the projector to start Part Two!

With the renewed interest in photography after the shortages of the war when film was difficult to come by, the camera shops in Kings Lynn and Hunstanton did well, and we opened another in Norwich. Ernest was the brains behind the organisation, and he also got the photographic concession with the USAF bases at Mildenhall, Lakenheath and Sculthorpe. There were two spin-off benefits from our mini film industry. Each Saturday night when the film wasn't being used on the 'circuit', we were able to show it to the family and our friends at home in the sitting-room, with the screen on the mantlepiece, a hole cut in the wall opposite, and the projector standing in the hall on the other side! The other benefit was that I became slightly more proficient at making films of farming activities and holidays. Some of the films were eventually used in television, but many were used extensively at local schools and Young Farmers' Clubs. Indeed two local schools, Helhoughton and Bawdeswell, who had enlightened and far-sighted masters, 'adopted' the farm at Raynham and made regular visits with their pupils, usually finishing up by seeing some of the films in the barn.

The other enterprises with which we were involved during that time were in Fakenham. We delivered milk to most houses in the towns twice a day, but there was no shop selling fresh milk and we thought it might be a good idea to open a delicatessen. This came about following a visit I made to the American PX when negotiating the USAF Sculthorpe base contract, as we supplied them with milk and dairy produce. There was an amazing variety of goods on sale there, which we hadn't seen in this country since the beginning of the war. I thought there must be an opening for such a shop in the town. We started by selling milk, cheese, yoghurt and other dairy products, but I think we built our reputation on hams which we started cooking once a week. We very soon found that in the delicatessen and on the milk round there was a demand which rose steadily to about fifty hams a week. Many American families were stationed on the base at Sculthorpe, but there were also a lot living in rented accommodation in the villages and they shopped in Fakenham. We aimed our specialist market, tinned escargots and exotic fruits (when we could get them), at these people and gradually the local folk were also tempted. The only site for a shop in the middle of Fakenham was Wainright's Music Shop, which had a very small tea-shop attached to it. I didn't really want the music shop and tea-shop, but the latter wasn't big enough for a delicatessen. So I bought them both, changed them round, and put the delicatessen in the larger shop, turning the small shop into a record and sheet music centre. We never sold musical instruments – pianos, cellos, violins or flutes – and I am afraid that the record centre was never a great success. Nor was the one we opened at Dereham. The delicatessen did very well to begin with, but for various reasons (not the least of which was needing the capital for other purposes) I decided to sell it. The person who bought it was a very nice chap, and I agreed to let him have it on a sort of hire purchase arrangement. But things went badly for him quite quickly, and suddenly we found that he wasn't available. He'd 'gone abroad' and had filed his petition in bankruptcy. As the Official Receiver said, it was an expensive way of buying one's experience.

Most of the dairy and shop enterprises were financed through the bank, and the capital amounts were paid off on the sale of each business as it came about. None of the businesses made very much money, but part of one of them – the dairy – showed a hefty loss which was paid off by the profits on the farm in future years. After I had bought the Heath Farm, complete with the dairy, from the other directors and farmed it for a few years, I sold it at a very acceptable profit.

All in all the twelve years after taking over the Raynham farm in my own right in 1946 were exciting and productive ones and brought me experience that was to stand me in good stead in later years. Even so, I had no idea in 1958 that within a year I would be launched into a quite different career that would occupy the majority of my time and effort for the next thirty years of my life.

Nose bleeds

a. Cotton tied tightly round the little finger or something tied tightly below the knee
b. Church key hung inside shirt in centre of back

Earache

Small onion warmed, covered with muslin and pushed as far as possible into the ear

From Grandma's *Commonplace Book.*

CHAPTER ELEVEN

Anglia Television

A casual encounter with Lord Townshend, my landlord, in the park of Raynham Hall early in 1958 was the prelude to events which were to change and shape my life for the next thirty years. He told me that he and a group of associates were working on an application for the franchise to transmit commercial television programmes to East Anglia. The application would be submitted to the Independent Television Authority, the Independent Broadcasting Authority as it is today. We could not receive television transmissions in our own area at this time, but in other parts of East Anglia reasonable pictures transmitted by the BBC could be picked up from London, and commercial television pictures from both London and Birmingham. The people involved in the venture were all very well-known nationally, mostly in the newspaper, publishing, film producing and theatre world.

During this conversation Lord Townshend asked me if I could help him by making a list of the local and national leaders in the farming industry, and those closely allied to it, whom I had met through my work as NFU delegate to London. I did this and a few weeks later he arrived at my house one evening with two very smartly dressed, obviously city, gentlemen – one very tall and the other comparatively short. I had been tractor driving all day and was still in my working gear, intending to take a last look at the cattle after supper, then have a bath and get to bed. During the introductions I learned that John Woolf was head of Romulus and Remus Films and Laurence Scott was the grandson of the great C. P. Scott, the chairman of the Manchester Guardian Newspapers and also of the Press Association. They wanted to talk about television, how it might be welcomed by people living in the area, and what sort of programmes might be produced. I remember remarking that as I didn't have a television set, indeed had hardly seen any television at all, I was probably not the chap to talk to. Lord Townshend said that he didn't have a set either, although his butler did and occasionally he watched his. We talked long into the night, and when they left they asked me if I would go to London and meet other friends of theirs who they thought might be interested in what I had to say. A date was arranged. I was to meet them in a plush theatre in the basement of one of London's smart hotels.

The purpose of this meeting was still not clear to me, but Lord Townshend asked me to repeat what we had talked about at Raynham, and take any props I thought might be useful. The next few days were wet and there was little we could do on the farm, so I borrowed a blackboard from West Raynham village school, marked out twenty-six squares on each side, and chalked in what might be happening on the farm season by season. The day before I was due to go to London I carefully wrapped up the blackboard in tissue and brown paper, to stop the chalk from smudging, and tied it securely with string. I went by train from Kings Lynn, the brown paper parcel stowed in the guard's van, and got to my west London destination a full two hours early! I asked for an easel and then unpacked the blackboard and waited in the small theatre. Eventually about fifteen people arrived in their smart city suits. Lord Townshend introduced me and I launched into my spiel which was, come to think of it, very similar to many of the talks I had given to the Bawdeswell and Helhoughton schools back in Norfolk. They were a very good audience. The first half of my board covered the first half of the farming year, October to April, and the other side (a bit smudged in transit) covered April to September. I had also taken some slides along, together with what must have been one of the smallest projectors made, and each slide corresponded to one of the blackboard squares. When I had finished they asked quite a lot of questions and seemed interested, and sometimes amused, by the answers. They thanked me for coming, we had tea, I wrapped up by blackboard (it had to be back at Raynham Infants by nine the next day) and made my way back to Norfolk. Lord Townshend saw me a few days later and said it had gone well, and one of his guests had commented that anyone who could hold an audience of that calibre for an hour deserved to get on. Perhaps it was my cavalry twills, sports jacket and brogues!

In June 1958 Lord Townshend told me that his consortium had been awarded the television franchise, and that the new company was to be called Anglia Television. It didn't occur to me then that I would have a future part to play in television; indeed there was no inkling of the tremendous impact the new television company would have on many people's lives. Lord Townshend said that the consortium had taken an option on a seventy-five-year lease from the Norwich Corporation on the redundant Agricultural Hall. Between the wars it had been used by various organisations, including the Army, the ARP, and the GPO for sorting mail. It had also been used as a roller skating rink, and pantomimes had been performed there. The famous Blondin once walked on a tightrope strung from one end of the balcony to another high up in the roof, pushing a wheelbarrow with his assistant sitting in it, and carrying a trumpeter on his shoulder. Or so my grandfather, who had been showing cattle at the Christmas Fatstock Show there, told me. The Agricultural Hall was a magnificent Victorian building opened in 1882 by Edward VII when Prince of Wales. Farmers had met there for cattle sales and horse shows, and had used it as a Corn Exchange. Mr Gladstone spoke there in 1886. As far as television was concerned, whilst not being the perfect building for conversion to studios, it looked right aesthetically, in the lee of the castle, in sight of the cathedral, and in the centre of the fine city.

Once the franchise was awarded, work started on the transmitter mast which would serve the new television region. It was sited at Mendlesham in Suffolk and had to be built on land 200ft above sea level. The mast was 1,000ft high, the tallest tower in Europe at that time, and nearly twice as high as the Blackpool tower. It was steel and weighed 180 tons and it took workmen one hour to climb up the 1,257 rungs inside its lattice-work construction. Fifteen steel cables kept it upright, standing as it did on a 2in steel ball.

Lord Townshend became Chairman of the new company, and Sir Robert Bignold, Chairman of the Norwich Union and former Mayor of Norwich; Aubrey Buxton, the well-known naturalist and ornithologist; Sir Peter Greenwell, Suffolk farmer and industrialist and Chairman of Ransomes of Ipswich; and William Copeman, Chairman of Eastern Counties Newspapers, joined the entrepreneurs John Woolf, Laurence Scott and Donald Albery (the prominent member of the famous London theatre family) on the board. To complete the formidable team were two academics from Cambridge, Dr Glyn Daniel, the archaeologist who chaired the famous *Animal, Vegetable, Mineral?* programme on television, and was elected Television Personality of the Year in 1955, and Dr Audrey Richards, an anthropologist and at that time Vice-Principal of Newnham College. Tom Marshall joined the company as Chief Engineer and one of his first problems was to design two studios in the Agricultural Hall that were sound and vibration proof. It was decided that all the technical equipment would be located at the front of the building, the whole of the centre section would be converted into studios, the services would be located at the rear, and the offices round the sides. The work had to be done within a year as the station was due to open in October 1959. While it was going on temporary office accommodation was used wherever it could be found and as close to Anglia House (the building's new name) as possible. It was calculated that a staff of about 300 would be necessary, 250 based in Norwich and the rest in London, as most advertising sales came from large businesses and agents with headquarters in the capital.

In August 1958 we were flat out getting in the harvest when Lord Townshend asked me to go with him to Norwich to check on the progress being made at the new studios. When we walked into the shell of the building I did not suspect that it was to dominate my life for the next thirty years. I had been surprised by all the events that had taken place, and was impressed by the transformation of the old Agricultural Hall, but I was stunned on the way home when Lord Townshend calmly announced that he wanted me to work with him and be responsible for the farming programmes. I spent that night, and many more, wondering how to start!

When offices at Anglia House became ready for occupation I found myself sharing with a charming lady, the new Personnel Officer, Brenda Monteath, an ex-Wren and very smart. We became firm friends, which was as well for our first 'quarters' were made up of a couple of desks and two filing cabinets squeezed into a passage. Brenda spent most of her time interviewing typists, secretaries, tea-ladies and all the clerical staff, while I employed my time visiting everyone I thought might be of use in a farming programme. The programme was to be called *Farming Diary*, and after thirty years it is still produced by Anglia Television. I met and talked to estate owners, landowners and farmers, the principals of farming companies, agricultural institutes, colleges and experimental farms, and the chairmen and managing directors of the suppliers of seeds and manufacturers of implements and spraying materials and fertilizers. The National Farmers' Union secretaries and the Farm Workers' representatives were all very helpful, their elderly members in particular. They had seen the great changes that had occurred since the Depression, and were at the heart of the farming revolution that was taking place and the new techniques that were being used. Six months of meetings and discussion resulted in lists and lists of people, places, and sources of information, and thousands of telephone numbers. I also took my 16mm camera with me and filmed anything that I came across that looked as though it might one day be interesting programme material. Little did I realise that I was breaking all the television union rules as there were very strict demarcation lines, especially about non-union members shooting film without a union ticket. No film was supposed to be shot without a full crew, which for mute film with no lights consisted of a director, a production assistant (known in the trade as a PA), a cameraman, assistant cameraman and driver. If lights were required a lighting man had to be there and in some cases an electrician (a 'spark') as well. If it was a sound film, a sound man was needed too, plus a boom swinger and cable puller – a total of eight to ten people. However, the local 'shop' was very reasonable and let me go on filming by myself until six months after transmission began, on the understanding that I was shooting only specialist material. However in June 1960 that was stopped and we had to fall in with the union agreement and only operate with a full crew.

Once I had compiled the lists of all the people and organisations I thought might be of help with *Farming Diary*, I asked Lord Townshend if it would be possible for me to visit a studio where I could see some television actually being 'done'. He arranged it and I set off on a tour of discovery around the television and film studios that were already operating. I went to Elstree, London, Birmingham, Edinburgh, Bristol, Manchester, Aberdeen and Southampton – anywhere where I could see television techniques being put into operation as, apart from helping to make a television receiver at school in 1936, I knew absolutely nothing about the 'nuts and bolts' of the business. At this stage it still hadn't occurred to me that I would actually present the *Farming Diary* programme myself. The company had been in touch with all the people who had experience in presenting farming programmes, including A. G. Street and Ralph Whiteman, but both were unavailable as they had signed contracts with the BBC for their farming programmes. It hit me like a thunderbolt when Lord Townshend said one day: 'You'd better have a go at it yourself. There are plenty of people who could do it but they haven't the farming knowledge that you have, and equally there are people who know about farming but can't put it over. You've done a lot of public speaking so I think you could get away with it!' It was arranged that I should have an audition and a camera test. It took place in the reading room at the Royal Hotel in Norwich, with one camera and the viewing panel squeezed into a small room adjacent with a television monitor to view my performance. The day before I had been given a script and told to learn it. I was to do a 'cod' interview with an actor who knew nothing about farming and, as I have always found it difficult to learn scripts, I gave my own interpretation of it. The interview with the actor was based on what I had told him about the subject the night before when we met in the bar. It turned out to be a 'hoot'. I heard later that the viewing panel next door had fallen about with laughter and wouldn't believe that it hadn't been a well- rehearsed double act. The final and unanimous verdict on my performance was that, as I hadn't been afraid to face the cameras and my head was the right shape – aspect ratio 4 x 3 – in other words round like an apple – I should be given the job of presenting *Farming Diary*.

Although I went to other companies' studios, read all the technical journals, watched as many programmes as possible, saw the production of plays for television and films for the cinema at Elstree and elsewhere, it wasn't possible to practise the art of appearing on the screen actually under live conditions. Whenever the opportunity presented itself I talked to people who were already appearing, like Richard Dimbleby, Norman Hackforth and Dr Glyn Daniel, but most of my experience before opening day on 27th October 1959 came from watching what happened from remote corners of studios or other locations, or in technical areas. In fact, anywhere where there was someone who would tolerate having a farmer around who wanted to learn the business. Because there had been virtually no television in the area before Anglia came into being, there were no local or locally-trained television personnel. If farmers, builders, accountants, motor engineers or any other professional people were needed, they could all be found. But in this completely new industry practically all the technical staff had to come from other parts of the country, mainly London and the Midlands, most of them with a background in film and the cinema. The new television skills and techniques were as unfamiliar to some of those who came to work in the new medium as they were to the few local people who were to join them. In later years formal courses in television skills and techniques were instituted in colleges and universities, but in these early days most people had to learn 'on the job'. In the beginning my problem was that I got any amount of advice from all quarters, from the few people who knew what they were talking about, and from a great number who knew little or nothing. The real difficulty was that there was no chance of practising, and in any case there is no way of reproducing the magic of a live broadcast, of going 'on air', knowing that you cannot withdraw a statement you have made or have a second go at the action. When it's live there's no second chance, and there's nothing like it to make the adrenalin run. Even after thirty years of broadcasting, with pre-recording established as standard procedure, my heart still misses a beat when the Floor Manager's voice announces, '4, 3, 2, 1, action'. We still treat every performance as a live broadcast.

The politically-minded pundits expected that a General Election might be announced for 1959. It was, and the BBC were well geared-up for Election Day and equipped to give coverage to virtually the whole of the country. ITV, with its federal make-up of franchises through a dozen or so companies, had never been presented with the opportunity of linked coverage over most of the country and some of the stations, like Anglia, were not due to be on the air at the actual time of the election in August. However, we were suddenly told by the ITA that even though Anglia wouldn't officially open until 27th October, it could be linked into the services of the stations already broadcasting if we were ready. The idea was that a network light entertainment show would be broadcast live one evening early in August, and this would be a 'dry-run' for the Election. The plan was that each company would feed material of a 'song and dance' nature into the network programme, just as reports on the political situation from selected polling stations would be fed in on Election night.

Because the Anglia studios were still unfinished it was decided that our contribution to the programme would have to be a live outside broadcast. Joan Kemp-Welch, a well-known producer with Rediffusion, was in charge of the Anglia insert. The format was a sort of country and western 'hoedown' done from a country farm location, and the Chairman suggested that because my farm was modern, and usually smart and tidy, Anglia's contribution should come from there. Joan Kemp-Welch and all the technicians duly came to see it and looked around. After a time she announced that it was a fine location but far too tidy, and could some scrap implements and old

Outside Anglia House 1959 on the old cattle market.

worn-out machinery, broken cartwheels, old gates and straw bales be brought in to make it look like a proper farm! After a lot of discussion she settled for a stack of baled straw in the middle of Raynham park, but then said that she wanted one hundred farmers dressed 'hill-billy' style to be the active audience and sing when required by the artistes. The problem of the audience was soon solved as the Fakenham Young Farmers and their friends entered into the spirit of the thing with great gusto, checked shirts, stetsons, cowboy boots and all! A 'hill-billy' band was engaged to supply suitable American 'hoe-down' music and the audience were instructed to cheer and react on the instructions of the director, through the stage manager. In addition to this several acts were brought up from London. The one I remember most vividly was half-a-dozen ballet dancers who were asked to perform a 'straw-ballet'. The poor girls and a couple of chaps had to go through their dance routine in the stubble of freshly-cut barley. For anyone who doesn't happen to have done this I must tell you that stalks of barley are very sharp and the girls' legs were literally lacerated to the calves with blood all over the place!

The show was called *Summer Song* – and we prayed for a fine evening. On the night the weather really came up trumps. A golden day turned into a fine evening with a magnificent sunset. Our turn to link into the network was, as far as I remember, at about nine o'clock. The local Pony Club, including our three girls, had been commissioned to gallop up and down in the background, going nowhere in particular, to create a suitable Wild West atmosphere. Rehearsals had taken all day. It was all very exciting, particularly as the barbecue had to be doused when a breeze got up just before transmission resulting in clouds of billowing smoke. It was certainly a 'baptism of fire' for the technicians. It would have been difficult enough if the signal had to be returned via micro-dish to Norwich some thirty-five miles away, but as the Mendlesham transmitter was not ready the signal had to be sent the whole 120 miles, via three dishes, through Barkway to Museum in London, where it joined the rest of the network covering practically the whole of Great Britain. It was a hot night with smoke and dust blowing around, and there were some difficult moments. Since then I have always had tremendous respect and admiration for the technicians and engineers who work in television. But from all parts of the country it was agreed that the whole operation had been a great success. Certainly the Fakenham Young Farmers and locals will never forget it!

Before we reached the opening day, throughout the summer of 1959 I got my first real insight into the razzamatazz of television. Aubrey Buxton (now Lord Buxton), who was in charge of Public Relations as well as preparing for the natural history programmes, initiated what he called the Conversion Campaign. During the Campaign people from Anglia visited every town and village, meeting as many local people as possible. The message was that Anglia Television would be opening on 27th October 1959 and, if they didn't already have one, now was the time to get a television set; and if they had a set already they should make sure that the aerial was turned to the new ITV transmitter. The television dealers and aerial suppliers were, of course, keen to assist and so were most of the mayors, council chairmen and civic dignitaries, schools, charity organisations, sports clubs and so on. In fact,

Bowler hatted, with secretary Jane Seymour 'driving' one of the first radio controlled tractors for *Farming Diary* 1964.
Camera: Ian Craig, Geoffrey Holsgrove.

there was a general air of anticipation and excitement. I think the single most effective weapon in the campaign was a helicopter, painted in the Anglia colours of yellow and grey, which toured the area dropping down as near as possible to the centre of the towns and villages where a hall had been hired, or a large marquee erected, so that the locals could come and meet their new TV people. They were given a sandwich and a sherry or coffee, and they heard something about the programmes that were to come. One of my jobs, as the regular film crews had not yet been appointed and because I had a camera with three lenses, was to be strapped into the open doorway of the helicopter and film a little piece of each location. It didn't work very well; although the quality was all right the rotor blades caused a vibration to the camera, which of course was hand-held on a monopod attached to my chest. It was great fun though and I wouldn't have missed it for the world.

My time between *Summer Song* and the opening of the Station on 27th October was spent almost every day, when the weather was satisfactory, with the helicopter and the Conversion to Channel Eleven Campaign. During the time that we were flying I was also able to do a certain amount of what I would loosely call 'research' for the farming programme. When we flew over

Norfolk, Suffolk, Essex, Herts, Hunts and Lincolnshire, I was able to see the different crops growing on the various types of soil from above and sometimes 'dropped in' on farmers I thought might be helpful for future farming programmes. At the same time we continually collected film and stills. It sounds naive, indeed daft over thirty years after the event, but I also rehearsed in front of a mirror almost daily. It didn't really help and was very silly, as I already knew what I looked like and, if anything, all it did was to confuse my already muddled mind. Practically everyone I met gave me advice, telling me what I should say on their pet subject and perhaps, more often, what not to say. Another stupid thing I tried to do was to learn and assimilate far too many statistics. However, I did learn the basic information about the size of the populations, and the density and acreage of crops in most of the counties that we covered, and found that this helped when interviewing people about their particular area.

Although *Farming Diary* was the programme Lord Townshend and I were most concerned with at this crucial time just before the opening of the station, there were many other programmes being prepared which became successful and popular. Two company directors were closely involved with drama production; John Woolf (later Sir John), one of the country's most successful film producers, and Donald Albery (later Sir Donald), head of a London theatre group. Dr Glyn Daniel was responsible for historical and archaeological productions; Aubrey Buxton, now Lord Buxton, was a full-time executive director from the outset, and he planned and produced all the natural history and wildlife programmes. Over the years he built up the now world-famous *Survival* wildlife unit. The News/Sport/Weather and locally-based light entertainment, including children's programmes, inter-town quizzes and religion were left to a team of producers, directors, editors and presenters who all worked together on the various projects which were decided upon at the Programme Planning Committee's fortnightly meetings.

On opening day, Tuesday, 27th October, electronic bleeps grew louder as the sweep hand of a clock face on the region's television screens pulsed away the seconds. At 4.15 p.m. the clock faded, a picture of the Mendlesham mast took its place and a voice announced: 'Anglia Television is on air'. The first programme was called *Introducing Anglia.* Drew Russell, Newman Sanders and Colin Bower took viewers on a tour of the region with views of the countryside shot from the helicopter. Then Russell related the history of the Anglia building and showed viewers the studios. In the newsroom Head of News, Peter Kennelly, and his deputy, David Thurlow, explained how stories would be handled; there were previews of some of the programmes which were to come, and finally Lord Townshend welcomed Sir Ivone Kirkpatrick, chairman of the ITA, who performed a simple opening ceremony. At 6.05 p.m. Anglia's first *News* went out and at 6.45 p.m. its first documentary, *Birth of a Regiment*, a fifteen-minute report of a ceremony in Germany a few days earlier when the Royal Norfolk Regiment and the Suffolk Regiment had been merged to form the first East Anglian Regiment. At 9.35 p.m. an Anglia production reached the whole country, fulfilling Anglia's promise to provide drama for the network; this was a play called *The Violent Years*, and it was presented under the 'Play of the Week' banner.

The second day brought the first edition of *The Midday Show*, actually transmitted at two minutes past one. This was to be Anglia's chief regional programme in the early days, on screen five days a week. Every day it welcomed to the studio a party of visitors from a town in the area; the first guests were from Haverhill in Suffolk. The programme included interviews with people of the region and also, on different days, items on records, books, films, motoring, gardening, shopping and pets, many introduced by the producer, Philip Bray. Music was provided by pianist Norman Hackforth, Anglia's Director of Music, with singers Roger Gage and Susan Hampshire, now the internationally famous film actress. There were six-and-a-half hours of locally produced programmes every week at the beginning. Earliest series included *Commentary Box*, which reported on the fortunes of the region's football teams on Saturday afternoons, and a fortnightly programme about life in Cambridge, introduced by Glyn Daniel, who already had considerable television experience and, of course, every Sunday there was *Farming Diary*.

Other series which followed during the course of the first year included *Let's Put Out the Light*, a late-night music programme presented by Norman Hackforth with singers, including David Kernan; *Anglia Presents*, a light entertainment series with Glen Mason; *Angles*, a series of film documentaries on places ranging from holiday resorts to missile sites; and *Arena*, a discussion programme with chairmen including Anthony Wedgwood-Benn and Brian Connell. There were also the plays, which continued to be networked – seven of them in the first year, and every one in the Top Ten – with *Lucky Strike* starring Gladys Cooper achieving third position.

Initially Anglia's programmes could be seen in 213,000 homes, mainly in Norfolk, Suffolk, Cambridgeshire and Essex, but engineering progress steadily widened the boundaries. By 1961 viewers in parts of Bedfordshire and Lincolnshire could also receive the service and it was available to 423,000 homes. Anglia's knight, the company's symbol, and the music which accompanied it on screen (part of Handel's Water Music arranged for the company by Sir Malcolm Sargent) became known far beyond the region. Originally the directors had thought of using Britannia as a symbol; then Lord Townshend saw the knight in Asprey's in New Bond Street. The knight had been modelled on a statue of Richard Coeur de Lion outside the Houses of Parliament, though it actually represented the Black Prince. It had been commissioned from a London firm of silversmiths by the King of the Netherlands in 1850 as a trophy for a sporting contest, but it was won by an Englishman who brought it home where it remained in the possession of his family until Anglia acquired it. The Bond Street firm made modifications, including the 'Anglia' pennon on the lance, and the knight stood in the reception area of Anglia House for almost thirty years until the company decided to introduce a new company symbol in 1988.

Chapter Twelve

Farming Diary

The first *Farming Diary* programme went out on 1st November 1959 and we were fortunate in having three splendid people: John Anderson was a senior man at the Ministry of Agriculture, Jimmy Coe, a friend I had known since I was a child and who represented the Farm Workers' Union, and Charlie Wharton, then in his fifties, who was a very well-known and go-ahead large farmer who represented the NFU (National Farmers' Union) and CLA (Country Landowners' Association). He is still farming today and although it is many years ago I remember the answer he gave to my first question. He said, 'I don't know why you're asking me that. You should know the answer – you used to be a bit of a farmer – once!' As I remember, it was a very gentle but far-reaching discussion about what the programme hoped to do. We wanted it to be technical and topical and aimed at farmers, but hoped it would be interesting to other people too. The second half of that first programme was a filmed report from the national sugar-beet demonstration at Driffield in Yorkshire. We had filmed it the week before, but we didn't have sound facilities at the demonstration and there weren't any facilities to dub a track on, so I did the commentary live from the studio as the programme was transmitted. It lacked the natural sound of machinery and it was on this programme that I learned how obtrusive the wrong sort of music overlay could be. From that day to this, we have always been very careful to get things at the right level if there are no natural sounds available.

Farming Diary was Lord Townshend's idea and was always his 'baby'. He was in the Control Room overlooking the studio for the rehearsal of the opening programme, and watched the transmission, and my début, from his office. His interest and enthusiasm for the programme never lessened, and he watched every edition avidly, always giving very forthright views on the results, whether it was praise or criticism. We usually had a phone call directly after coming off air at two o'clock and, if there was more to be said than just 'OK', we had to attend an inquest on Monday morning.

All the early farming programmes were transmitted just after lunch on Sundays. The majority were live outside broadcasts. This meant a major operation and involved the use of an enormous vehicle called the 'scanner', which contained virtually all the same equipment found in the studios, confined in a much smaller space. The director, production assistant and vision mixer sat in front of a bank of approximately five monitors which showed pictures from the various sources. Also in the scanner were separate areas for the technicians controlling the quality of the picture output from each source, the men controlling lighting, and the sound balancers. All this was very carefully fitted into a vehicle the size of a very large furniture van. The scanner was accompanied by other trucks carrying the rest of the technical equipment and electrical generators. But that was by no means the end of the circus. Because of the curvature of the earth's surface and the natural undulation of the land, the signals had to be 'bounced' by large dishes in order to get them back to the transmitter. These dishes were placed on the highest points practical, usually a church steeple or water tower. So, as well as the scanner and the crew, there were sometimes three landrovers carrying the dishes, scaffolding and ladders, and pulling their own generators. The dishes, of course, were rigged the day before, but at the moment of transmission everything had to be exactly co-ordinated. It was always a hazardous and tricky exercise involving anything up to thirty people; and this didn't include the survey team, who went ahead days before and arranged the locations, and made certain that high tension cables were avoided and that the vicars would agree to having dishes stuck on top of their church towers!

A stalwart of the *Farming Diary* team from late August 1959 was Ron Downing. He came from Associated Rediffusion, where he had been directing a programme called *Farming Year*. The nature of the content of this programme had made Ron realise that London was not for him, and that he would like to live and work out of the capital and in a rural area. He explained this to Lord Townshend during an interview at Anglia's London office, and got the job of director on *Farming Diary*. Ron told me years later that Lord Townshend had told him that day to keep his eye on a young fellow called Dick Joice as he thought that I might have a future as a programme presenter. The first time Ron was introduced to me I asked him what farming experience he had. He said, 'A certain amount for *Farming Year* which is a schools programme, but otherwise not a lot!' My response was, 'Well, if you can admit to not knowing a great deal about farming, then I certainly can admit to knowing virtually nothing about television! However, I reckon we will make a good team!' And I was proved right. He is a man I have always had tremendous admiration for. He prepared the scripts and directed all the early films and, after the first year, the outside broadcasts as well. The early OB's were directed by the late Geoff Rimmer, who had the official title of Anglia's Outside Broadcast Director. Ron Downing has only just retired from Anglia where he became a highly respected programme director and colleague.

Getting a half-hour programme together each week with a small team may not sound too taxing, but it filled every available minute. The live OB programmes seemed always to leap from crisis to crisis, but this complicated operation involving more than thirty people, three cameras, and all the other paraphernalia, usually came together just in the nick of time. Conditions were often difficult and I well remember a programme on celery-growing from Littleport in Cambridgeshire. The soil there is absolutely black and that day the rain fell from leaden skies so filming was extremely difficult for the camera crews – none of whom were used to sliding about in fen soil on a wet day in wellies, oilskins and sou'westers. We kept them going on coffee and encouraging words, but after transmission they still had to 'wrap-up'. It took about four hours to clean up all the heavy equipment, and we had to bring in caterpillar tractors to get the heavy scanner back onto hard ground.

For those involved nearly every programme had its funny moments, although at the time they usually didn't seem funny. The programme we did from the AI Centre at Beccles is, I think, among the most amusing. Sex in any shape or form, even with cows, was a very delicate subject to handle as the details had to be submitted to the ITA for approval before transmission. A great deal of correspondence and discussion took place over the suitability of this particular topic, and they finally agreed that we could do it. The restrictions imposed meant that we could not show a cow actually being inseminated, and we certainly were not allowed to show the collection of semen from the bull. We got round it by using a blackboard with a rudimentary diagram of a cow. I stood in front of this with a pointed stick, like a schoolmaster, and gave a rough indication of what happened. I filled up the rest of the time in discussion with an eminent scientist from Cambridge, who was an expert on the subject. He talked on and on about blood lines and improving milk yield and hybrid vigour, while we walked slowly past a row of bulls' heads looking out over small doors! We followed this with pictures of the office and, whilst we were talking about the complexities of their records, the viewers saw a man taking a telephone call – presumably from the owner of a cow in season – and another jumping into his car complete with vacuum flask which may have contained the semen straws, and tearing off into the distance!

One very unusual *Farming Diary* programme came from the home of the now famous 'bootiful' Bernard Matthews. Bernard, who started with just one clutch of turkey eggs, acquired the magnificent, but long unoccupied, Jacobean Hall at Great Witchingham and converted it into a turkey factory. He hatched turkeys in incubators in the bedrooms and used the downstairs rooms for processing them into oven-ready birds, but not, I hasten to add, before he had covered up the unique wall decorations and doors with hard-board so that they weren't damaged by the birds. For our Christmas programme in 1960 Bernard (again after careful covering) packed the marvellous staircase of the Hall with live turkeys. It was a tremendous start to the programme, which ended with a turkey dinner and a demonstration of cooking oven-ready birds. On that programme Bernard said that he would change the habits of the buying public, so that turkey would no longer be just a Christmas delicacy but an everyday dish. And he has done just that, the world over.

After transmitting the Bernard Matthews story during Christmas week, we decided to include a little 'leg-pull' in the programme scheduled for Sunday, 1st April. I have to admit that the BBC, with their earlier item on harvesting the fruits of the spaghetti tree, probably influenced us in making a very complicated little film explaining a new way of growing mistletoe (which, of course, is a parasitic plant usually growing on apple trees). We had met a Dutchman who had invented a new type of plough, which was really not unlike the old mechanical giro-tiller or steam-driven Derby digger, and having done the serious item and in order to make it look more authentic our Dutch friend agreed to act as the principal presenter in the 'con'. The programme then took the shape of a visit to a secret location where this very large Dutchman explained in broken English that he had devised a way of treating sprigs of mistletoe so that, when plucked from the trees and planted in the soil, they would grow into mistletoe trees. He explained that they needed to be grown in a mixture of peat and sawdust from trees grown above 10,000ft in the Bavarian Alps, and irrigated with a solution of fossilised plankton and water from the Andes. We spent days planting out an acre of mistletoe sprigs for the film, and the viewers saw shots of the plants growing. The 'pay-off' came back in the studio, where there was a bench with four boys sitting on one side and four girls opposite them. overhead was a continuous belt with pieces of mistletoe tied to it. As they passed above the 'testers' the youngsters kissed. An adjudicator, again the Dutchman, sat at the other end and, according to the intensity of the kiss, he either passed or rejected that particular sample of misletoe! It was all presented very seriously and I ended by saying I hoped that everybody had a good day and would be joining us the following Sunday. Believe it or not there were quite a number of calls asking for more details, some obviously with tongue-in-cheek. But one lady, a Mrs Labouchere, came to my house and I think would, if necessary, have paid for the information and the address of our friend the Dutchman. Incidentally, the programme finished with him singing a ('cod') mistletoe song from old Amsterdam, and collapsing into a chair with a gin glass in his hand and an empty bottle of Bols standing on the arm!

Other *Farming Diary* programmes reported on things like safety and accident prevention, new designs in machinery and buildings, and visits to experimental stations and universities, with crop reports and explanations of new varieties. The great majority, of course, were filmed in East Anglia, although if there were good reasons we travelled much further afield in Great Britain and occasionally went abroad.

Our first trip overseas was to the Hilleshog sugar-beet research station at Malmo in Sweden, and we got a dispensation from the ACTT (Association of Cinematograph Television and Allied Technicians) to go without an official ticket-holding cameraman. After lots of meetings between management and unions they agreed to allow me to shoot the film on the basis of its being highly specialised material, needing an expert with sugar-beet knowledge! I offered to join the technicians' union, but it was argued that I should be in the actors' union as I was a presenter. So eventually they settled for me shooting 'specialist' material by mutual agreement. Ron Downing was the director and our wives acted as PA's, again after much argument with the local 'shop'. The Swedes are renowned for their hospitality, and if we didn't know this before we went we certainly did afterwards. We all worked extremely hard for four days and got some very good and interesting film, but the evenings were, to say the least, a trifle blurred. In fact, after the proprietor of the 'Stakette' restaurant, just outside Malmo, found us having a mock battle with the swords and wearing the armour which decorated the walls of his restaurant, he threatened to call in the police and we had to beat a hasty retreat in a taxi, leaving an extremely generous tip. The worst moment though came the next morning when I was woken at four with a breakfast of five fried eggs. I thought I had asked to be called at five with absolutely no breakfast!

The two most important filming trips abroad made during the early years of *Farming Diary* were to America in 1962 and the USSR in 1964. In October 1962, with Geoffrey Holsgrove as cameraman, I went to America with a party of journalists and farmers to make a film contrasting East Anglian farming methods with those in America. We arrived in Milwaukee and, as the trip was sponsored by Colmans Agriculture, our first visit was to the Quaker Oat Research farm. This was followed by the Schlitz brewery, then on to Madison and the University of Wisconsin to see the research being done on dairy and poultry farming. The following two days were taken up with visits to farms, before arriving at our final stop in Chicago. Here we allowed ourselves a couple of days off from lectures, discussion groups and very intensive indoctrination into the American way of doing things and impressing people! We enjoyed the experience, and came back with plenty of good film from a purely farming point of view, but I was left with the feeling that one day I really must return to America to see the place and meet a few people in a more leisured and less competitive atmosphere.

The most memorable *Farming Diary* trip abroad for me was to Russia in May 1964. This time the entire party of fifteen were journalists. Geoffrey Holsgrove was on camera again, and we were the only people representing

British television. The trip had been offered by the sponsors of the British Agricultural Exhibition of Industry which was being held just outside Moscow in the grounds of the USSR Exhibition of Economic Achievements. As well as accommodating the British Exhibition in its 540 acres, the site held 300 pavilions showing the achievements of all branches of industry and agriculture in the Soviet Union. In farming terms the sheer vastness of the USSR, covering one-sixth of the world's land surface, is awesome. The figures we were given claimed that there were 9,200 state farms in the country, each of 25,000 acres, and 39,600 collective farms of 15,000 acres. At that time when 'glasnost' and 'perestroika' were remote and unthinkable concepts, we were very closely watched, information was censored, and we were shown only what the Russians wanted us to see. They were, however, extremely friendly and generous, and the party was provided with a charming young lady (the wife of an architect) who was a very good interpreter. She was even more skilled at answering, or usually not answering, our searching questions.

The British Agricultural Exhibition was opened by Mr Christopher Soames, the Minister of Agriculture, and literally dozens of British firms exhibited including all the large ones like Fords. There were also many specialists in agriculture, many of them from the Anglia region. The most prominent (although not so well-known in those days as he is now) was Bernard Matthews. Even then he stole the show, for on his stand he had a very, very large turkey weighing 56lb as the centre-piece of the display. At the preview of the first day's itinerary, we were told that Mr Khrushchev himself would in all probability be visiting the exhibition. Bernard told me the evening before that if Mr Khrushchev came anywhere near his stand he was going to hand him the large turkey as a gift from Great Witchingham, Norfolk. I said, 'You'll be arrested by the KGB if you do.' Mr Khrushchev *did* pass his stand, and Bernard didn't heed my warning. He simply handed the short, very stout, Soviet leader the huge turkey. Taken by surprise the Soviet premier clutched it and continued to hold it for several minutes, whilst various interpreters tried to explain that this was for his Christmas dinner. His omnipresent bodyguards, though very much on edge, were completely nonplussed. Bernard, of course, got world coverage in the press and on television and radio for his audacious act, and he wasn't arrested!

After several exhausting days in Moscow, where we were taken to see all the usual tourist attractions and enjoyed a memorable visit to the Bolshoi Ballet to see a performance of Swan Lake, we departed by Aeroflot in an Ilyushin 104 for Tblisi in Georgia. The plane was a jet and as modern as a Boeing of the time. We couldn't understand why the plane taking us on this two-and-a-half hour journey was packed with Muscovites, all with large attaché cases cluttering up the stowage. There were strange, but useful, racks above each seat, complete with brass knobs, that could have been designed

Bernard Matthews presents a 56lb turkey to Mr Khrushchev at the British Agriculture Exhibition, Moscow 1964.

for a Victorian bus, or bedstead. The passengers used these for their cases. We later discovered that on the return journey all those attaché cases would contain fruit, which was almost unobtainable in Moscow. Oranges in Moscow could cost up to 5s 0d each at this time, and it was a viable proposition for enterprising men and women to fly to Tblisi and bring back a couple of cases of oranges, pay the £17 return fare, and still make money. In fact, *Oranges at £5 a Dozen* became the title of the film we made when we got back.

During our time in Tblisi we visited a collective farm on the outskirts of the city where there was an enormous poultry unit which, although not big by today's standards, seemed huge to us then. The unit housed over a quarter of a million birds, on a big acreage in that marvellous Georgian climate so suited to viticulture. The charming 6ft 6in tall chairman of the collective invited us all to his house for lunch, which began at one o'clock and finished at five. The courses were varied and numbered at least a dozen. Each one was followed by a special drink and I have to admit that after the first hour none of us were worried about the content of the next course. I have a note in my diary saying that out of the fifteen journalists present, only three were upright at the end of the meal! As an 'almost teetotaller' I managed to stay on my feet, but the last farewell drink was from a very special polished cow's horn and it had to be quaffed in one go. That would have finished me, so I resorted to pouring most of it down my shirt. I have vague memories of lugging Geoffrey into the bus, but we all went back to the hotel 'sodden' in more ways than one!

The next day we visited the Maxim Gorky state farm, a well-known showpiece, which consisted of 4,500 acres of mixed crops including arable, fruit, vegetables and livestock. Their target yields, however, were very much lower than the actual yields being achieved in England at that time. The cows were a Friesian type and looked fairly well but a great number had got, or at some time in their lives had had, severe mastitis. Although they had quite modern milking machines each milker was only expected to milk twenty cows. The farm was managed by Victor Isiof and an agronomist called Vladimir Popkov. They were splendid, hard-drinking chaps. The labour availability by British standards was at least four times what we would consider an economic and viable level but, as the interpreter pointed out, the people were available so they were used. There was, therefore, no unemployment. This visit, too, finished up with a gargantuan meal, but most of the reporters by then had learned their lesson. I had the feeling that the Russians thought we were a bit prim, but that amount of alcohol two days' running would have ended in 'intensive care'.

There were obvious shortages in the whole country of many of the consumer products we take for granted, and from the time we arrived at Moscow airport throughout our trip we were constantly badgered for biro pens and shoes, being offered roubles or small buttonhole emblems in exchange. People also desperately wanted to buy clothes, though not mine as I wore very conventional grey flannel trousers and a sports jacket. But Geoffrey, who was younger and always up-to-date, had a very modern and desirable wardrobe. He told some of the students from the universities who spoke a certain amount of English that he would sell some of his clothes and shoes before going back to England, and they came to the hotel the night before we left. As this sort of activity was frowned upon by the authorities Geoffrey went off in a taxi with them to find a less public place for the 'trading'. I was convinced that he would be abducted and that we should never see him again. It was real 'cloak and dagger' stuff, with an exchange of clothes for roubles and Geoffrey returning in a long, sad Russian mackintosh with little else underneath, having sold his shoes and most of his top clothes. For the boots that he bought in Norwich for £3, he got £15 worth of roubles, but his Marks and Spencer cowboy-type shirts were the most popular items and fetched the highest prices. The problem then was to get the roubles out of the country, as all our money was examined on entry and any remaining was counted on departure. Undeterred Geoffrey devised a very complicated system of changing roubles for dollars at one end of the cashier's desk in the hotel, and then swapping these for pounds at the other end! Perhaps the reason why we got away with Geoffrey's enterprise was because the officials were more concerned about the film we had taken – indeed they carefully checked every roll against the list recorded by the Customs officials when we came into the country. The interpreter also submitted a list to the authorities of what she had seen filmed.

Getting the flavour of how ordinary people lived was difficult, if not impossible. We were told that every Russian had the right to have five-eighths of an acre of land on which to grow whatever he pleased and market it wherever it was feasible to do so, but we were not taken to one of the peasants' markets which are dotted around Moscow. On the last morning, however, when the surveillance was relaxed and I think they thought they could trust us, we went for a walk and got into one of these stockaded markets simply by nonchalantly walking past the guard. Success was short-lived though because as soon as Geoffrey took out his camera from under his coat, they were after him and we were chased out. It was also the ambition of every journalist to try and get to see inside the home of a Russian family. We were taken to see show apartments, but never the ordinary homes. One evening, in a cafe near the university, we sat at a table with two Russian girls who were learning English. They could speak a little of our language and, after buying them a coffee and cakes and talking to them for a long time, we asked if they would like to be taken home in a taxi. They said 'yes' and off we went. Our idea was that if we found out where they lived we could just arrive at the place the next night and say we had come for coffee. When we all alighted from the taxi at their apartment block they pointed to a window about six storeys up and said that was where they lived. They shook hands with us, thanked us, and disappeared into the building. We were obviously not meant to follow them, but we carefully copied down what it said on the plaque on the wall of the building, confident that we would find it again the next evening. When we got back to the hotel and Geoffrey was able to look at the words closely he realised that what we had copied down meant no more than 'Please cross here'. He had taught himself a smattering of Russian before the trip, and it was to come in useful in more ways than one!

Intourist put us up at the Ukraine Hotel in Moscow. It was a huge new skyscraper building, similar to a New York hotel vintage 1930. The furniture and decor was very heavy and dull with all 'mod cons', but many of them not working. There were no bath plugs in some bathrooms and telephones were often out of order. Strategically placed on each floor was a lady in her sixties, sitting at a table and apparently in charge of all hotel personnel on her floor. These ladies were actually there to record visitors coming and going and seemed to note everything, from a request for soap and a bath plug to who was in which room. The hotel staff all wore a black uniform and I didn't find one person who spoke English, which made communications difficult. If you did want to make a request you were handed a pad and pencil to write down what you wanted and then asked to wait, either whilst a long conversation took place on the phone, or the member of the hotel staff disappeared down the stairs for what always seemed like hours. We soon found that it was easier not to ask for anything and fend for ourselves. Some enlightened people had taken bath plugs with them. Others, like us, 'found' one in another bathroom and then hung on to it. The food was adequate, but dull, cool and a very long time in arriving. Meals in Russia seemed to take up an immense amount of the day – perhaps this was how they managed full employment. The work was shared by everyone available to do it, regardless of efficiency in the deployment of labour – in fact Parkinson's Law in reverse. But the Russian people seemed content with their Communist lot, queuing and waiting, and waiting and queuing for everything. GUM Stores, a very big and ornate supermarket, always seemed full even if people didn't actually seem to be buying much. Bearing in mind the language difficulties, and in spite of some obvious differences, I found the Russians to be courteous, helpful, cheerful and very curious about us. Many of them I felt were suspicious of foreigners, and perhaps the sombre ladies on each floor of the hotel were rightly suspicious about the disappearance of their bathroom plugs.

During the whole time we were in the USSR we hardly had a meal at which fresh vegetables or fruit were offered. Potatoes, we thought, were reconstituted from dry or powdered and then cooked, ending up as a sort of rissole. Turnips and cabbages were presumably fresh. The fish was very good, but there wasn't much of it. Meals were served to us only on the presentation of coupons, which we obtained in England together with our flight and hotel tickets. Geoffrey nearly starved. He's a very fussy feeder, and only used about half of his meal tickets. I don't know how he did it, but he persuaded the chap in charge of the hotel restaurant and the manager of the hotel shop to swap his coupons for jars of caviar. Caviar was comparatively cheap out there but very saleable in this country. The Customs officials at London Airport on our way home were intrigued to know why he had very few clothes in his case, but lots of jars of caviar. I cannot remember the explanation he gave, but knowing my friend Geoffrey it would have been convincing! Incidentally, I wouldn't like to give the impression that Geoffrey wasn't law-abiding. He really didn't like Russian food and neither did I. In fact, after six days my 'plumbing' clogged up through lack of fruit and I became so constipated I found difficulty in moving around. I asked Geoffrey to go out and find some fruit, telling him that I thought I would die if he didn't. Always resourceful, he succeeded and came back with two oranges which cost him a pound. (I have always been relieved to know that he thought I was worth it!) He also went to the local hospital and came back with a small box of pills which he said were 'purgadomskis'. Anyway, after an orange and a couple of pills I was back to normal . . . with a vengeance.

Geoffrey was always a marvellous and entertaining companion on all our farming trips, but perhaps the moment I enjoyed most happened at the party given by the British Ambassador in Russia during our visit. The Ambassador had invited the Russian Minister of Agriculture, Ivan Volovchenko, and a number of Russian reporters to meet the British press. The party was held at the British Embassy and the tables were decorated with red flags with the hammer and sickle, interspersed with small Union Jacks. It was Geoffrey who noticed that the Union Jacks were all upside down, and he solemnly dismasted them from their little flag poles and reversed them! The Russians were bewildered.

The *Farming Diary* trips and reports from abroad were all very exciting and the viewers seemed to like them, but our 'bread and butter' programmes were obviously from the Anglia region. We soon realised when getting the *Farming Diary* team together that we would need another interviewer, a sort of 'outside reporter' or 'leg man', and I remembered John Slater from Nayland in Suffolk. He was one of my fellow pupils in the 'Remove' form at Culford, and he had always seemed to me to be a lot brighter than the rest of us. He was a quiet, thoughtful and likeable person; a farmer's son, and destined to become a farmer himself. He was also an excellent sportsman and took part in many Suffolk activities in the sporting world. I went to see him and he agreed to 'give it a go'. A couple of programmes later we brought him into the studio and could see from the start that he would fit the bill. He not only knew his subject well, but he was also a complete contrast to me. Had he been a Scotsman he might have been labelled 'dour': he was actually quiet, unshakeable and confident, and not quite so ebullient as me!

As it is transmitted on every Sunday throughout the year *Farming Diary* has always been able to cover a wide variety of subjects, and there have been many interesting and eminent participants. Early on we visited John Slater's Saddlebow Farm, which had not long been connected to mains electricity, and talked about new methods of irrigation. A few weeks before that John had been to Foxfield in Berkshire and, in his first interview, had talked to John Fall about a new early-weaning system for calves. There was an outside broadcast from William Chapman's farm at Martham (he was an authority on cattle rearing and fattening methods), and we also visited Jim Prior (now Lord Prior) at his farm near Lowestoft. One programme was devoted to a Brains Trust Forum on farming and agriculture. Charles Wharton, Jim Prior, and Arthur Mitchell, editor of the *Farming Weekly*, were on the panel, and an audience of young farmers put the questions to them. We also made several visits to the Boxworth Experimental Station just outside Cambridge, the Easton School of Agriculture near Norwich, and Brooms Barn near Newmarket, and the famous Norfolk Experimental Station.

One of the early programmes that I remember with pleasure was really a dramatised documentary. It was called *The Hand that used the Plough*, and it was written by Dick Gilling, a very well-known and respected writer. In the documentary we talked to many of the old ploughmen, and they gave us their reactions to the new methods. One of the nicest remarks about *Farming Diary* came from one of these old ploughmen who, just before we were leaving, said, 'Now when that cum on don't cut it tew short. Lets see thum par of hosses leaving the headland one side of the field and plow roight acrorse and tun round and cum all the way back agin.' I replied, 'Well, that would take more time than is available, and in any case you've seen that happening almost every day of your life.' He said, 'Yes I know and thass why I loike seein it Sunday arternoons as well!'

Through the years many people helped on the technical side of *Farming Diary*; they are too numerous to mention, but I must include Geoffrey Scott. Geoffrey had an extremely pleasant way with him and a nice voice, and he came to Anglia when the station opened, as a stagehand. He worked on many programmes, *Farming Diary* included, putting up the sets, moving chairs and packing props away; but I noticed that he was always very interested in the programme content as well. One day he asked me what the chances were of coming onto the *Farming Diary* team as a researcher. His qualifications were that he came from a farming family and had been to agricultural college. To my surprise, when I put his name forward he was accepted. I was only surprised, I must add, because I didn't think the company would allow me to have any more help. Geoffrey stayed with us for about three years, and did quite a lot of commentaries on films and an occasional appearance. I was very sorry to lose him, but when his father died he was more or less summoned home to run the farm at Reydon in Suffolk. About that time also he met a beautiful Swedish girl called Karin. I heard afterwards that she had given him an ultimatum: either he could come home and farm and marry her, or he could stay in television and she would return to Sweden. They are a charming couple, now with a grown-up family, and they still live in Suffolk. When Geoffrey was in the Farming office he was joined by Colin Ewing. For a time they worked together on the programme, but when Geoffrey left to farm Colin took over and became editor of the programme content, later becoming the director and 'sometimes' presenter. Colin went on to make many memorable and award-winning *Farming Diary* programmes, until he was promoted to Assistant Programme Controller for Anglia Television. Since 1988 he has been Deputy Managing Director of the Broadcasting Division of the company. Another well-known face, who appeared as a presenter in 1963, was John Jenkins from Cambridge. I am not certain how much television experience he had before joining us but he had certainly done quite a lot of radio work in Scotland and was well-known in the upper echelons of farming politics, particularly in London. In fact, he was a man right at the centre of things. When an unbiased political opinion was needed about farming we usually asked Jim Murray, the well-known political correspondent, to come up from Westminster and, sometimes together with local people, report on whatever issue was at stake in Parliament.

Farming Diary proved to be as exciting – and hardworking – as anything I had yet been involved in, but in May 1960 the company decided to produce a new magazine programme for the region and they asked me to present it. It was to be called *About Anglia*.

CHAPTER THIRTEEN

About Anglia and After

The new regional news-magazine programme *About Anglia* began in May 1960, and ran for half-an-hour after the ITN news on Tuesday nights. Transmission was quickly increased to two evenings a week when the first programme ratings emerged with figures indicating that it was on the way to being popular and successful. The early portents held true. *About Anglia* went from strength to strength, and in September was extended to four evenings a week, and then five. The programme brought together the regional news, which had always been shown in the early evening, and magazine items from the *Mid-day Show*, which had always been shown every week-day at lunchtime. Items of local interest, plus reports and information on natural history topics, cookery, medical matters, Do-it-Yourself, sport, gardening and the weather were all included. It wasn't long before the time allowed was also extended and the programme ran from 6.05 p.m. to 7.00 p.m. A programme of this length and diversity, transmitted on five nights a week, needed to have a big team of people working on it. I was the first presenter, and the first newscaster was Newman Sanders, who later became Anglia's Education Officer. The original team also included many people who cut their teeth on *About Anglia* and then went on to become familiar household names. One of the first to join was Bob Wellings, who had been at Cambridge University and was seen at the Footlights Theatre by one of the senior people in the company. He became a great personal friend of mine, and the viewers loved him. There were also: Chris Kelly, now with the BBC and very well-known all over the country; Anne Gregg, our first lady presenter, now a national figure; Valerie Pitts, who married Sir George Solti; John McGregor; and Dick Graham. David Dimbleby worked for *About Anglia* in 1960 during his summer vacation from Oxford University: and other famous names included Kenneth Robinson and David Frost, who spent a short time in the *About Anglia* newsroom as a reporter after leaving Cambridge. He has pulled our leg about it since, as some management executives at Anglia didn't consider he had a future in television when they first saw him on the screen and his contract wasn't renewed. David, of course, proved them all wrong, going on to earn an international reputation in television, and a lot of money.

Apart from the few items which were transmitted regularly on a certain day of the week, the running order of *About Anglia* was flexible. The nightly local news bulletin which followed the news from ITN in London was, however, sacrosanct, and usually lasted about fifteen minutes. The programme had its own news-collecting service on the top floor of Anglia House in offices close to the *About Anglia* office. The News Room staff consisted of the Head of News, his deputy, and several sub-editors, the copy-takers and secretaries, and a number of researchers out in the field. Technically the programme was serviced by the film, stills, and clipping libraries, the music and engineering departments and all the other departments within Anglia. Every evening the news department presented to *About Anglia* a 'package' of hard news for the bulletin. The *About Anglia* team liaised closely with the news team at all times, especially when there was an item of sufficient gravity or interest to be enlarged upon after the initial outline had been given in the news bulletin. A visit to the area by the then Prime Minister, Sir Alec Douglas Home provided an opportunity for both news and feature teams. His official visit was covered on film by the news department, but we were also able to persuade him to come to the studio before he went back to London. Here he did two 'live' interviews, each of about twelve minutes duration; one with Brian Connell on the general national and international situation, and the other with me, on farming, as Sir Alec farmed extensively in Scotland. If I had any qualms about doing the interview I needn't have worried, for Sir Alec was an extremely easy man to talk to with a fine sense of humour, and he is very knowledgeable on farming matters. In fact, he seemed happier talking about farming than about the political and international situation. I remember I began by saying 'Sir Alec, you must have had enough of politics for one day – how are your sugar-beet?' He visibly relaxed.

Most evenings *About Anglia* followed a set pattern from Monday to Friday. After the news section we would have a predetermined item on a subject like gardening, cooking, or Do-it-Yourself; then there were motoring hints, advice on medical and legal matters and sport on Fridays, with a shorter sports report on Monday after the weekend fixtures and events. The items came from a variety of sources: the news department, the papers (daily and weekly) and magazines. The news 'stringers' (often professional photographers, and some with their own news agencies) would ring in with items, or we would ring them if we heard of anything happening in their area which we wanted them to investigate for us. Members of the public would also sometimes contact us about a story in their area.

The weather forecast was always a very important part of the Anglia service and came at the end of the local news bulletin. An accurate weather forecast is vital in our area, with its many miles of coastline and farming and fishing industries. Anglia Television was the first independent company in the country to provide an extensive weather service, and to be linked directly by facsimile machine to Bracknell in Berkshire, the headquarters of the Meteorological Office. The forecast was presented by the late Michael Hunt who joined *About Anglia* in 1961, after more than twenty years as a meteorologist with the RAF and Air Ministry. Although he used all the most sophisticated aids available, Michael also seemed to possess a natural ability to predict the weather, and he presented it in a way that was interesting not only to farmers, fishermen and those who depended on the forecast for their livelihood, but also to the region's many visitors and holidaymakers. He always gave a report on conditions in the North Sea, and received first-hand reports from the captains of the ferries which plied between the east coast to the Continent. Michael was a man of tremendous enthusiasm and warmth of personality, and he soon established a following of appreciative and interested viewers whom he never failed to respond to when approached for help or advice. This was nowhere more evident than in the support he gave to the region's schools.

It would be impossible to mention any but a few of the thousands of items shown in the *News* and *About Anglia* during the thirty years it has been running, but it's worth recalling that occasionally we were able to include foreign inserts of local interest. In 1961 a team travelled abroad to Amman to cover the wedding of King Hussein of Jordan to a Suffolk girl, Toni Gardiner of Chelmondiston, near Ipswich. Unfortunately for me I had to stay behind as I was then introducing the programme every night. However when I was in America and Russia for *Farming Diary* I was able to record a few lighthearted pieces for *About Anglia.*

Police Call started in January 1963. Its object was to involve the public in helping the police and it involved a great deal of co-operation with the Norfolk County Police, and later with the police in other counties and towns in East Anglia. It became one of *About Anglia*'s longest running regular features, but I cannot say that I enjoyed presenting it, particularly when the anonymous threatening letters began to arrive. I was very relieved when the producers decided that my face was too jovial and not serious enough to appeal on behalf of the police for help in solving crimes, and I was able to hand over to John McGregor.

In 1962 the *About Anglia* team decided to hold a Christmas party in the studio. The idea behind the party was to link the men who manned one of the lightships out in the North Sea with their families, wives and children, as they would be on duty over the holiday period. The first problem we faced was that the lightship in question (the Smiths Knoll, which was permanently anchored twenty miles off Great Yarmouth) didn't have a television set on board. The second was that our camera, sound and lighting equipment was so heavy that it wasn't practical to take it to the light vessel on the Trinity House tender when it made its regular service visit. We decided, therefore, that only two people would be able to go. So a few days before Christmas a cameraman and I, with a silent camera, boarded the tender at Great Yarmouth in a howling gale and bobbed our way out into the North Sea. After about three hours (which seemed more like three weeks!) we arrived at the Smiths Knoll lightship. In those days the Smiths Knoll was manned by three permanent crew, who were relieved at intervals. We greeted them with their Christmas presents and fare, including a turkey donated by Bernard Matthews, plum puddings and all their personal presents from their families. Neither the cameraman nor I felt at all like filming – or the lunch of cold roast beef and fried bubble and squeak and beans which we were offered. After lunch we speedily got on with the job of filming the men at work maintaining the light, engines and generator etc., and made for home as daylight was beginning to fail. As the little boat chugged its way back to Yarmouth it rapidly got darker and our nausea increased, until by the time we arrived we both felt extremely sick! We had also delivered a television set donated by Anglia to the lightship, together with the necessary aerial, and a few days later an Anglia engineer went out and fixed the aerial to the mast, and made sure that the set would receive pictures from Tacolneston.

Now all appeared to be ready for the party and our link-up. An hour-long programme had been planned for Christmas Day afternoon, which included interviews with the families of the crew aboard the lightship. On the appointed day tables in the studio were laden with Christmas fare, there was a Christmas tree, and a conjuror had been engaged to entertain the children. The plan was to show the film we had taken of the men at work on the light vessel with a commentary from me, and then to transmit pictures of the wives and families in the studio which the men would see aboard the lightship. We had also set up a radio telephone link so that while we were transmitting still pictures of each individual man he could talk to and see his wife and family at the party together with all the viewers. All went well until the moment arrived for the radio link-up with the lightship. I explained what was going to happen and said, 'When I pick up this telephone I should be through to the lightship'. I put the receiver to my ear and said, 'Hello is that the Smiths Knoll lightship?', and the voice of an Anglia telephone operator answered saying, 'Good afternoon Anglia Television, who do you wish to speak to please'. I said, 'Um . . . er . . . I am supposed to be through to the Smiths Knoll light vessel', to which the operator replied, 'Do you have their number? We have no Smith or Knoll here'. Obviously something had gone wrong so I put the receiver down, apologised for the hitch, and said very loudly, 'I hope some engineer will put us through shortly. We will try again in a few minutes', and asked the conjuror to entertain the children. Ten minutes later virtually the same thing happened, except that now I was through to an engineer who said he was on the cliffs at Runton on the east coast of Norfolk trying to link up! More red-faced apologies and promises from me to the viewers, were briskly followed by interviews with the children. After a decent interval, I tried the phone again but with the same result. One by one I talked to the wives of the men on the light vessel, and asked them what it was like to be a lightshipman's wife, what their hobbies were, and what they had bought their husbands for Christmas! At this point the programme time was running out, and I made one last shot, pleading with the engineers to try and get me through to the Smiths Knoll light vessel, only to be told by a GPO engineer in Norwich that there was nothing he could do and why didn't I try Trinity House in London! Out of time, all I could do was apologise profusely, particularly to the wives and children in the studio for our failure to make the promised link. I wished the viewers happiness for the remainder of the day and the New Year and said goodbye. On came the advertisements before the next programme and at that moment the phone rang: it was the senior person on the Smiths Knoll lightship who said, 'Good afternoon – is that Anglia Television? I thought we were going to talk to our wives!'

The main object of the features in *About Anglia*, was to balance the news content of the programme with reports and items of more general interest to our viewers. Let's face it, most news is bad news for someone and when we had to report on fires, rail, road, and plane crashes, or floods, (most of which went in at the beginning of the programme) we tried where possible to finish on a lighter note. On many occasions, of course, it *wasn't* possible and one had to finish seriously with words to the effect, 'That's all for this evening. Let us hope that the news is better tomorrow'. Giving news of tragedies which we knew must have heart-rending effects on those involved didn't leave us entirely unaffected. Some evenings when the programme was over and I was on the way home in the car alone I would think of a better way of presenting an item, and often if the news had been particularly heavy, and a large proportion of it bad, it took a long time to stop thinking about it and put it out of one's mind. The reverse was the case, of course, on those nights when there was good news to report, and on the majority of occasions we usually found something to smile about.

We deliberately tried to lighten the situation in January 1963, the year of the 'big freeze'. Night after night we were talking about accidents on icy roads, aeroplanes unable to take-off, trains running late, shortage of fodder for livestock, and frozen pipes everywhere. Even the North Sea shoreline was frozen and birds and wildlife were badly affected. It all began to get a bit dreary. I cannot remember whose idea it was, but someone in the department suggested that we should take the OB unit and all the technical equipment necessary to Wroxham Broad, which was completely frozen over for the first time in living memory, and present *About Anglia* on ice. We did

About Anglia on ice, live from the Norfolk Broads, winter 1963.

the programme from the centre of the broad where the ice was 2ft thick or more below us. We even took my desk as I was the only one of the team who couldn't skate, and I sat in the centre of the broad whilst the rest of them skated from interview to interview, keeping within the arc of the lights, and obviously having a great time. Even our resident chef at Anglia was there, barbecueing! This all took place on a Friday evening and was such a success that we planned to repeat the location again on the following Monday, but over the weekend the weather broke and the ice began to disappear. In fact, the follow-up to that story was the flood!

Sometimes we were able to make use of quite unexpected occurrences. On one occasion, I was having lunch in the canteen when the chef told me that they had a problem at the back door with a tramp who was going through the wastebins looking for food: the chef had been asked by a member of staff if he could make the old boy a sandwich. We happened to be a bit short of material for *About Anglia* that evening, so I said to the chef, 'If he's still there, I'll come and see what he looks like. He might have a story to tell'. He was there, and he certainly had a story. We kept him at Anglia all that afternoon, listening to his tales, and I interviewed him on that evening's programme. He told us that he walked everywhere with his girlfriend, and he had many amusing anecdotes about their lives, not only wandering through England, but also on the Continent. He had a strong Irish accent and was very convincing and articulate. There was an immediate response from the viewers after transmission: many people telephoned about the item, and some posted money. We kept this for him, as he had told us he would be coming back in a few weeks. I always felt that he had an idea that he would appeal to the viewers, and that money might be the result. After his third visit to the studios, I thought it would be a good idea to do a very long interview with him and edit it into fifteen five minute films. This we did and the series *On the Road* was born. It didn't occur to us until much, much later that no one ever seemed to see our tramp actually 'tramping'. But someone did swear that they had seen him driving a very smart car – with his girlfriend just outside the city.

Another chance encounter produced an absolute gem of a chap. On reflection it seemed he was heaven-sent: he certainly appeared from above. I was working quietly in the office one afternoon when I heard strange noises over my head in the false ceiling. 'Engineers', I thought, for in Anglia low ceilings conceal labyrinths of wires and electrical 'plumbing'. Then there was a bang and a hole appeared in the ceiling followed by the lower half of a boot. Before I could say anything a voice in beautiful Norfolk said, 'Cor, blast – that was a nerun – cum 'ere you little bugger'. I waited. The foot withdrew, but the voice carried on. 'If thers anyone down there I'm sorry about you workin but I've lorst my ferret. I'll be down directly'. I waited again, and sure enough after a few minutes a short chap appeared at the door, covered in dust. He was wearing breeches, leggings and boots, a Guernsey and a shooting hat. Hanging by a strap from his shoulder was a crudely-made box, and in his hand a stick. He said, 'Sorry if I disturbed you but I lorst my ferret in yar roof. I'm Jack Rumsby, the rat catcher, and there's an old doe rat up there who wouldn't go for my bait so I thought I'd sus her out with my old ferret. Now I've lorst her amongst all those wires and I hent caught the rat yit. I shell hatter put her box up there and hope she'll recognise it as hom and cum back laater on'. I asked him why he didn't put some food in the box? 'She usually eat rabbits guts', he replied, 'I suppose you hent got a lot of them about here' I said we hadn't. He leapt onto my desk and put his box through the hole in the ceiling and said he'd be back. I went to the studio and started rehearsing for the evening show. About five o'clock I was told that one of the people who should have been appearing on *About Anglia* that evening had had an accident. He had gone to the doctor and wouldn't be coming. I rushed up to my office to see what stand-by material we had, and there was Jack, still making ferret noises and patiently waiting under the hole in the ceiling. On the spur of the moment I said, 'How would you like to come on *About Anglia* and tell me about being a rat catcher?' 'I wouldn't mind', he said, 'cept that since I joined the Council offishly I am a Rodent

Interviewing Sir Alec Douglas-Home on a Prime Ministerial visit to Norwich.

Operator – thet say so on my van. Hev I got toime to go hom and change?' 'No', I said, 'we're on air in under an hour – you're all right as you are'. The programme started and after the news and weather I announced that we had a very special and unusual guest, and told the story of how earlier in the day the foot had appeared through my ceiling. Then I put the first question: 'How long have you been a Rodent Operator or as you were known, a rat catcher?' Jack looked at me and said, 'Are yew goin to pay me for doin this?' I can't remember the rest of the interview, except that it was full of fun, and Jack chaffed me like this from beginning to end. I invited him to appear on the programme several times, and each time he was extremely funny and full of interesting tales about his life. Incidentally, when we got back to my office after the show, his old ferret was back in the box with the tail, four feet and a few other parts of the rat.

Two other favourite people who appeared from time to time on *About Anglia* were Mrs Marjorie Daynes of Mattishall, Norfolk, and Mrs Runnacles of Wickham Market, Suffolk. They were both cooks. Mrs Daynes came in to demonstrate 'old-fashioned country cooking', which she had learned as a girl when in service: and we filmed Mrs Runnacles (who had a similar upbringing and initiation into adult life) at her café at Wickham Market. Mrs Daynes was a mature lady of short stature and looked the part of the real old-fashioned cook she was. She had a round, florid, chubby face and strong, well-scrubbed, hands that were masters of anything to do with catering. Her hands could knead dough or skin rabbits, but they were also capable of icing a Christmas or wedding cake with the most complicated and delicate design. Mrs Daynes always appeared on the screen in the traditional light blue cook's dress, spotless white overall, apron and white hat, with no make-up or jewellery, of course. She was a great and natural talker. In fact, keeping the item to time was always the biggest problem with her as she never stopped talking. She was usually at the studio very early, always arriving at twelve for rehearsal at 2 o'clock. We found the answer was to take her to the canteen, and before you could say 'cheese grater' she was through the serving counter and into the kitchen. After the initial shock the chef and staff got used to her and eventually accepted that she was a very strong-willed, good cook and, as it were, one of them. She sometimes forgot on live transmissions that the viewers had not been in the Anglia canteen, and neither had I. Trying to sort out what she had done that morning in the canteen, what she had done in rehearsal, and what she was supposed to be doing on transmission was quite a problem and usually resulted in an 'over-run'. Indeed, sometimes we were left with no time at all to finish the item.

One such memorable occasion occurred when she had enjoyed a particularly exhilarating time in the canteen before the programme helping the chef to make the Anglia Christmas puddings, brandy and all. She had chosen to demonstrate stuffed cod that evening, and the viewers were later treated to pictures of Mrs Daynes sort-of wrestling with the large fish, eventually chopping its head off, disembowelling it, scraping and cleaning it out, and then proceeding to make the stuffing. She gave instructions in slow and deliberate tones, saying that she didn't believe in 'all this ready-made stuffing', *her* way was to prepare her own using herbs fresh from the garden and eggs just laid. Unfortunately, as she was taking so long I had to gently move in and say, 'Well I'm sorry we must leave Mrs Daynes and her stuffed fish, but I promise we'll pick it up again tomorrow night'. At this point the cameras were still on Mrs Daynes, who at that precise moment dropped the fish on the floor, bent down to pick it up and disappeared from view. There was so much laughter and hilarity going on in the Control Box that when the director, trying to make himself heard above the hubbub shouted 'roll end credits', someone pressed the wrong button and up came a picture of the continuity announcer looking distinctly startled at seeing himself suddenly appear on the screen. I kept my word, and after the news the next evening there was Mrs Daynes, standing serenely behind her table upon which lay the half-stuffed cod. We had told her not to hurry too much but to keep it moving, and she did. This time she finished early and I thought I would have to 'pad' out a bit. I was wrong. Mrs Daynes turned to camera, and with arms folded below her ample bosom, pulled herself up to her full height and addressed it square on. She then proceeded to tell the viewers that the cod episode was all my fault and that next week she was going to show everyone how to make Norfolk Dumplings, 'cos her dumplins were as light as love'. After that I could only say that I was sure they were, and there was no doubt that she would be back next week. As we started packing up Mrs Daynes offered pieces of the stuffed cod to the crew to taste. We all dutifully ate it, even though it had spent two days in the hot studios and a night in the stores cupboard, and was certainly well past its eat-by date!

We first encountered Mrs Runnacles when we were filming the water mill at Wickham Market, which was still grinding corn in the old traditional way with stones. The miller was Mr Rackham, very articulate and totally dedicated to his mill. It was a super day and when it came to lunch-time, instead of going to the pub, we decided on Mr Rackham's advice to go to a small café-cum-take-away in the village. There we found Mrs Runnacles, doing all the cooking for her tea-room in an old-fashioned wall oven. It turned out that she was renowned for her Suffolk Rusks and she also cooked her own sweet pickled hams. I shall never forget that picnic on the banks of the mill pool, eating fresh rolls, delicious ham and Suffolk rusks. We went back to Wickham Market a few days later and filmed the splendid Mrs Runnacles, who was not only a marvellous cook but also an astute business woman. Soon after the film was transmitted all her paper bags were printed with the legend, 'Mrs Runnacles' special home-made Suffolk Rusks as seen on Anglia Television', and a banner was hung right across the window of her shop carrying the same message.

In March 1965 we passed our 1,000th edition of *About Anglia* and I began to think that I was going to be the oldest man to say, 'Good evening, and welcome to another edition . . .' So I asked if it was possible for me to ease down and let someone else introduce the programme. It was agreed that Bob Wellings and John McGregor should take over and that I should be given the title of Head of Local Programmes. My new position meant that each month I had to go to London and attend the Programme Planning committee. When the original Programme Controller left shortly after the company opened he wasn't replaced, and instead a Programme Planning Committee was formed under the chairmanship of Sir John Woolf. Its members were Lord Townshend and Aubrey Buxton; Peter Holmans and Ken Elphick (who were responsible for all programme scheduling in co-ordination with the other network companies), Brian Connell (as programme adviser) and me. This worked very well, but in later years the Authority decreed that we should have a Programme Controller like all the other ITV companies, and Arthur Clifford joined the company from Tyne Tees. Arthur and I became good friends: a good job we did as our responsibilities overlapped a great deal. He was a colourful and charismatic man, and one of the best writers I have ever worked with, a real 'wordsmith' with a great deal of experience from his days on newspapers. His writing made compulsive reading in every sense of the word, and he was a great 'ideas' man. He also had an explosive temper which when lost, often resulted in a typewriter or telephone disappearing through the window into the courtyard below. Paradoxically Arthur had a very gentle and kind nature, and these outbursts only occurred as the result of frustrations connected with the job. I learned a great deal from him about putting facts together on paper. One of his favourite sayings was, 'When you have written a news item or article, go through it, cut out at least half the words, and it will be about the right length'.

My retirement from *About Anglia* and new responsibilities as Head of Local Programmes coincided with the opening of a new transmitter at Sandy Heath in Bedfordshire in July 1965. The new transmitter meant that Anglia programmes would be received by the whole of that county and also large areas of Hertfordshire and Northamptonshire, and, for the first time, parts of Buckinghamshire and Leicestershire. Peterborough, Kettering, Northampton, Bletchley, Hitchin, Letchworth and Stevenage were among the towns which were able to receive Anglia programmes as a result and the occasion was celebrated with a programme called *Opening Night, Channel Six*, presented live from a new civic centre at Dunstable. It was compèred by Rupert Davies and included Ron Moody, Janie Marsden and Johnny Hart; there was ballroom dancing, and the first heats were held of a new contest designed to find the most beautiful girl in our region, *Miss Anglia*. In December 1965 the boundaries of the Anglia region were pushed still wider when the Belmont transmitter opened in Lincolnshire. This beamed Anglia programmes to the whole of Lincolnshire and to parts of Yorkshire, Derbyshire and Nottinghamshire. The number of homes that could receive Anglia was nearing a million. The company opened offices in Hull and Grimsby, and there was a small rudimentary studio for filming interviews in Hull. Vic Birtles looked after both offices, and sent film and copy by despatch rider daily to Norwich. Without the Humber Bridge the journey was often hectic, and even though there were ferries that plied across the water between the two places, the journey by road round by Goole to Norwich took over three hours. The people living in the new territory of Lincolnshire, South Yorkshire, and parts of Derbyshire and Nottinghamshire, were used to watching programmes from Tyne Tees Television and ATV and I was given the job of mounting a promotion campaign to persuade people to re-orientate their aerials and sets to receive Anglia programmes. It took approximately three months to visit every town and village of any size to 'beat the Anglia drum' and meet the dignitaries and heads of important businesses. A small aeroplane was put at my disposal and by using various private air strips and landing fields I was able to get to most places within an hour or so of leaving Norwich. We had twenty-two landing points throughout the area and knew practically every taxi driver by his first name.

The task of converting people from watching signals coming from the west of the Pennines to ours from the east was not as difficult as I had at first expected. The extended coastline to the east and the fact that the whole of the area was predominantly agriculturally orientated was greatly in our favour. We were, after all, a company transmitting from the heart of a big rural area with strong coastal connections, unlike Tyne Tees and ATV who were serving a largely city/urban industrial area. The net result was a great boost in viewing numbers. Nearly ten years later in 1974, and after new franchise allocations in various regions, the Independent Broadcasting Authority redefined our 'patch'. Up until then, where the Anglia and Yorkshire Television borders had overlapped around Humberside both services were available to the viewers in these areas. The IBA decided that the Belmont transmitter should be given to the Yorkshire area. The decision brought a storm of fierce protests from viewers, which were supported by local organisations and Members of Parliament of all parties. The Authority remained unmoved, and the decision held – to this day parts of North Norfolk receive their television programmes from Yorkshire.

My position as Head of Local Programmes meant that I was responsible for overseeing the production of news and locally originated and produced programmes. My office was in the centre of the building at the top of the stairs, with a small outer office for my secretary, and I adopted the 'ever-open-door' policy as far as my relationship with the rest of the Anglia staff was concerned. Both doors – my secretary's and mine – were always kept open unless a very private conversation or meeting was in progress. People soon got the message that I was quite happy to listen to a suggestion or a problem, but if the conversation wandered from the point they were left in no doubt that the meeting was over. In the whole of my twenty-five years with the company, give or take an odd 'temporary', I had only four secretaries. I cannot speak highly enough of them. I shall never know how they kept up with the constant ringing of telephones and the comings and goings of frantic programme people, to say nothing of having to put up with a farmer who invariably arrived at the office before anyone else, never knew when to stop, and couldn't spell. They were all intelligent, efficient and supportive, and I have been lucky to work with them. This was a busy and productive time and I soon discovered that being responsible for the running of a television station was no nine-to-five job. It was, however, very stimulating working with so many different creative people. Then in 1967 the Chairman called me into his office and told me that at a meeting the previous day a proposal had been unanimously passed that I should be invited to join the Board. I remember thanking him very much but telling him that I wasn't certain that I would have the time to attend some meetings, which took place at Anglia's London office, Brook House, Park Lane.

Lord Townshend replied, 'You will have the time because we have decided to have alternate board meetings in Norwich'.

Working life was becoming increasingly busy, and the pressures were considerable. My responsibilities as Head of Local Programmes and as an Executive Director on the Board took up most of my time, but in 1967 I also began to make the series of *Bygones* programmes, which were to continue for the next twenty years. The *Bygones* programmes were a spin-off from the years I spent presenting *About Anglia*, when I began to use items from our collection of bygones to ease my way through unexpected hitches or under-runs. The programmes brought together two of my chief interests: the collection and the preservation of old craft implements, machinery and other paraphernalia. It was a great pleasure for me to be able to share these interests with so many people through the medium of television.

Warts

a. Rub the wart with raw beef and then secretly bury the beef
b. Rub the wart with castor oil
c. Squeeze on the juice of the milkwort plant

From Grandma's *Commonplace Book*.

CHAPTER FOURTEEN

The Collection: *Bygones*

I cannot remember a time when I didn't collect things. I was born with a naturally acquisitive and inquisitive nature, always wanting to find out how things worked and where they came from.

As with most country boys my first ever collection was of birds' eggs and small mammal skulls. Collecting skulls was a grisly business. Once you had found the dead animal – rabbit, hare, stoat, weasel, rat, mouse or frog – it was necessary to boil it until all the flesh came off and then bleach it in the sun. Stuck on a card the skulls made an interesting exhibit! Today, of course, egg collecting is illegal. Like the rest of my school friends I also collected marbles. During the twenties and thirties most children played marbles and the competition was keen. The game was played on a flat piece of concrete, the tarred road or a barn floor (in fact, wherever marbles would roll) and the object was to knock your opponent's marble out of the field of play. When this happened his marble became yours. Most boys and girls had a marble bag to keep their trophies in. These were usually made of cotton, about 6in long and 4in across. A slip-noose top pulled the opening of the bag together, leaving a loop which was tied to your trouser belt. Genuine marble marbles came in a variety of plain colours, brown, blue, yellow, green and so on, but the glass marbles were those most sought-after. These were sometimes called 'alleys' and were made of clear glass with wavy coloured lines running through them. They were often larger than the plain ones. I can't remember all the rules of the game but most children prized their cache of marbles.

In the autumn we turned our attention to conkers, collecting the shiny brown horse-chestnuts as soon as they had fallen from the trees. Each conker had to be strung, baked in the oven, and soaked in vinegar to harden it enough to smash your opponent's conker. His score was then added to yours. There was no material gain in this game, save that you finished up with the champion conker that was unbroken at the end of the season. I don't remember girls playing conkers. They probably had too much good sense, as the swinging missile on its 18in piece of string could, and did, result in many a black eye. Conkers, like tiddlywinks, required a certain skill, but collecting cigarette cards relied only on knowing people who smoked. Most cigarette manufacturers put a card in each packet. They were usually made up into sets of fifty and were 3in long and 1½in wide. On the card face there was a picture of a king, cricketer, footballer, railway train, castle, motor-car, film star, battleship or aeroplane, and the details of the person or object were printed on the back. The more up-market brands of cigarettes sometimes contained sets of international flags. The designs were beautifully woven onto a piece of silk and enclosed in a small packet of transparent paper, with a card giving details of the country or origin. These were called Stevengraphs and were highly prized. The first step for the collection was to find out the brands of cigarette smoked by father, brother or acquaintance and make certain they saved their cards up for you, then it was off to the tobacconist to get an album appropriate to your collection to stick them in. The children in large families with lots of brothers and sisters who smoked were at an advantage here, although I do not remember women smoking as much as the men

Anything mechanical always interested me; speedometers, clocks, steering wheels and instruments from old cars. The latter were difficult to come by, but as I spent a lot of time in Mr Richardson's scrap-yard at Fakenham I could occasionally acquire a gem for a 'bob' (shilling) or two. Mother didn't take too kindly to the steering wheels, radiator badges, car mascots, door handles, window winders and hand-brakes hanging as ornaments in my bedroom, but they were all made of brass, copper or aluminium and I thought they were wonderful – and still do. I also loved small brass bushes and ball bearings: the precision with which they were made fascinated me. I remember on one occasion taking my mother's sewing machine to pieces: she was so relieved when I got it together again and it still worked. She must have been quite impressed though, as it prompted her to buy me a machine that had been dropped and broken – and I got that to work too. For the rest of the working life of her sewing machine, until she gave up using it, I was the only one who was allowed to service and adjust it. That machine is now in the Holkham Bygones Collection.

When I left school I started collecting horse brasses, bells and plumes from harness and then moved on to bigger things like car wheels, brass oilers, grease caps, steam gauges, brass whistles from steam engines, and the beautiful old candle and paraffin lamps from horse and pony carts and traps. During these years horse equipment was being replaced on the farm. It was either converted to tractor power or worn up, but on some farms it was allowed to rot away in the corner of a field or cartshed as it became redundant. One day my father announced that he was about to have a fire and burn some of his old horse-drawn carts, drills, wooden-baulked harrows and elevators. I asked him if I could have the money from the comparatively small amounts of cast iron, steel, brass and aluminium salvaged after the wood had been burnt if I broke them up. He agreed. It took a lot of my spare time, a hard chisel and hammer, and several black thumbs and fingernails, to extricate the metal from the wood. All the wood was unceremoniously burnt and the metals (cast-iron, aluminium, brass and copper) were carefully sorted and taken to Mr Richardson's yard. He weighed each type of metal and paid me. Included in the vehicles and implements broken up was a very large W & G ex-First World War army lorry. Most of the engine was aluminium and there was a great deal of brass. It accounted for most of the money I received, which came to the princely sum of £7. However, I didn't go home with the £7 for standing in Mr Richardson's yard was a very early circa 1860 two-man operated hand-pump, which had been used at one of the stately homes as a fire pump. All the mechanism was made of brass, with a large pressure cylinder (tennis-racket size and pear-shaped) on the top made of copper. It had four wooden wheels and pony shafts. Mr Richardson relieved me of five of my seven pounds and I went home very happy with weeks and weeks of work in prospect, taking the fire pump to pieces, polishing the brass and copper and painting the chassis and wheels fire-engine red. I kept it in the cattle feeding house in the 'dungeon' with my beloved pigs, and it was several weeks before I got round to telling my father what had happened to the proceeds from breaking up the old implements. We didn't realise then that the fire pump would become very valuable, and it is now almost unique. We still have it in the Collection and it looks as magnificent as the day it was made, about 1900 by Shand Mason.

Not all Father's discarded implements were smashed up, and I took quite a lot of them with me when I moved to Raynham and stashed them away. During the Raynham years I also began buying, usually for a few pence, any craft tools I saw for sale, and became fascinated with the strange tools and implements that craftsmen used in their different trades. It is amazing how many different hand-tools were used by the various craftsmen. Although they were basically similar to each other, there was usually a very slight difference. This was often a modification by one particular man when he needed it for a special job. Gradually I built up sets of tools connected with most of the local country crafts, like those of the carpenters, blacksmiths, wheelwrights, joiners, plumbers, well-sinkers, leadsmiths, glaziers and stained glass window-makers, moulders and casters, harness-makers and leather workers. I also managed to find examples of the tools used by craftsmen making items for the domestic market, such as peg-makers, tinsmiths, candle-makers, hatters, coffin makers, basket weavers, and many more. As I acquired items I hung them up in groups on the barn walls at Raynham. People who came to the farm seemed fascinated by the old implements, and would often contact me and let me know when there was a sale in their village where there were items I might be interested in. On one memorable occasion I heard that two old gentlemen, the Bailey brothers, who had worked the Barney brickworks all their lives, were packing up. I went over and saw them and, after an interesting and enlightening chat, bought all their brick-making equipment – barrows, moulds and two pug mills – and also the 1930 Ford lorry which had carted all the clay from the clay face to the works and from then on to the kilns. Printed on the lorry's licence disc, and signed by the Chief Constable, was the message 'Exempt from tax. Permission to drive five miles from Little Barney Post Office only'. It still runs beautifully.

Later, I got more and more enthusiastic and started acquiring stationary engines, small motor cars (mostly two-seaters), and horse-drawn vehicles and implements; but my ultimate ambition had always been to own a traction engine. I solicited the help of my old friend, George Cushing, and he told me that there was a Fowler 7 nhp General Purpose traction engine for sale, somewhere in the Fens, north of Kings Lynn. We went to see it and the owner, Reg Palmer, said he wanted £120 for it. It seemed like a fortune at the time and we didn't buy it, but said we might go back. We did – four times – during the next month. The first time we bid £50 for it, and on each visit we gradually increased the bid until finally we reached £100. Reg accepted, and I achieved a life-long ambition! Now I had to call on another old friend, Harry Bushell, who lived next door to George at Thursford, to help to get the Fowler home, and naturally he told me just how big a mistake I had made in buying it. *Margaret*, as we named the Fowler, had lived for forty years in the Fens and had been filled with water from the fen dykes, which meant that all her tubes needed renewing, and there was a good deal of wastage in the firebox. Harry did all this work for me and charged, by today's standards, a very small amount of money. We then cleaned her down thoroughly and gave her an exact copy of her original livery, a dark gloss green boiler, black firebox and chimney, all lined out in gold, and red wheels. What a magnificent sight she looked. I suppose it was enlightened self-interest that prompted me to name her after my wife – the trouble was I had to name the three engines that followed *Miriam*, *Jennifer* and *Carole*, after our daughters.

Small things as well as large interested me. Many years after buying the Fowler I went into an antique shop in Needham Market one day and, rummaging through a box-full of pudding basins and kitchen-ware, I came across what looked like a glass scent bottle, about 6in high, and beautifully cut to a very elegant shape. It had a small hole in the top which could have taken a tiny cork stopper. The sides of the hole had not been ground, so it had not had a ground glass stopper as scent bottles usually do. When I asked the proprietor about it he said it was a scent bottle, but it was no good as it had a hole in the bottom. He told me he had paid 5s 0d for the box of junk and that I could have the lot for 7s 0d, glass and all. Luckily for me, I had remembered seeing a much more ornate version of the little glass item in a museum and recognised it as a toddy lifter, used at hunt meets to serve drinks to those on horseback. The host's butler or a groom passed amongst the mounted horsemen with a large bowl of hot toddy held in the crook of his left arm, using the little glass decanter as a pipette, to refill the riders' glasses. This feat was achieved by plunging the pipette into the liquid, allowing it to fill through the bottom hole, with the thumb placed over the top hole to trap the liquid inside. He would then reach up, take his thumb off the top hole and release the liquid into the rider's glass, usually without spilling a drop. Special stirrup glasses were also used by riders to the hunt, and they were always beautifully cut. They were just like ordinary wine glasses with a long elegant stem but no foot, just a round knob to stop it sliding out of the gloved hand of the horseman. There was no point in having a foot on the glass when there was nowhere to stand it on a horse! After use the stirrup glasses were collected and kept in a special mahogany rack with holes in it, like a miniature egg rack. I have only ever found one stirrup glass. It was being used by a watch repairer to keep the tiny parts of a watch together on his bench and protect them from dust and moisture, by standing it upside down on a piece of blotting paper. He was kind enough to sell it to me saying that a wine glass with the foot broken off served his purpose just as well.

With collecting, of course, there are sometimes real disappointments, and I shall never forget buying the Clepsydra, which is a water clock. It was in a sale and I really thought I had found something, for through the dirt and grime on the brass plate at the bottom the words 'Glemson Anno Dom 1691 of Ye Towne Wakefield' were legible. The dial goes from 1 (in the usual place) to 12 (where on today's clocks it is 6), and starts again with 1 (where 7 now is) and goes round to 12 (at the top). The action works by filling the brass cylinder with water, then a float on the end of the chain pulls the hand of the clock round as water drips from the brass cylinder into the square reservoir on the bottom of the woodwork. The rate of leakage of water is regulated by a small valve behind the name plate, and this controls the speed at which the hand goes round. No allowance is made for evaporation, changes in temperature, spiders using the reservoir as an oasis, or even freezing up, but I suppose it gave some indication of time. My big disappointment came when I found one exactly like it in York Museum labelled 'Copy of an Early Victorian Household Device – a fake, not genuine'.

One of the most interesting and unusual, indeed unique, bygone items I ever bought was the Wolseley-Siddeley Landaulet 1907 motor car, especially built for Queen Alexandra when she and King Edward VII were in residence at Sandringham. I was told that it was on offer by someone who had seen it in the showroom window of a car business in Hunstanton. It had been there for some time, and little interest had been shown in it. After looking at it I made an offer and I must admit was very surprised when it was accepted. It just wasn't generally appreciated at that time that these rare motor cars would become valuable collector's items. This one in particular was to become very special because of its royal connection, and the fact that it had only done a few thousand miles. It was also in near-perfect condition as it had been stored for many years in one of the heated coach houses at Sandringham.

While the car was in my possession it wasn't used very much, but went out occasionally to rallies and it took my daughter, Miriam, to and from Raynham church on her wedding day. Short-sightedly, I, too, sold it as it was depreciating in my unheated cold, damp barn – and in any case I needed the money. But there was a sequel. Twenty-five years later when the Bygones Collection was safely installed at Holkham Hall, Lord Coke bought an almost identical car, a 1904 Wolseley-Siddeley, which originally belonged to the third Earl of Leicester at Holkham. I had tried to find this car some years earlier for the fifth Earl of Leicester, who had asked me to locate it. It had been sold between the wars by the original owner, the third Earl, to a garage owner at Brancaster on the north Norfolk coast. He had used it as a taxi in that area and eventually, when it broke down, it was relegated to his garden, where children played in it and the hens even used it as a roosting place. After the fifth Earl had commissioned me to find it I paid the elderly garage owner a visit, only to learn that the car had been sold – he thought to a collector in Scotland. This seemed to be the end of the trail, but to my great surprise almost twenty years later I heard that a restorer in Cambridge had brought it back from Scotland and renovated it to its original condition. I went to see it and found that he had made a beautiful job of it, and managed to persuade Lord Coke, heir to the Estate to buy it back for Holkham. It now takes pride of place in the Collection.

The story doesn't quite end there, but goes back again to 23rd May 1933, the date of my brother's twenty-first birthday. On that day Lord Leicester – the third Earl – came to Testerton in this yellow and black Wolseley-Siddeley. My parents had invited the five landlords of the estates on which Father farmed and all his employees, altogether 125 people. After photographs all the guests sat down to a high-tea in the big barn at Testerton. The gargantuan meal of roast beef, salt beef, tongue and pickles, then loads of plum pudding and cream, was followed by a dance in the evening and a great deal of beer. The ladies drank cider. I was brought home from school at Bury St Edmunds for the day and spent most of the time with Lord Leicester's chauffeur, admiring the car, sitting in it and talking to him about it. After the meal and the speeches the VIP guests left. Lord Leicester came to his car and found me sitting in the open front seat next to the chauffeur. Noticing the badge on my school blazer he asked me a lot of questions: where my school was, if I had come home for the day, was I interested in motor cars, and if so would I like a ride in the Wolseley-Siddeley? I accepted with alacrity, and he told me to get in the back with him. Whilst the chauffeur was cranking it up, he showed me the beautiful interior folding tables, the

A small part of the *Bygones* collection in the old stables at Holkham.

small extra folding seats and the speaking tube, which he blew into, making a whistle 'peep' near the ear of the chauffeur in the driving compartment. He then gave the order, 'Please drive on', and away we went. After a couple of miles he asked the driver to stop, and took a shilling from his waistcoat pocket and gave it to me. He told me to save hard and perhaps one day I would be able to buy myself a car but in the meantime I would have to walk home! I think he knew I'd have walked home without the shilling just for the pleasure of a ride in what was then, and still is, one of the most beautiful cars ever built. I'm so pleased that after all its subsequent experiences it is now back home at Holkham once more.

My passion for collecting objects from the past was to lead me into two new and different ventures in later years, which I could not have foreseen. One I have already touched on; the establishment of all the bygone items in a permanent display, open to the public at Holkham Hall. As the collection grew and became more catholic and diverse, the problem of storing it all in suitable conditions became more acute. It had had several 'homes' since its beginning in the Testerton farm barn in the late twenties. In the early forties I moved it to the Raynham farm, and later moved it again to Castle Acre where I now live. All the while it was growing and at Castle Acre, although under cover, everything was housed in very cramped conditions where it couldn't be seen properly. Then one day Lord Coke, heir to the present Earl of Leicester, who administers the Holkham Estate, came over to ask me about a specific bygone item that he had seen somewhere. I told him that I thought I had one of the objects he was interested in, and we went into the old buildings, which had once been cowsheds and bullock boxes, to try and fid it. Locating it was difficult, and as we searched I asked Lord Coke whether there might be anywhere at Holkham that would be more suitable to store it all. Out of this chance discussion emerged the idea of moving the whole collection to Holkham and setting it up on permanent display in the disused stables, coach houses and grooms' quarters in the grounds.

Holkham Hall is one of the most beautiful Palladian mansions in the country, set in a 6,000 acre deer park, open to the public and attracting thousands of visitors each summer. It was a perfect place for the collection, where it could rub shoulders with some of the Leicester family coaches, cars and harness that had survived from the past.

My step-daughter, Zara, agreed to set up the collection in its new home, and to become its 'caretaker' at Holkham. She was a qualified general and cardiac nurse working at the London Heart Hospital, but she had already decided that she would like a change and a break from nursing. Lord Coke offered her the use of a little house on the Estate and together we erected and set out the various displays in the old stable complex. Most of the tools and objects were in good order as we had cleaned and preserved them over the years, and wherever possible we had kept up the original paint and livery on all the engines and vehicles. Zara made clear labels for the displays giving the correct name of each item and describing its use, and in order to do this as attractively as possible she took a course in calligraphy. The whole effect was judged a great success by all and we opened the Bygones Collection to the public in the Spring of 1979. Zara worked hard during the next few years, constantly changing and refurbishing the displays from items kept in store, so that there was always something fresh and interesting to see. She arranged a series of craft displays and demonstrations, helped to 'steam' and drive the engines, and talked to and welcomed many of the early visitors. She was tireless in her efforts to establish and publicise the Collection, and very successful. Visitors and local people alike came in ever-increasing numbers. After five years at Holkham Zara decided to resume her nursing career and Inigo Monk, a name at the very top as far as theatre design work is concerned, now looks after the Collection. He is well-qualified to keep the displays and designs up to the very highest standards with his professional experience of display work.

Holkham Park is always open for people to leave their cars and walk in the grounds or picnic. The Hall itself and the Bygones Collection opened for only two days a week in the early years, but now both are open five days a week.

The other, and in fact, earlier 'spin-off' from my passion and enthusiasm for memorabilia and objects from times past, was the *Bygones* television programme. Like most people in television, certainly in the early days, I had

The 1904 Wolseley-Siddeley at Holkham with Lord Coke driving.

a horror of 'drying-up' on air. That terrible moment when you have what is called in the trade a 'micro-sleep'; you can't even remember your own name, and you freeze. A lot of people make a great success of using autocue. The programme script, either written by the presenter or for the presenter by a researcher, is first typed onto a endless spool of paper. The spool is then attached to a gadget which revolves just below or to one side of the camera lens, so that the presenter can read the script while apparently looking straight at the camera. I never liked autocue, particularly as sometimes it had to be worked by the presenter himself on a foot pedal – toe down for forward, heel down for backwards. I did try it on rehearsal once or twice but always found great difficulty in co-ordinating my eyesight and brain with my toe and heel, and often found it was going backwards or I had lost my place. I soon discovered that it was easier for me to use notes as prompts, and tried not to make it too obvious. I even used to write the name of the person I was interviewing on the palm of my left hand, so that I could casually glance down if my mind suddenly went blank.

Most of the regional news-magazine programme, *About Anglia*, was ad-libbed in the early days, certainly the links between the various items were. The floor manager, who was always close to the lens of the camera giving signs with his hands and fingers, counted down the number of minutes and seconds remaining for each item, All independent television programmes have to start and finish on the second because the commercials come up at pre-determined slots. Presenting, therefore, was, and is, a complicated business, as you have to be aware of the signs from the floor manager while at the same time carrying on an interview. I remember one evening that we came near to a catastrophe. The programme had gone very well, the interviews had come out on time, the film hadn't broken, none of the high-powered bulbs in the studio had gone 'pop', and I had been given the wind-up signal from the floor manager telling me that there were thirty seconds left and I only had to thank everybody and say goodnight. Suddenly, with a look of absolute horror on his face, the floor manager gave me the sign which meant 'stretch' (his hands in a silent clapping motion, and then holding up the fingers on one hand to let me know how much time there was to fill). Nobody can describe how long two minutes are when you have absolutely nothing to say! By a strange coincidence, as I was going into the studio for rehearsal that evening, someone had walked into the reception area at Anglia and left a potato shaped like a duck. The receptionist had given this to me and I had put it in the drawer of the desk at which I sat to present the programme. When confronted with the floor manager's 'stretch' sign I opened the drawer, took out the potato, held it up to the camera and said, 'Of all the millions of potatoes dug up in East Anglia I bet there are not many that resemble a duck'. And then continued to waffle for another sixty seconds, until I could say, 'and that's all from *About Anglia* this evening, etc'. That evening I vowed I would never again be left with nothing to grab when such an occasion arose. So I took into the studio a selection of objects, like Victorian skirt clips, pie funnels, toddy lifters, any unusual item from the past, and when an opportunity presented itself I would use one of these objects to get through a tight spot. Apart from receiving a lot of dog, frog and rabbit-shaped potatoes after the first incident, we soon found that there was tremendous interest in these items – most of which came from my bygones collection. Looking back to 1961 I suppose that this actually was the start of the *Bygones* programme, as we eventually set aside a regular ten-minute spot in the *About Anglia* programme for these strange objects. 'Bygones' was not a term in everyday use in those days. It was a term used mainly in the museum world to describe everyday objects from the recent past, not antiques but no longer in present-day use. In 1967 we chose the word for the title of a half-hour programme about old crafts, buildings and collections of unusual objects. *Bygones* ran for twenty years and became a household name, and many of the items we continued to show resulted in a great deal of interest from the audience. The Rockfish Gap apple peeler was an outstanding example.

The 1917 'Titan' as found in 1960.

The 'Titan' rebuilt at demonstration pulling four-horse drag, 1965.

The mechanical nature of small kitchen apple and peach peelers had always intrigued me. My interest in them began when I bought an apple peeler on a stall on Norwich market in 1960. It was very rusty, not quite complete, and had 'Little Star 1910' printed on it. I thought little more about it until 1971 when I was in the USA making a *Bygones* film, and we happened to pass a threshing engine standing outside a little log cabin with a small store attached. We stopped to look at the engine and the owner came out, corn cob pipe, straw hat and all. He soon found out that we were interested in his collection of bygones, which were scattered about everywhere and beyond description. It was a paradise of agricultural equipment, as well as domestic appliances and dairy utensils: you name it, it was there, including some old apple peelers similar to ours. When I asked the owner if he would sell us one of the 'Little Star' variety as we had an incomplete one at home, he said, 'Nope, but you can buy a new one'. He disappeared into the store and after much searching came up with almost identically the same thing – new, unused, and in its original box complete with instructions. The only difference was that the new one was called the White Mountain Apple Peeler, and it was made in Antrim, New Hampshire, USA. Of course I bought one, and when I got back to England mentioned it on the programme. We were inundated with letters and telephone calls, particularly from the good ladies of the WI who made chutney. I gave them all the address of the Rockfish Gap Country Store, Afton, Virginia and told them the cost, $4.95. I often wondered how long the stock lasted and how the rural owner of the country store reacted to requests for apple peelers from across the Atlantic!

The only other sort of peeler I could find in the store was a very intricate piece of machinery for peeling peaches. It worked on a similar principle to the first mechanical apple peeler, but was more sophisticated because of the soft nature of the fruit. In order to cope with this the manufacturers had made the three prongs holding the peach on the revolving spindle of much thinner wire, with one of them spring-loaded, so that the prongs actually grasped the stone inside the fruit. The other difference is that the cutting knife revolves as well as moving to the contour of the peach, unlike the fixed blade used for apples. It works very well as long as the fruit is not over-ripe. Apparently, in Florida in the early part of the century, hundreds of people were employed in the peach canning factories all using similar, individual, machines. Incidentally none of the machines works on potatoes unless the potato is very symmetrical and just the right size, which potatoes usually are not. Another coincidence occurred around 1970 when an American firm brought out a re-print of the 1897 Sears Roebuck catalogue (rather like Gamages or Harrods catalogues in this country) and featured in it was the apple peeler from Rockfish Gap country store – the price, 40 cents in 1897. In the description of it the advertisement claims that you can pare, core and slice an apple with one hand in five seconds. I can vouch for this.

As a result of the *Bygones* television programmes, we were also introduced to many types of kitchen mincers for meat, suet, and so on, and an ingenious device for stoning cherries. The cherry stoner does separate the flesh from the stones, but it is a very messy machine to use. The same applies to raisin stoners. My mother used a raisin stoner when preparing mincemeat for the annual festival of the first batch of mince pies for Christmas (which carried on weekly until Easter and beyond). That too, was a very sticky, messy business: one of the tasks that I imagine people were pleased to see the end of with the advent of seedless raisins.

Many kitchen items that we discovered were 'puzzles', until suddenly the truth dawned. But the hot-cross bun marker was not difficult to identify; it was a simple wooden cross used to mark the hot, spicy buns. (This, of course, was used in the days when buns at Easter were not just lumps of dough with an odd currant lurking!) The same goes for all those different pastry jiggers, used for marking pastry and making pretty little indents round the outside of pies and tarts. Some jiggers had the added refinement of tweezers on one end, to pinch the pastry together. Not so long ago, at a rather pathetic sale of cottage furniture and effects belonging to an old lady who had died, I bought a box of kitchen cutlery, not for the contents, which were mostly well-worn spoons and bent forks, but for the handsome box with a centre carrying handle. When I got it home and had sorted through the contents, I was about to throw away an old piece of wood when I realised it had been used, probably for several decades, as a 'food-mixer'. It was simply a piece of a stem cut from a tree and by the set of the branches it looked like holly, which when peeled is a lovely white wood. The cook just twirled it between the palms of the hand to beat and mix ingredients together. It must have been used by the dear old lady a great deal as the bottom of the hard wood, where it came into contact with the basin, was completely rounded and the shaft had finger marks worn into it. I suppose it was this that sparked my interest in the many methods and tools that have been traditionally used for beating up cake mixes in the kitchen, and I finally finished up with a collection of literally scores of whisks, beaters and 'swizzles'.

Other items shown on the programme which intrigued both us and the viewers included a device with a handle section holding five axles on which are 2-3-4-3-2 small wooden balls. This machine, it was claimed, 'made the fat fall off ladies' hips'. It cost 2s 6d in 1924, and I've often wondered if it worked for men. The patent wasp gun is another interesting nineteenth century gadget. Made of metal it was presumably 'baited' with honey or jam smeared onto the plate on the end of it. The 'gunner' waited for a wasp to settle, pulled the trigger, and 'wham' – one squashed jammy wasp. This must have been a handy item on a picnic.

Often the most exciting thing about collecting bygones is the research that leads to the strange facts about an unusual piece of equipment. The lark lure was an item that foxed us for a time. The bottom half of it was a mystery. It is made of wood and is pointed at one end, with a spindle sticking out of the other which is slit about half-way down. For years we thought it was part of a toy, then one day I saw exactly the item we had in Edward Pinto's book on *Treen*, except that his illustration showed that the missing part was a curved piece of wood, inlaid with tiny pieces of glass. When the string is pulled it turns the spindle and the curved piece of wood spins round. When the string reaches its full length of travel, the momentum of the wooden cross-member winds it back ready to be pulled again: the same principle as a Yo-Yo. According to Pinto, the insatiable curiosity of larks, and their attraction to anything glittering, makes it easy to bring them within shooting range.

Sugar nippers or cutters are always interesting, and people often think they are castrators. They came in a variety of sizes. Hand models, were used at table, while the larger sizes and heavier iron nippers mounted on wooden blocks were used in the kitchen or in grocers' shops. Until the early years of the present century white sugar was generally made into cones or 'loaves' about 36in high, and weighing about 14lb. These were made by pouring a saturated solution of the cane sugar syrup through a funnel. As the solution dripped through, it crystallised on the outside and gradually set, until the funnel could be inverted and removed, leaving behind the characteristic sugar cone. Large households would buy whole cones wrapped in blue paper, but smaller amounts could be bought from the grocer in the form of pieces broken from the sugar loaf. It then had to be crushed into smaller pieces for table use, or powdered with a pestle and mortar and possibly sieved as well to make it fine enough for cooking. A bygone item which is a favourite of mine is the 'Arthur Pneumatic Patent Variable Shower'. It really works, and is especially refreshing when used on hot days, outside, in a hip bath. All that is necessary is to plunge it into a bucket of cold water, place the thumb and finger over the two holes in the handle, swing it aloft, remove the thumb, and down pours six pints of water.

These days, I'm afraid, many collectables have either been worn out and thrown away as junk, or have become so sought after, that it is very difficult to collect them compared with the ease with which we did it a few years ago. When cataloguing the Collection for Holkham it surprised me to discover that between 1938 and 1978 I had put away over 4,000 items ranging from bodkins to traction engines, most of them classed as 'junk' at the time, and deemed to be of no future use except for scrap. My hope is that the many series of *Bygones* programmes have helped to tell part of the story of our past, and that the Collection at Holkham Hall will continue to do so for generations to come.

Demonstrating Victorian portable shower in the hip-bath mother used for us.

CHAPTER FIFTEEN

The *Bygones* Programmes

During its twenty-year run, the *Bygones* series was produced by a small unit (in a very small office!) consisting of a director, his production assistant, a researcher/writer, my secretary and me. We were very fortunate in the directors allocated to us. They were all gifted and sensitive, each with a different approach and all had the enthusiasm and ability not only to get the best out of the programme participants but to control me at the same time! Ron Downing, who first directed me in *Farming Diary*, was an old hand and one of the most patient men with whom I have ever worked. Michael Edwards who successfully rose through the ranks and was promoted director after years as floor manager, knew only too well the sort of mistakes I was liable to make. Geoff Weaver too, who started as a research writer had a real flair for finding interesting and unusual old characters from his beloved Suffolk countryside. David Kenten was one of the original film editors with the company when it started and, it is true to say, was a real wizard at editing film, which together with his general knowledge of the film industry, particularly the national film libraries and archives, was a great asset. It was he who brought in John Huntley, the film historian, who not only enlivened many programmes with fascinating archive film but also stepped into my shoes and presented the programme during my stays in hospital. Wendy Witham, the production assistant, kept tabs on everything: studio bookings, film locations, arrangements for transport, hotel bookings, meals, requisitions for facilities, booking people for studio interviews and sorting out expenses. It was she who had to ensure that all the departments in Anglia were co-ordinated to do their bit on the correct day at the precise time, in exactly the agreed sequence! The mind boggles at the thought of how many things could go wrong but thankfully usually didn't! We had our ups and downs and disagreements but the standard of professionalism was so high amongst the eight hundred members of staff at Anglia, that I don't remember a single occasion when a programme wasn't transmitted due to human error. There were incidents of mechanical failure in the early days but the engineering genius usually got round the electrical or mechanical bugs in the system. The rest of the *Bygones* team consisted of my secretary,

Stanley Mayhew driving a sail reaper (c. 1895).

Stanley Mayhew and Jimmy Knights scything wheat (from the film 'The Harvest')

Harold Smart driving the clipper (1890) with Stanley Mayhew raking the cut crop to one side. ('The Harvest')

Pam Kelly, her predecessor Sally Jordan and myself. How those girls put up with a dyslexic old farmer, bristling with ideas and enthusiasm, who usually arrived at the office by seven-thirty in the morning, I shall never know – but they did!

We were a small, successful production team, thanks to the back up of an ultra efficient band of people from all the other departments.

One thing I am certain about, is that we never over-rehearsed, for the directors soon discovered at recordings, that, like many other presenters I usually gave the best performance at the first attempt. This is why I liked live shows – warts and all! The adrenalin flows and you know you only have one chance.

Occasionally we came across a subject that deserved a longer slot than the seven to ten minutes usually given to an item in the half-hour magazine format of the weekly *Bygones* programme. These 'specials' as they came to be known, usually ran for thirty minutes or even longer. The team thoroughly enjoyed making them because they took a much closer look at some aspect of country life, usually through the eyes or memories of elderly people who had been craftsmen in their younger days.

One film that I remember with particular affection was *The Harvest*, recalling through the reminiscences of Suffolk farm workers who were in their eighties and even nineties, how the harvest was gathered in the early days of this century. In those days, the only power on the farms was man, woman, horse or bullock. There were virtually no tractors. The old boys described how the welfare of the whole village depended on the harvest, and how everyone joined in and enjoyed it. The horses played such an important part in the life of the community that they warranted a special programme called *The Horseman*. It was devoted entirely to working horses and the men who looked after them.

The growth and demise of the railways was covered in a charming half-hour programme and showed how the railways opened up East Anglia before the motor car and died because of it. *Muddle and Go Nowhere* as the film was called, described the rise and fall of the Midland and Great Northern Railway. After the development of the railways and general opening up of trade to the area, many East Anglian men with little prospect of employment in the winter, left the farms and went up to the Midlands to work in the maltings, earning additional money to supplement their meagre wages at home. Hardly any of them were still around in the seventies but fortunately a few were still about in Suffolk, so we managed with the help of Geoff Weaver to get them to retrace their steps back to the Midlands as they had done a lifetime before, in a special programme called *Going to Burton*. Never again will this opportunity occur to recall history, for these splendid old chaps were the last to actually take part in this annual exodus.

Another railway man, Arthur Randell from Waldersea in the Fens, was a professional mole catcher and a great friend of mine for many years. He wrote books about the Fenland railways, mole catching and country lore. He often appeared on the programme, as did Jack Rumsby, the 'rodent eradicator' and George Lamb who had worked for me at Raynham since 1947 and was by ancillary trade, a peg maker. Pegs being very important in the days when linen was pegged out on the washing line before the days of the tumble dryer.

We spent a very interesting five days in the Lake District near Kendal and as well as covering the manufacture of the famous Kendal mint cake, and a snuff mill, the oldest working mill in the country, we filmed a spale basket maker – in fact, the last spale basket maker, Myles Newton. (Spale baskets were used extensively by the dock labourers at east coast ports when unloading the colliers in the days before mechanical unloading conveyors). Indeed, we were actually filming him making a basket right through from the splitting of the wood to the finished product, when, after trimming off the handle, he suddenly said as he threw it down in front of the cameras, 'That's the last and I'm the last, so it's all finished' and he never made another one!

And there were many more; locksmiths, key-makers, clog makers, a rope walk, items with carpet experts, jewellers, clock makers, stone-wallers, seed breeders and a sagger-makers-bottom-knocker, which with a word from our

Engine Driver

Playing trains.
The Nene Valley
Railway, Peterborough.

Signalman

Opening the gates.

promotion department had our viewers guessing for weeks before the item was shown. (A sagger-makers-bottom-knocker is the chap who breaks the moulds when the ceramic objects come out of the kilns in the potteries!) We went abroad whenever we felt it was justified and the budget allowed. The subjects were usually linked with our area, for instance: up to about one hundred years ago men used to fish on some of the north Norfolk coastal beaches, trawling their nets with horses. The practice came to an end early in the century and we only found one person who claimed to remember it. However, it turned out that on the coast of Flanders in Belgium, they still practised the skill. We found them at it, filmed them, and enjoyed super fish washed down with wonderful wine.

During the last war on the royal farm at Sandringham, they processed flax into linen yarn. They packed up after the war but we found that the process was still carrying on in the same bygone way in Ireland, so David and crew went and filmed it and covered the world famous Butterfant horse fair at the same time. The Netherlands was a rich source for film, easy to get to and

Guard.

very similar to parts of East Anglia. After all, it was a Dutchman, Vermuyden, who drained our Fens.

We found the splendid open air museum at Arnhem a joy and also a paper mill: one of the oldest working machines in Europe. One of the highlights from overseas was filming the world famous museum at Williamsburg or as they prefer to say in the U. S. the 'restoration' of the eighteenth century state capital of colonial Virginia. What a splendid job they have made of it! The whole town has been rebuilt and looks exactly as it must have done in the latter part of the eighteenth century. Beautiful town houses line the pea-shingled streets, there are no wires or modern street signs and dotted around are all the little shops and tradesmens' warehouses, with the various craftsmen actually at work at their trade or profession – even wig makers, milliners and silversmiths. Sheep graze the parks, the militia are in the garrison complete with court house and stocks outside. There is no evidence of electricity or motor power on the streets, just traders with hand carts, horse carts and extremely elegant carriages. As visitors, we stayed in one of the many small town houses, though we had to go along to a nearby period hotel for breakfast.

Most of the films we made are here for posterity, a few Anglia assisted by helping to finance various projects in return for the film rights. One such project was the building of an exact replica of Sir George Caley's first ever 'Heavier than air machine to fly and carry a man'. The original did this in 1852, at Sir George's house at Brompton Manor in the Yorkshire dales. The late Ken Fripp built the replica from Sir George's original plans and Derek Piggot, the well-known glider pilot, for this exercise became the test pilot and actually flew it. Up until 1852, the only man-made object that had got off the ground carrying a man, was a hot air balloon. The Caley glider looked rather like a winged sailing dinghy with a wheel on each side, one on the front and a tail skid. The small amount of wing control was by a tiller. On the day that it flew in 1852, the pilot was reputed to have been a coachman. The entire complement of household servants and gardeners are supposed to have turned out to drag it to the top of one of the hills and then rushed down, helter-skelter, towing the plane until it took off. According to a 'note' scribbled on the wall of Sir George's workshop, it flew for 141 feet and crashed leaving the pilot with a broken leg and saying words to the effect that he was hired to drive horses and coaches, not fly boats!

Although our 1974 machine looked exactly like its 1852 predecessor, we did have a car to tow it off from a small airfield at Southdown. The first attempt with the intrepid test pilot, Derek, at the tiller and cameras all over the place, wasn't very successful. It did fly – just! It got off the ground and rose about twenty feet for about one hundred yards. As he stepped from the crumpled mass of wood spars and canvas and twine, Derek said 'I think we need a few adjustments to the tiller!' But we did fly. I shall never forget the expression of elation on his face.

The director of the film was Harry Aldous, himself an ex-wartime flyer and another of Anglia's first film editors. He certainly captured the excitement as 'She' (as it was known) flew again. After repairs, subsequent attempts were made to fly 'She' but as she had to be towed, flight was always limited by the runway length.

In the early 1970s we heard that there was a move afoot to build a replica of George Stephenson's famous railway engine Locomotion No. 1 to mark the 150th anniversary of the opening of the Stockton to Darlington railway in 1825. A small bunch of enthusiasts led by a splendid steam buff, Michael Satow, begged, borrowed and bludgeoned firms, including Rolls Royce, to build an exact copy. We were lucky enough to be in at the beginning and the whole story was filmed from its inception as part of a series on industrial archaeology directed by Forbes Taylor. I was linking the series and had the honour of being one of the first to drive the newly built replica at the

Beamish Open Air Museum in September 1975. The original Locomotion No. 1 is in the Darlington North Road Station Museum.

About this time, a very different kind of bygone, in the shape of the 200 year old former workhouse at Gressenhall in Norfolk claimed my attention and in due course that of the *Bygones* film unit. For some time, a group of interested people had been trying to persuade the powers that be, that Norfolk needed and should have a Rural Life Museum. Gressenhall was near enough to the centre of the county, the building was no longer to be used as an old people's home, so why not turn this large bygone, with its historic interest and its adjoining farm, into the museum that everyone agreed should reflect Norfolk rural life and agriculture over the centuries.

Leading the group of enthusiasts was a very old friend, a well-known farmer and agriculturalist with the Ministry of Agriculture during the war, Dr Harold Hudson, at this time chairman of the County Education Committee. He was lobbying the County Council to renovate the old workhouse and trying to get as many local bodies as possible interested in the project. After many meetings with people who promised to support the idea, we decided to 'take the temperature' of local people by holding an open meeting in Anglia's largest studio on 7th March, 1975. It was well advertised and with a 'casual mention' on the screen the previous evening, we got a packed audience. There was only one dissenting voice – from the local Rate Payers Association. The rest were one hundred per cent in favour – beyond our wildest dreams – and voted to form a 'Friends of Gressenhall' group to start fund raising for the project in the hope that the local authorities would support us.

The reorganisation of local government in 1974 had brought all the museums in Norfolk into one museums service under its director Francis Cheetham who backed the proposed newcomer up to the hilt. So, to cut a long story short, in 1975 by agreement with the Norfolk County Council, Beech House, Gressenhall, built as a 'House of Industry' in 1777 for the Mitford and Launditch hundreds became the Norfolk Rural Life Museum with Bridget Yates as curator.

It seemed only fitting that a descendant of the great Norfolk agriculturalist 'Turnip' Townshend, the present Lord Townshend, should become president of the 'Friends'. In his foreword to the 'Friends' appeal brochure, he wrote disarmingly 'I learned only recently that it is almost exactly 200 years ago that one of my ancestors took his wife to see the then recently completed "House of Industry" at Gressenhall. I also discovered that the reason they went was to assure the local objectors to the project that their worries were unfounded.' If there were any local objectors in the 1970s they must by now be mollified by the tremendous success of the museum which has grown steadily over the years and attracts visitors from all over the country – indeed, the world.

Filming George Lamb – Pegmaker.

From that first meeting at Anglia the 'Friends' have grown too. The first secretary (at the time, my secretary also) was Gillian Shephard. Dr Hudson became treasurer and I was asked to be chairman. A great deal of work followed, not only fund raising but also much needed practical help by way of cleaning engines, cataloguing objects, restoring the gardens. Many local and county organisations lent a hand; the Women's Institute furnished a cottage dating from the early 1900s; the Industrial Archaeology Society cleaned and restored engines and the Mid-Norfolk Guild of Spinners, Dyers and Weavers laid on many a 'sheep day' which proved very popular. The latest achievement is the opening of the adjoining 170 acre Union Farm to visitors to demonstrate the famous four-course rotation of farming crops which is still the basis of good farming practice throughout the world – a fitting place, since Norfolk is where Turnip Townshend of Raynham and Thomas William Coke of Holkham pioneered the system over 200 years ago. Gillian Shephard left us soon afterwards to become a County Councillor and eventually Member of Parliament for South West Norfolk, but many of the original 'Friends' including Gillian, and many more recent 'Friends', are still working for and watching their 'Baby' go from strength to strength.

It must be the hope of everybody who produces information programmes for television and radio, to have the experience that I had a few years ago. At a money-raising event in the house and garden of a friend who lives in north Norfolk I was surprised to find that one of the exhibits contained a selection of local photographs, taken mostly in the first quarter of this century. They were pictures of people and places very close to the village of Castle Acre near Swaffham. Obviously they were of great interest so I asked where they came from and was told that they were taken by a lady, Viola Farley, née Grimes. She lived, strangely enough, in the same parish as myself. I knew of her, but had no idea that she was once a photographer, taking pictures mostly for the local newspapers. So I went to see her and was in no doubt that I had arrived at the right house for all the way up the garden path were glass plates, which had obviously once been photographic plates, now doing duty as mini-greenhouses for growing lettuces. The emulsion had long since weathered off and the pictures therefore were lost for ever. But I found Mrs Farley, whom I had often seen busy in her garden. She was only too happy to talk about her past experiences as a press photographer and to let me see what negatives she still had intact.

Today, even the cheaper cameras have instant development, automatic built-in exposure meters and flash, zoom lenses and on the more sophisticated models automatic wind-on film. In fact you hardly have to point the camera at the subjects, and with the multi-picture cassette many pictures can be taken so increasing the chances of a good one. By the law of averages if you take enough, one is almost bound to be good. Not so in Viola Farley's day – all negatives were on glass slides and these had to be loaded into wooden carriers in the dark and handled very very carefully. It obviously took much more skill to produce a quality picture with this large cumbersome equipment than with today's small pocket-size compact camera. But she did it; the composition of her pictures is superb, the quality sparkling and her technique has stood the test of time. It must be remembered that, having taken the pictures, she had to hurry home to the dark room, develop and print them and then cycle to the railway station, or sometimes the post office, to get them to the newspaper for the next edition.

Many of her best studies are of old people with faces full of character but she also caught the fun and enthusiasm of youth. She was particularly good at action pictures; her horses in draught really look as if they were dealing with a heavy load. Country-born and bred, she captured the farming seasons for posterity and recorded some now defunct local activities that are never likely to return, such as flint knapping at Grimes Graves or gathering wild mushrooms and watercress. Most of the plate glass negatives were in heavy boxes in cupboards throughout Mrs Farley's house – even under her bed. We finally got them all together and Anglia bought the entire collection from her. Some were used to make a television programme *Pictures from a Village* and these and others were later published in a book of the same title. After this the plates were donated to the County of Norfolk to remain part of its photographic archive.

The many instances of this kind where Anglia has been able to record and preserve the past have given me enormous pleasure. Soon after this Mrs Farley, by now very old and frail, died and her house was put up for sale. One of the people who came to look at it was a chap called Graham Martin who was a millwright and, as it turned out, looking for a derelict mill to buy and restore. It was pure chance that we met and he asked me if I knew of such a mill. I didn't but soon afterwards he found a tiny overshot watermill in the nearby village of Foulden and asked me if the *Bygones* team would be interested in filming the process of rebuilding it. It was in such a derelict state when he found it, that it was unrecognisable as a mill and even had an ash tree thirty feet high with a three foot girth growing straight up through the middle of it. The roof had long since disappeared. As it was an overshot wheel and therefore underground, the peaty fen soil had preserved not only the iron-work of the wheel but also the gearing and single pair of grinding stones. Graham and his wife Gloria not only restored it to its original state but now have it grinding corn into flour as it did 200 years ago. It took them three years during which Anglia filmed the story from the time he removed the ash tree to the first bag of flour to be ground.

CHAPTER SIXTEEN

Full Circle

On the surface I seemed to be enjoying more than one man's fair share of success in the sixties, with a satisfying career in television and success in the farming and business enterprises with which I was involved. But these years were also marked by bereavement and unhappiness within the family. After twenty years of marriage Margaret and I had separated, and I was living on my own in a flat in Norwich. In March 1968 my brother Jack died from a heart attack. He had previously undergone an exploratory operation, and had been warned that it would be wise to lose weight and cut out physically strenuous activities. But it was still a great shock when he died suddenly on 23rd March at a Masonic ladies night, leaving a wife, three sons and a daughter. A further blow to the family came on 2nd August when Tony Priest, my youngest daughter's husband, also died suddenly from respiratory failure. Tony was twenty-six years old, Carole twenty. They had been married for only twelve months and had been living with Margaret at Hall Farm, East Raynham, where Tony had a pig breeding and fattening unit. For most of his life Tony had suffered from asthma, and he had had a very bad attack in the middle of the night from which he didn't recover. Four months later, on 11th December, my father died at the age of eighty. It was about this time that Margaret and I agreed that we had outgrown our relationship and decided to divorce.

These were years of great emotional stress. I was the sole surviving executor for my brother's estate, and executor with my sister for father's estate. My mother and Carole were both in need of emotional support and Carole's affairs needed to be sorted out. Life was moving at a very fast pace, particularly as my divorce was granted on 4th February 1969. Carole soldiered on with Tony's pig unit for six months until it became obvious that the most sensible thing to do was to cease trading and sell the stock. In November 1969 she married Peter Smith, who was in the vegetable growing and marketing business locally with his father.

It was during the difficult time between 1967 and 1969 that I started work on the house and farm which later became the home that I share today with my wife, Jean. I was talking to Lord Leicester one day in 1967 when he mentioned that he had for many years been trying to sell a small watermill on the River Nar in the village of Newton by Castle Acre. He had been unable to find a satisfactory purchaser because of the restrictions he insisted on placing on the property: it was always to be kept intact as a mill and millhouse and could not be converted into a cafe or similar premises. As the asking price was to my mind comparatively low I bought it, thinking that rebuilding it at weekends would be a therapeutic exercise which would also get me away from the pressures of television. However, it didn't work out as I had planned, as it was over twenty years before I was able to get around to rebuilding the millhouse and refurbishing the machinery inside the mill. Fortunately a small farm only a few hundred yards from the mill, and also belonging to the Holkham Estate, became vacant six months later so I bought that too. The farmhouse which had originally been two cottages, needed modernising. This was done and an oak panelled study, an extra bedroom and bathroom were added. In July 1969, and before the rebuilding of the farmhouse was completed, I married my present wife Jean, who had worked for the BBC in London and Norwich and also at Anglia Television. We came to live at Mill Farm and built a completely new set of farm premises, as there were no outbuildings to go with the land. Nine years later, at Michaelmas 1978, we were also able to acquire more of the surrounding land. We now have a small, but very convenient working unit of 250 acres in the valley of the River Nar on the outskirts of Castle Acre, one of the prettiest villages in the county.

By 1970 Anglia had introduced a policy of regularly sending people to the recently opened BUPA Medical Centre in London for a complete medical check-up. It was a new concept in preventative medicine and each patient had to work through a very comprehensive set of tests. The Centre was equipped with all the latest technology. Before undergoing all the clinical tests and examinations I had to sit in a small booth confronted by a television set which flashed up questions. Answers were given by pressing a 'yes' or 'no' button, and if by any chance you contradicted yourself the machine would simply say, 'Oops, we'd better go back to question whatever it was and have another go.' The idea was that the machine wasn't influenced by the way the questions were answered. The information gained, together with the results of the clinical reports, was then fed into a computer and the results sent through to the company doctor. If there was a need for further diagnosis, appropriate action with specialists was taken. In 1970 and 1972 everything seemed to be all right as far as I was concerned, except that in 1972 the computer suggested that I have a test every year. I wondered why. In 1973 I was told that I must see a heart specialist as soon as possible. I did and was told that I had a heart condition, described as 'severe calcific aortic stenosis affecting a congenitally bicuspid aortic valve'. In laymen's terms, my aortic valve wasn't working properly and was causing problems when I was under stress. I was advised to slow down, cut out stress, lose weight, and generally try and ease out of the rat race of modern business. I remember asking what the alternative was, and being told, 'Start imagining tomorrow without you here.' The chairman and senior members of the Anglia board were made aware of the situation and I was told to take a sabbatical, wherever possible hand over my administrative duties, and generally wind down.

I took heed of the warnings, handed over my job as Head of Local Programmes to Philip Garner, who had been my assistant, and cut down on the driving. However, I still continued to attend board meetings, and present the *Bygones* programmes. As a form of relaxation therapy, Jean and I started to acquire a few animals at Newton. The first arrivals were four Hereford X steers: Arthur, Redvers, Diggory and Feckless. They were followed by a small flock of Jacob sheep. At first this change of pace seemed to hold the situation, and a visit to Dr Sam Oram, one of the top heart specialists in Harley Street, in July 1974 was reassuring.

In 1975 we decided to go to Jersey for a long weekend. I had kept in contact with John Rondel and his family who used to ship cattle to me in the 1950s. I still loved the Jersey breed but hadn't imagined that Jean would be immediately besotted with these pretty, little doe-eyed animals. We finished by buying three in-calf heifers – the idea being that they would carry their calves back here and in due course bring them up as single suckler calves, any surplus milk going to feed the pigs or other bought-in calves. Determined to do the whole thing ourselves, we borrowed a cattle float and drove to Castle Donington airport to meet the newcomers off the plane. After hanging about for the ministry vet to sign them out we finally arrived home about 4.00 a.m. They seemed none the worse for the experience and settled down very happily in the new stalls we had built for them.

The first to calve was Design's Royal Pierrette: Griselda to us, one of the most beautiful animals I have ever owned. She was a real friend and milked well, giving enough for her calf and for us, not only to drink but to make butter and cheese. She supplied us thus for over thirteen years and went peacefully to the great island in the sky from her favourite bit of pasture where she looked so beautiful. Of her calves, one born on my mother's birthday was named after her, Rose May and one of *her* calves (Griselda's granddaughter) born on Christmas day had to be called Merry of course! When I found her at 6.00 a.m. on Christmas morning and woke Jean, I never expected to see anyone giving post-natal treatment to a freshly calved cow in her nightie and wellies! Griselda and Rose-May were very relaxed about the whole thing and Merry is still milking well in her new home with the Dade family at Wisbech St Mary.

However, despite the steady routine of life with the animals various incidents during the next two years made us realise that things weren't really improving. In January 1975 I had the first real 'pass-out'. It happened after running across the garden pulling a long hose. I suddenly had an attack of nausea and dizziness, and felt I must lie down. But in fact I passed out. Not long after that I chased one of my neighbour's peacocks out of the garden and the same thing happened. One wet morning the following year, I had finished milking the cow and was carrying two pails of skimmed milk to the pigs, which were kept several hundred yards away, when I realised that I was going to pass out. As it was still raining I crawled into one of the pig arks recently vacated by a sow who had just farrowed, and lay down in the straw. I came round minutes later, and found myself being nuzzled by ten little pigs who couldn't understand why their mother's bed was not occupied by her complete with milk bar! It all happened once again when I was in London to attend an international television conference. I had been given the wrong address and was late and harassed by the time I arrived at the venue. I hurried into the building, only to discover that the lift wasn't working and I was faced with climbing seven flights of stairs to the room where the meeting was being held. I finally made it, walked into the room, made my apologies, and sat down. Five minutes later I slid gently from my chair on to the floor. The last thing I remember hearing was an Indian gentleman who was sitting beside me saying, 'Oh my goodness gracious, we must get a doctor'. The upshot of all this was that Dr Oram told me that the time had arrived for serious consideration to be given to fitting a new heart valve. For various reasons they decided it was best not to do it straight away, but ordered me to take things even easier.

Taking things easy has never been something that comes naturally to me. In the same year, 1976, I decided that having been used to a reasonable-sized farm all my working life and being less busy at Anglia, I would like to increase my acreage. Tithe Farm, Grimston, about eighteen miles from Newton, came on the market in August 1976. Agriculture then was in quite a buoyant state and profitable, so I decided to bid for it even though it meant borrowing a large amount of capital. In order to buy the farm I had to sell something, so Heath Farm, Fakenham, was put on the market and sold in October, which together with the sale of my share in Joice and Hill, went a long way towards buying Grimston. The rest of the money was borrowed. I think it gave Jean a shock, and perhaps some other people as well, when at the sale in Kings Lynn, Tithe Farm was knocked down to us. Privately, I too wondered how I was going to manage! But what was done was done, and Dick Burgis took over the management of the farm in his usual efficient way.

For a year or so all went well but the deterioration in my physical condition often made me wonder whether I had done the right thing. After the first complete year at Grimston, land values took off – in fact doubled. This coincided with the advice from the doctors to take it 'even easier', so I decided to take whatever profit I could make and give up Grimston. The farm was sold privately eighteen months later for double the price I had paid. Although parting with Tithe Farm was sad, it did remove the overdraft at the bank – what a feeling of relief that was!

In May 1977 I saw Dr Oram again. He was of the opinion that things were slightly worse with my heart and sent me to Kings College Hospital for an exploratory operation which was very unpleasant. It was started by pushing a large catheter through a vein in my right arm, up to my heart. This showed a picture of the aortic valve working. Next, another catheter was pushed through my groin into the other side of my heart. That wasn't too bad and it was interesting to watch from the operating table. Then I was told that the next bit would be uncomfortable. An iodine solution was going to be injected into my arm which would immediately be pumped round my body by my heart. I was warned that I would probably feel a burning sensation in my extremities. It was not a sensation but excruciating pain in my feet, fingers and at the top of my head. I asked afterwards if that was the reason I had been tied to the table but no, that was in case I needed to be turned over if drastic action was required! I remember commenting that if this was what having a valve fitted was like, I didn't think much of it! I was assured that the valve replacement would be done under general anaesthetic and I wouldn't be aware of anything. After several more consultations, I was asked to present myself at Kings College Hospital in London on Friday, 5th August, for Mr McArthur and his team of ten, to perform the operation.

I was in a very old-fashioned part of the hospital, which, being a teaching hospital, was full of very young student doctors and trainee nurses. Many of the nursing staff were from the Far or Middle East: so too were the patients. Oil rich and ill: their families squatted outside the doors of their private rooms.

The pre-op performance was exactly as shown on those television hospital dramas. I had to give all my details again to the almoner; give my permission to operate, hopefully ensuring that they chopped the right piece off the right chap! Further details required included who to inform when it was all over and somewhat optimistically, which newspaper I wanted to read in three days time!

On the Saturday, between my tests, baths and the male nurse with the lethal selection of razors, I went to the hospital chapel for communion. I thought it might be a prudent long-term move, although I had mentioned the operation to Him now and again for some time.

Saturday night would have been very long if I hadn't by chance found some of the local emergency services wavelengths on my shortwave radio. It made me realise that there were many people worse off than myself – people whose houses had been burgled or burnt down, people homeless and drunk, or giving birth!

At 6.00 p.m. on Sunday the dreaded notice 'NOTHING BY MOUTH' appeared on the door followed by a jab in the thigh. It was 8.00 p.m. on Monday 8th that I regained consciousness to be told by Sister Paula that the operation had been a success. I became aware of a man in a bed opposite me, wearing a face mask, with tubes sprouting out of him and an oscilloscope dot blipping away on the wall above his head. I thought that I wouldn't like to be in his shoes, his bare chest was stitched-up and heaving heavily; he looked so uncomfortable. I gradually became aware that I couldn't move or talk but wasn't particularly worried. It didn't occur to me that the chap opposite looked exactly like me!

During the next twelve hours I drifted in and out of consciousness, becoming more aware of the discomfort of the breathing tube and the dryness of my mouth. I tried to indicate this to the nurses. I could move my left hand (my right hand had tubes strapped to it) and I tried to write H_2O on the paper that the Chinese nurse had brought in to me. I managed to form letters resembling 'drink'. My efforts were rewarded, a block of ice, carefully held by tweezers, was placed on my lips. I found out afterwards that the nurses had been doing this all the time! When I wrote 'fruit gums' on the paper I still got ice!

I was still worried about the man opposite, he'd gone yellow and his dot was blipping slower and slower. I kept counting my fingers to see if my brain could still function. The staff were in constant attendance, paying special attention to two large red drain tubes from my abdomen, using chrome pliers with small wheels which squeezed out the excess of fluid.

Later I had a visit from Dr Davies the anaesthetist. I was informed that my heart was working well and that I must start to breathe by myself. He started to draw the tube from my mouth. The tube seemed unbelievably long. I tried to take deep breaths but choked, it was very painful. Dr Davies said that was very good and to do it again! I was given oxygen and felt my lungs expand in fits and starts and I thought my stitches were going to burst. I was told to relax and go to sleep. I woke about midday. Jean and her daughter Zara were with me, the chap opposite was still there and I could now see beds on either side of mine each of which contained a fellow sufferer strapped to tubes and monitors and blipping machines. Jean and Zara told me that the sheep, cows, cats, dogs etc were all OK at home and that the operation had gone according to plan. I drifted back to sleep and don't remember them leaving. Sister woke me that evening to tell me that some more of my drain tubes were to be taken out. She asked me if I would mind a freshly qualified nurse taking one tube out 'to practice'. Apparently there is an art in 'tying-off' as the tubes are removed. I said I was sure it would be a pleasure. It wasn't. It hurt much more than when Sister did it! The young nurse was full of apologies. I assured her that with more practice she would improve! Sister then told me that at one stage of the operation I had reacted to a blood transfusion and they had had to change the plasma as I came out all blotchy.

In the evening I was taken to a new room but I don't remember the move. I awoke at seven o'clock next morning to look out of the window at a splendid chestnut tree. I had a cup of tea – bliss! The notice on the door now read 'LIQUIDS ONLY'. I realised that the tubes were out of my hand and all orifices so I asked for a razor (electric) to shave myself – well sort of – but I felt much better for it!

Mr McArthur and his retinue visited me later that morning and showed me my old heart valve in a jar. My first reaction was 'if my life was depending on that, thank God I have a new one!' Mr McArthur informed me that I now had a Bjork Shiley Tilting Disc Valve. He was pleased with the operation and explained that I would probably have to take anti-coagulant warfarin (rat poison) from now on. I would be on antibiotics for a time and could have pain killers as long as necessary. I should exercise gently, just walking about, starting with short journeys round the room. I could sit out on the balcony too, as and when I felt able.

It was a great joy to know that I didn't have to use a bedpan! My blood pressure, temperature and pulse were still being taken every hour and my chest was very sore. My next visitor was a physiotherapist with a machine to get fluid off my lungs. It was a very painful process and not very successful. The congestion on my lungs seemed to be getting worse, making breathing difficult and full of pain. Shortly after the physio had left, the Rev John Wright arrived wearing his white surplice and carrying his portable altar. I received the sacraments. Before it was over, I had an emotional breakdown. I wept profoundly and it was a great relief for all that heaving and sobbing broke up my phlegm and cleared my lungs. I could breathe again. It must have been divine intervention for the physio suddenly reappeared with her machine to have another go at me.

Jean and Zara arrived at noon to find me sitting in a chair. It was wonderful to see them but I found I couldn't talk for long, I kept dozing off. I was still sore but not in such pain, except when I coughed.

It was when the nurse was making the bed, at about four o'clock, that disconcertingly I discovered that I couldn't speak or form words. My mouth and limbs were not obeying the instructions from my brain. I remembered when Father had a stroke, these were the same symptoms. I pressed the red button. Doctors and nurses flew in from every direction. Good job they realised what was happening for I simply could not tell them. I passed into unconsciousness. Thankfully I came to about an hour later and was back to normal and able to speak but I had had a minor stroke.

Routines began to develop over the next couple of days. Friendly ladies would arrive with menus, asking what I would like to eat. I usually requested fruit juice, fish, and cream caramel. I exercised my arms frequently but although it hurt, the movement helped my breathing. I was still on sleeping pills and pain-killers but when I decided to do without them, I woke up very stiff and had to roll painfully around to get going. When I couldn't sleep, I listened to my short wave radio. Nurses often came in for a chat and a laugh and rarely changed shifts without coming in to say cheerio – very comforting.

By 13th August I was getting adventurous. I started to pare my own grapefruit! I had been given enough fruit from people at the London office to set up my own stall! I very carefully dissected every little piece of skin on the grapefruit: I found it very relaxing and therapeutic. Jean was constantly looking in and giving me Symphytum for mending bones because the 'Black and Decker treatment' from my Adam's apple to my navel wasn't healing very well.

On Monday 15th, I decided to tackle the stairs. It was easy going down. Going up was more difficult. Fortunately the stairs were next to the lift shaft so I could complete the journey without exerting myself. Mr McArthur and Dr Oram arrived together the next day, along with a dozen Egyptian students. I was asked to say in my own words what the operation was like. I gave a ten minute lecture after which Mr McArthur commented 'If you make it sound that good, they will all want one!'

Two days later I was told I could go home. I thought someone was pulling my leg! It wasn't a joke, and I really enjoyed my breakfast of grapefruit and bacon and eggs! Before leaving I wanted to find the intensive care unit to say goodbye and thank you. I walked down six short flights of stairs and was surprised by the size and complexity of the operating theatres and intensive care units. Six patients were being operated on that morning. The nurses gave me a box of buttered almonds. Apparently I had talked about buttered almonds whilst under anaesthetic! I said my goodbyes but I shall never be able to thank the surgeons, doctors and nurses enough.

It is amazing that exactly one month after the operation I was back at Anglia House, recording an interview for the 4,000th edition of *About Anglia*. I had one or two more butterflies in my stomach than usual! My diary for 9th September reads, 'Today is one month since I came round in intensive care following the operation. Can't believe it possible that I could have made such good progress or feel so much benefit so soon. In fact I begin to feel like my old self'.

The 'plumbing repair' succeeded in making my body machinery, not as good as new, but certainly ninety per cent better. I had had my big warning and realised that in future I must take things much more easily. The experience also reminded me that the future wasn't going to go on for ever. So, from 1977 onwards, life took on a completely different meaning and I knew that I was fortunate to be enjoying the best of two worlds. I continued to have a certain involvement with Anglia presenting a series of *Bygones* and other special programmes about people, places and crafts and also continued the interesting work as a member of the Anglia board. Apart from presenting the *Bygones* programmes each year we published a series of small booklets connected with the programmes. I was also very busy with the farm and in 1978 Lord Coke agreed to let us have some extra land from the Holkham Estate adjoining the small piece I had already bought at Mill Farm. This enabled us to have our first harvest at Mill Farm in 1979. At the same time Lord Coke also agreed to make the disused coach houses and stables at Holkham available to house the Bygones Collection. The conversion for this project occupied a great deal of my time and energy until opening day in Spring 1979. I also managed to give myself a hernia, caused by lifting concrete blocks. So it was back to hospital for a short spell to be repaired. It was the second time I had succeeded in rupturing myself lifting heavy weights around the farm, and I made a solemn resolve that I would never again use man-power for any serious lifting when every possible mechanical lifting device that attaches to tractors is available for the purpose.

Jean took to farming like a duck to water, an analogy very close to the truth for our house is within a hundred yards of the River Nar and is constantly surrounded by many breeds of duck. She feeds them daily and they breed profusely, and every now and again we have to find new homes for some of them. Recently when the mallard population had reached about fifty I decided, after the mating season, to take twenty drakes up to Denver near Kings Lynn and turn them out onto the marshes. We had great trouble in catching them because, although many were tame and could be picked up, a lot more couldn't. We eventually succeeded in getting twenty of them into the crates and I set off for the Wash. I released them onto the marshes, left a bag of wheat to be fed to them by a kindly fenman, and drove home, calling at Kings Lynn on the way. I arrived back an hour or so later to find all twenty drakes sitting happily on the doorstep, obviously wondering what being put into crates and taken somewhere else to be given a feed of wheat was all about! Jean was very relieved to have them back and is still feeding them – too much.

The land that we took over when we moved to Mill Farm was part of a much larger farm and there were no farm premises attached to it. One of the first things we had to decide was what sort of new farm buildings we should erect. It would have been nice to build traditional Norfolk flint buildings, but that was too expensive. The least conspicuous alternative seemed to be to use custom-built premises using greeny-brown modern plastic sheet. When the largest building was erected it stood out like a sore thumb against the surrounding countryside, but now after ten years the small plantations of trees we planted have screened it. We also replanted some of the old thorn hedgerows dividing the small paddocks close by, which has helped the new building blend into what now looks like an old established farm. For me, one of the most important buildings on the farm has always been the workshop. We built an extensive one at Mill Farm, with welding facilities, drills and lathes, saws and planers and all the modern machinery necessary for keeping the wheels turning.

I have always enjoyed making and repairing machinery and for many years have been an active member of the Model Engineering Society's branch in Norwich. Traction engines are my other mechanical passion, and the two interests came together when I asked David King to make a scale model of the Marshall General Purpose engine like the one my father had, and the one I own. I had always happily carted our own traction engines (weighing 15 tons) about to rallies and shows, but it had become a very costly business and David, who is a very close friend of mine and one of the best engineers in the country, agreed to build the model traction engine. He built it in five-twelfths scale and it weighs just under a ton. We transport it on a trailer behind the Range Rover. One night I was coming home from a Model Engineering meeting with another friend of mine, Harry Bushell, when he said, 'You've got a good workshop, why don't you build a threshing drum to the same scale to go with the engine that David is building?' I remember saying that I wasn't sufficiently skilled to do it. But Harry's idea started me thinking and in the end with a lot more encouragement from Harry and David, I finally ordered the necessary wood to build the drum. I don't believe I really expected ever to finish it, but I realised that it would be therapeutic as much as anything else, and the fine tolerance lathe work that was necessary would keep my fingers nimble. The project occupied many hours of my time in the workshop over the next seven years and as I saw the drum take shape my keenness increased. One of the difficulties was that there were no detailed working plans for the Marshall drums built at that period, around the 1920s. The plans were all destroyed during the war when the Marshall workshops at Gainsborough were blitzed by the Luftwaffe. I owned the drum that my father had used, and it stood outside my workshop. Steadily, piece by piece, I took it apart, made a rough sketch of every component, multiplied each dimension of that component by .417 which brought it into five-twelfths scale. I then pre-fabricated each component in metal or wood, reproducing an exact scale replica of the Marshall threshing drum, as David had done when he built the traction engine. I was able to do much of the work in the traditional way using lathe and milling machines for the metal and bandsaws and morticing machines for the woodwork, together with the necessary hand tools. When I turned my attention to the four wooden road wheels, I decided to make a pattern of the centres, which were metal, and have four cast in aluminium. I then cut out and fitted the forty-eight spokes and twenty-four felloes. I took the wheels to John Gapp, one of the last working wheelrights in the country, to shrink on the metal bands to pull each wheel segment together.

George Cushing and self with *Fowler*.

Harry Bushell.

David King and self with *Tigger* at Holkham.

My three friends from whom I learned the true majesty of steam.

Replica 5/12 scale model of 1924 Marshall traction engine made by David King and drum made by me. Chicken driver shows scale.

Flushed with success after completing the threshing drum, I decided to make a straw pitcher or elevator. There were several makes to consider and I chose to make a replica (at the same five-twelfths scale) of the elevator that had been used with my father's drum. The original had been made by Harry Bushell when he was a young man. Workshop activities came to a halt at this point, however, when I stupidly got my left hand caught in the hydraulic mechanism of a plough, which – not to put too fine a point on it – filleted the hand as you would a fish! Jean rushed me to hospital with the odd pieces that were completely or very nearly severed, but unfortunately the first repair operation didn't go very well. It was at this point that a brilliant young surgeon, Trevor O'Neill, took over. He virtually took the hand to pieces and made a splendid repair. Six months later after long hours of physiotherapy it began to work again, and I decided to try it out and give it plenty of exercise by building a chaff cutter to complete the threshing outfit. I chose to make a Maynard and was able to borrow the remains of an original chaff cutter which hadn't been used for thirty years. It had stood out in the Fens, rotting away, and after we brought it home on the trailer to Castle Acre it disintegrated. But at least I had all the metal parts from it, plus a few photographs, to make the replica. Eleven years on, the threshing outfit driven by David's engine (which took him two years to build) is now very much admired at the occasional rally and at Holkham where it spends most of its time. The biggest compliment I think David and I ever had was Harry's remark when the outfit first ran, 'She's alroight boi, she look roight, she sound roight and she smell roight – in fact I'd loike to hev a bottle a scent outer her!'

During the six months 'arm in the sling period' I recorded another series of *Bygones* programmes which was almost the last batch. After twenty-five years the time had come for me to give the studio a rest. At the risk of sounding immodest I must say that the decision didn't appear to be accepted too happily by the viewers. We received literally hundreds of letters wanting to know why there were to be no more *Bygones* programmes. Three years later we are still getting letters from people asking for information about individual items, and many of the people who visit the Bygones Collection at Holkham ask why the programmes finished. I usually give the answer, 'Everything becomes a bygone some day – that's why they should be looked after!'

For Jean and myself, since the day we married Mill Farm has been the hub of our activities and centre of our life. We have shared its running, and we have shared the work. The farm has 130 acres of quite hilly, third grade arable land skirting the Nar valley, and 120 acres of water meadows with the river running through them. To keep it as least capital intensive as possible we grow only two crops in a two-thirds, one-third rotation of barley and peas. A small (200 ton) under-floor cold-air blowing system has been incorporated in the buildings to keep the grain and peas in condition.

Now that our last Jersey cow has gone, we have acquired two British White and two Salers heifers – no milking but we hope some young pedigree stock to sell on in due course. The Salers are an up and coming beef breed and the British Whites which were near extinction in the early 1970s are now lower down the Rare Breed Survival Trust's 'risk' league table owing to the improvement in numbers over the last decade.

Our main cattle enterprise varies according to the prevailing market conditions. We buy in bunches of steer or heifer calves, yard them in the winter and run them out on the water meadows through the spring, summer and autumn. Parts of the water meadows are suitable for hay and this is fed back to the cattle in the winter. We also feed reject carrots from my son-in-law's vegetable enterprise, and use barley straw for litter, which is returned by the plough to the land for the subsequent crop. We have kept a few elderly Jacob sheep mostly for fun and pullovers. Kept in such small numbers the animals certainly give no profit, but they are all friends and each has its own Christian name. We share the management of the farm. I do the early morning stint and last look at night and Jean does the afternoon session. A local chap, Peter Wright, who was actually born at Mill Farm when his father had it as a smallholding and who is now self-employed, helps us with the heavy work and is a good all-rounder. He loves the farm and regards it as his home territory.

In 1988 the government announced their plans to deal with surplus production on the farms and the huge amount of excess food which was going into expensive store. The scheme the government introduced is called

'Set-Aside', and farmers are paid to cease production on all or part of their farms: the present rate is £80 an acre per year over a period of five years for not growing anything, but keeping weeds cut. If a farmer feels so inclined he can also take an extra payment for sowing the land down to non-competitive grasses, keeping them cut and generally managed and so increasing the habitat for wildlife, birds in particular. To do this, he also has to allow public access to the land in question. We decided to take part in the scheme and everything was arranged through the Ministry of Agriculture and the Countryside Commission by the Norfolk Farming and Wildlife Advisory Group (FWAG). At the same time we decided to plant six acres of deciduous hard woods in the shape of three small broad leaf forests. The main crop is oak but there are also sweet chestnut, beech and ash. The periphery of each of the three woods is made up of a variety of species including hazel, spindle, willow, poplar, crab apple and holly. Running through the centre of the farm are the remains of a lovely ancient double-fenced leafy lane. The lane is very narrow and once much longer and obviously used for horse transport. Where the banks have been removed on each side of the lane, we have replaced a total length of about a thousand metres with live fences. The plants include hawthorn, blackthorn, hazel and hornbeam. We have also planted a few hard woods amongst them, like ash, beech, oaks, mountain ash and holly. It is good to think that in fifty years time, if all is well, they will be here for the next generation to enjoy, together with the oak forests which we hope will restore in part the vanished landscape of earlier days.

So from farming, as I first remember it, with mostly man-and-horse power and virtually no mechanisation, through to the food shortages of the forties, during the war and afterwards, when with more mechanical power, artificial fertilisers, selective weed killers, pesticides and fungicides, we farmers were given every encouragement to achieve the maximum output, we are now being paid to replant the forests and hedgerows we pulled out and to reduce cereal, beef and milk production. It seems we have turned a full circle.

N
EAST RUDHAM
TATTERFORD
A148
TO KINGS LYNN
HELHOUGHTON
RAYNHAM HALL
THE PRIORY
MILL FARM
THE CASTLE
THE MILL
PEDDARS WAY
A1065
ALL SAINTS
NEWTON-BY-CASTLE-ACRE
CASTLE ACRE
TO SWAFFHAM